CLOTHING & CRAFTING OF GODEY'S LADY'S BOOK 1861

CIVIL WAR PERIOD
VOL I

LELE SIMMONS
Copyright © 2018 Lele Simmons
All rights reserved.
ISBN: 0692068600
ISBN-13: 978-0692068601

DEDICATION

To John, my loving husband, who's support and guidance I couldn't live without.

CONTENTS

Chapter 1   JANUARY 1
- Chitchat Upon New York & Philadelphia Fashions For January ... 2
- New Styles of Aprons ... 7
- Novelties For January ... 9
- Crafting & Needle Works ... 13
- Embroidery Designs ... 21

Chapter 2   FEBRUARY 23
- Chitchat Upon New York & Philadelphia Fashions For February ... 26
- Seasonal Fashion Plates (Black & White) ... 28
- Children's Fashions ... 31
- Hoops and Farthingales Philadelphia February 1861 ... 33
- Novelties For February ... 36
- Crafting & Needle Works ... 39
- Embroidery Designs ... 47

Chapter 3   MARCH 49
- Chitchat Upon New York and Philadelphia Fashions For March ... 50
- Seasonal Fashion Plates (Black & White) ... 53
- Short Hair For Ladies ... 58
- Spring Bonnets ... 59
- Novelties For March "Juvenile Fashions" ... 60
- Crafting & Needle Works ... 65
- Embroidery Designs ... 71
- Dress Pattern ... 73

Chapter 4   APRIL 79
- Chitchat Upon New York and Philadelphia Fashions For April ... 80
- Spring Fashions ... 83
- Children's Fashions ... 89
- Novelties For April ... 91
- Spring Bonnets & Headdresses ... 93
- Crafting & Needle Works ... 95
- Dress Pattern ... 100
- Embroidery Designs ... 101

Chapter 5   MAY 104
- Chitchat Upon New York and Philadelphia Fashions For ... 105

May
- Seasonal Fashion Plates (Black & White) — 107
- Description of Dresses Worn at the Late Drawing-room Reception of Her Majesty Queen Victoria — 109
- Novelties For May — 111
- Crafting & Needle Works — 114
- Embroidery Designs — 119

Chapter 6 JUNE — 123
- Chitchat Upon New York and Philadelphia Fashions For June — 124
- Seasonal Fashion Plates (Black & White) — 127
- Description of Dresses Worn at the Late Drawing-room Reception of Her Majesty Queen Victoria — 130
- Novelties For June — 132
- Crafting & Needle Works — 135
- Embroidery Designs — 143

Chapter 7 JULY — 145
- Chitchat Upon New York and Philadelphia Fashions For July — 146
- Summer Toiletts For the Street and Watering Places — 149
- Novelties For July — 154
- Patterns From Madame Demorest's Establishment — 155
- Breakfast Caps & Summer Bonnets — 157
- New Styles of Aprons — 159
- Crafting & Needle Works — 161
- Summer Dress & Mantle Pattern — 164
- Embroidery Designs — 165

Chapter 8 AUGUST — 167
- Chitchat Upon New York and Philadelphia Fashions For August — 168
- Seasonal Fashion Plates (Black & White) — 171
- Novelties For August — 174
- Patterns From Madame Demorest's Establishment — 176
- Crafting & Needle Works — 177
- Embroidery Designs — 181

Chapter 9 SEPTEMBER — 183
- Chitchat Upon New York and Philadelphia Fashions For September — 185
- Seasonal Fashion Plates (Black & White) — 187
- Novelties For September — 189

- Patterns From Madame Demorest's Establishment — 191
- New Styles of Aprons — 193
- Crafting & Needle Works — 195
- Embroidery Designs — 197

Chapter 10   OCTOBER — 199

- Chitchat Upon New York and Philadelphia Fashions For October — 200
- Seasonal Fashion Plates (Black & White) — 203
- New Styles of Aprons — 205
- From Madame Demorest's Magazine De Modes — 206
- Novelties For October — 209
- Crafting & Needle Works — 213
- Embroidery Designs — 217

Chapter 11   NOVEMBER — 219

- Chitchat Upon New York and Philadelphia Fashions For November — 220
- Seasonal Fashion Plates (Black & White) — 223
- Caps & Bonnets — 228
- Headdresses — 230
- Novelties For November — 231
- From Madame Demorest's Magazine De Modes — 232
- Crafting & Needle Works — 235
- Embroidery Designs — 241

Chapter 12   DECEMBER — 243

- Chitchat Upon New York and Philadelphia Fashions For December — 244
- Seasonal Fashion Plates (Black & White) — 247
- Bonnets For The Season — 251
- Aprons — 252
- Bridal Finery — 253
- Novelties For December — 254
- Crafting & Needle Works — 258
- Embroidery Designs — 264
- Definitions — 266

Foreword

I decided to create this book due to my interest in clothing fashions of the Civil War period. I am a seamstress and I love sewing period clothing and found that reenactors take this subject very seriously. I realized that I needed to do my research in order to create the desired effect. While researching I realized that Godey's Lady's Home Journal was exactly what I needed to use for my education. The books were hard to come by and expensive. I am a little old school, in that I like having a book, as opposed to having to go online every time I wanted to look something up. Fortunately, I was able to purchase the Godey's Ladies Home Book in its entirety on microfilm. While studying the images, I thought it would be great if I could pull out all of the information regarding clothing and fashions for each year. So I decided to make a five volume set for the Civil War Period

This is my first attempt at creating a book and it has been more complex than I first imagined. It has also been very rewarding. I truly hope that the content I have included will enlighten and reward you as much as it has me. Included, are all 12 color plates for the year, black and white plates, knitting, embroidery designs, and any written articles pertaining to the fashion trends for the year.

Just as a side note on spelling and grammar I would like to state that I tried to keep the original writings just as they were in the original text. I found that many of the French terms used were italicized and I tried to follow suit with the same formatting as the original writers.

I found it difficult to understand some of the terms used when referencing these articles of finery due to the defunct terminology, so whenever possible, I researched definitions of the words I didn't understand and have listed them in the definitions pages. I hope this is of some use to you.

CHAPTER 1
JANUARY 1861

DESCRIPTION OF FASHION-PLATE FOR
(Reception and Evening Dress)

Fig. 1 - Dress of blue *glacé* Silk. There are two skirts: The lower one trimmed with ruches of ribbon, placed in clusters of three, at a little distance apart; the front of the upper skirt has a trimming to correspond, placed *en tablier*, while the three puffs form with it a tunic, the puffs are caught to their places by garlands of apple blossoms and grass, the upper one, that on the corsage, and the coronal for the hair, are with the simple foliage of the tree.

Fig. 2 – Dress of rich mauve reps, the skirt and corsage quite plain; the richness of the silk, and of the cape and sleeves of Pointe Duchess, worn with it, being all sufficient. This style of corsage presents a decided novelty, and is very elegant. Hair in full raised puffs; coronal of purple Marguerites, without foliage fastened with a knot of ribbon to the left.

Fig. 3 – Dress of violet and *white gage d' Indie* in stripes; trimming, a ruche of white satin ribbon. Square corsage; sleeves with one puff and a frill

Fig. 4 – Simple and elegant dress of green crepe, over green silk; the bouffantes of the skirt, corsage and sleeves caught up by ruches of white crepe. Chatelaine of Cape Jessamine blossoms, without foliage; cluster of the same on the left of the skirt; drooping wreath to correspond, mixed with foliage

Fig. 5 – Dress of tulle over silk. The double skirts have alternate puffs of tulle and violet crepe; the upper skirt has a broad bouffante of violet crepe edged by a puff of lace, and caught at regular intervals by oak leaves in gold, the acorns being in real gold. A cluster of the same forms the bouquet *de corsage*, while a flat Norma wreath of leaves and acorns is arranged in the hair.

CHITCHAT UPON NEW YORK AND PHILADELPHIA FASHIONS JANUARY

Our Fashion plate naturally leads to a few more items on the subject of evening dress.

First, as to the width and shape of the skirt: "ill made crinoline, worn under ridiculous or wretched toilets, had inspired some ladies who have a strong dislike to anything ugly or common, with a desire to diminish the fullness of dresses and return to the Greek or Roman tunics, but the change was soon found to be altogether impracticable;" is the flat of the Moniteur, to which admirable counsellor we are also indebted for the following valuable suggestion as to the arrangement of the amplitude of evening dress draperies, on which their peculiar elegance so entirely depends.: To secure all possible gracefulness in ball dresses the plaits at the top are made wide and then doubled again, and without cutting the stuff to a point; but three points of gores are added at the bottom of the under skirt, one between the widths at each side, and one behind. These points make the lower part of the skirt spread well, and form a train. The front of the skirt is always made shorter to give freedom to the feet. Again, as to the sleeve: the bell-shaped puff is quite as much in favor as ever; it is always becoming to freshness and youth. Where the arm needs more concealment, a puff and flounce or two wide flounces may be worn, falling nearly as low as the elbow .In material, the widest liberty of choice is given. For young ladies, tulle, white and colored crape, gauze, Tarleton, and other diaphanous fabrics, are the most suitable. Still, the rich silks in stripes of contrasting high colors, in *moiré*, and particularly watered silks, in stripes of large and small waves, or brocaded silks with plain grounds, and Jacquarded figures, seem to be most sought after. They are more costly, but more enduring; they range in price from $4 to $14 and $15 a yard. We have seen one of plain Magenta and pure white, in stripes two inches wide, of oriental richness and luster; the same may be said of many of the brocaded silks, especially where gold, scarlet, green, and crimson are brought out upon modes, black, mauve, or any plain decided ground. Among the richest fabrics, however, velvet has regained its place, especially uncut velvet, or velours *epinglé*; the rich shades of crimson and fuchsia colors, and, in fact, all prevailing tints are to be found. Velvet requires very little addition to its elegance. Rich lace is its most suitable ornament. We quote two French styles for making up velvets, which have novelty to recommend them; "An Ornament on the sleeves of a very pretty nacarat velvet dress made by Mme. Bernard, one of our first rate dressmakers, should be noted. The ornament was formed by a broad gold band, and the body of which was high, was fastened by gold buttons. The skirt, quite plain and long behind, was eleven yards round. " Another dress by the same maker was made of light peach-bloom velvet, with a plain skirt, a low body, short sleeves formed of large *beret* of velvet, arranged so as to leave at intervals, hollows, in which was seen a large puff of white satin. The body has draperies arranged contrariwise, reproducing the ornaments of the sleeves, that is to say, in the intervals left by the waved plaits of velvet white satin puffings were visible. This new fashion, which it requires the pencil rather than the pen to represent intelligibly, is most happily effective. In a splendid ball given in Paris, one of Gagelin's Pompadour costumes, worn by a youthful bride of remarkable beauty, attracted much notice. This costume consisted of a skirt of green silk looped up in two places on each side by white and pink chicories forming ribbon. The front of this skirt, which was in the apron style, was white satin decorated with white and red roses. The body had a white and pink bertha, rounded behind, and beginning in front from the point of the body. The sleeves were white and pink chicory on one side, accompanied by roses on the other, and two large white marabout feathers.

A charming ball cloak made of quilted satin, white outside and pink inside, with a milkmaid's hood, profusely trimmed with white and pink chicories, served to complete this toilet, so fresh and youthful.

In the wedding outfit of the bride just alluded to, among the splendid articles of all kinds, many of which had been obtained from Gagelin's were two French Cashmeres, such as had never been made before. Their colors, quite novel, are as lasting as those of India, and their patterns, absolutely unique, presented a wonderful relief.

It will be noticed that necklaces have now regained their old place in popular favor for evening dress.

For all light tissues, flowers or foliage in bouquets, wreaths, agrafes, etc., are the most suitable ornaments. A parne of flowers is often almost as costly as one of gems, and includes a whole set — wreath for the hair, bouquet *de corsage*, and sprays for the skirt of the dress. A parne of these fragile but exquisite ornaments often costs from $15 to $100, if ordered from the best French houses; but their delicacy is so exquisite as to outrival nature. They may be set in any form most becoming to the wearer. It is absurd to wear a coronal, when a drooping wreath is more becoming, merely because people tell you "round wreaths are the most fashionable:" our steel-plate illustrates this; and the best articles mount a wreath for the face that is to wear it. We may notice among the infinite varieties of styles and blossoms a round headdress of convolvulus, with drooping branches all round, as well as the agrafes of the dress, which came from the celebrated flower manufactory of Tilman, 104 *rue de Richelieu*. Another headdress composed of China rose-color auriculas, divided into small tufts, accompanied a dress of China rose-silk. One, very light, was made of clematis and orange-bloom: it presented on the forehead a narrow but rounded cordon, which increased in volume behind. Another was composed of periwinkles, white lilac, and waxed orange bloom. Both were masterpieces of taste. Bouquets to match, of an elongated form were placed at the side of the waist. Mme. De Laere had also supplied a delightful coronet, formed of pale blue cornflowers on the right, wheat ears pointing upwards on the left, and behind, a large tuft of wheat ears and blue flowers. Last of all one of cherry-color wild roses and white lilac, extremely fresh and graceful.

When the dress is of a heavier fabric, the ornaments for the hair, which are now so popular, in gilt, etc., are very suitable; also, headdresses combining velvet and flowers of the same material, velvet and gilt, etc.

For a dress of cerise and white, for instance, large cherry-color roses with fancy foliage, daisies, lilac velvet pansies and gold anemones. A large gold torsade encloses it on one side, and a bunch of white lilac hangs down on the other.

For a cherry-color dress covered with a white tulle tunic, a coiffure presenting a cherry velvet torsade fastened by three gold buckles, and terminated on one side by a tuft of white frizzed feather, on the other by a large bow of two loops blended with another of gold cord, the two long tassels of which hung down on the shoulder. Lastly, for two toilets of court mourning, the following headdresses: A bandeau of black and violet velvet powdered with gold stars and accompanied by two tufts, one very compact, of silk violets, and the other of black and violet bows mixed with gold threads. A torsade of wide mallow ribbon blended with black lace, and fastened at the side by an agrafe of wheat ears in silver. Plain dresses continue to be made of thick tissues such as druggets, terry velvets, and poplins. Ottoman velour is perhaps the favorite material for street dresses, and offers a sensible, suitable resistance, for once, to the mud and mire which last year fringed the rich floating flounces of costly robe silks. The corsage is almost invariably round, with a belt; the sleeves are often plain, slit up to a certain height, and buttoned behind the arm with large buttons like those on the front of the body. These buttons are continued down the front of the skirt in the cassock or empress dresses, which are quite plain in front, and laid in wide plaits behind and at the sides.

The dresses of our best establishments spread out and fall in a peculiarly graceful manner, owing to a new arrangement most happily imagined. Another kind of sleeve is narrow at top without gathers or plaits and wide at bottom with a turned up cuff showing the satin lining edged by a ruche. At the top of the arm there is a fancy shoulder knot with tags. These shoulder knots as well as the *Fourragéres*, the frogs like those worn by hussars, ornaments in the guipure style, badges and medallions made with the crochet, the fichus, and berthas of the same kind mixed with jet, are all worn more or let on rich plain goods.

In our notices of Mrs. Scofield's bonnets the past month, an error occurred in the mention of the bridal hat. The ornaments were a barbe of rich blonde, a branch of orange flowers and buds, with a light plume of marabout to the right. A novelty in the cap was a papillon (butterfly) in velvet and gold, on the right temple.

Short, full feathers — these butterfly ornaments, long grooved leaves in velvet the color of the bonnet, golden ornaments, macaroons in steel, pearl, and gilt, are among the chief ornaments of the velvet bonnets. The drawn brim in velvet is one of the chief novelties, as for instance, a royal purple brim, tulle cap crown, encircled by a wreath of purple chrysanthemums with golden centers. Velvet cape covered by a frill of blonde. As to colors, fuchsia, rose des Alpes, mauve, royal purple, pale and very deep green, all the clarets and maroons with deep blue, will be among the most popular. Of course the bonnets can be made as plain as desirable: one has infinite choice, and a person with good taste may combine the best points of two or three in her order. The blonde cap is optional: brides of black lace and plaiting's of ribbon, or plaited bands extending from the forehead to the cheek are substituted in many, and an attempt will be made to do away with the cap altogether. The satin linings put on with a colored cord or piping, betokens this, and foreshadows the style of next spring's straws.

Our notice of Genin's furs must necessarily lie over another month, owing to the crowd of information accumulating at this season of the year.

CHILDRENS FASHIONS

Fig. 1 – Boy of four. Skirt and vest of bright barred poplin; little jacket of plain gray poplin

Fig. 2 – Street dress for a very young child. Warm cloak of cashmere, embroidered in silk or braid; white satin hood, with a ruche and loops of ribbon inside the brim

Fig. 3 – Coat dress for little girl, in dark blue merino. The front has a plastron or flat tablier application of the same material, trimmed with braid alone, or braid and fringe, according to fancy

Fig. 4 – Lad's blouse and trousers in dark kerseymere; Renfrew cap in black cloth

Fig. 5 – Dress of scarlet merino plain and full; Cloth paletot with wide sleeves trimmed with plush gray fur collar. Beaver hat, with velvet bands and bows, and a *plume de coque* to the left

Fig 6 – Boy's Raglan of dark cloth, with oval buttons. Renfrew cap in gray; blue neck-tie

Fig. 7 – Little girl's coat dress of plain poplin, a pearl gray shade. The chemisettes and cuffs are of blue satin, quilted in diamonds. Round hat of blue and black barred velvet.

THE VALENCIAN

This graceful and truly classic *sortie de Bal*, or opera cloak, is made of white merino and bordered with a gold passementerie and tassels. The combined effect is admirable, while the richest sweep of the material produces an effect which is peculiarly statuesque and dignified. Made in suitable material, the same fashion is greatly in favor for the promenade.

From the establishment of G. Brodie, 51 Canal Street, New York
Drawn by L.T. Voigt, from actual articles of costume

WALKING-DRESS FOR A YOUNG LADY

Made of Steel-Colored Poplin; trimmed with Magenta-colored velvet and buttons. The velvet is crossed at intervals by squares of the poplin, having a button in the center, which makes a very stylish trimming.

THE EVELYN

Made of plain colored merino, and trimmed with very bright silk or poplin

OPERA HOOD

Still another style, this is of split Zephyr, of any bright contrasting colors; the balls are passed through a single thread and form a chain, with a new and pretty effect.

NEW STYLES OF APRONS

THE ZEPHANIA

The Zephania is suitable for silk or wash goods. It can be made of colored cambric, scalloped with white, and braided with Marseille's braid.

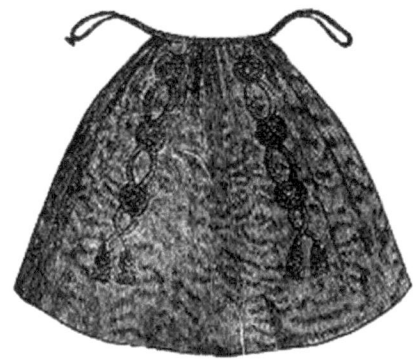

THE JENNY

The Jenny is made of black *moiré* antique, and trimmed with cords and tassels caught at intervals by rosette buttons.

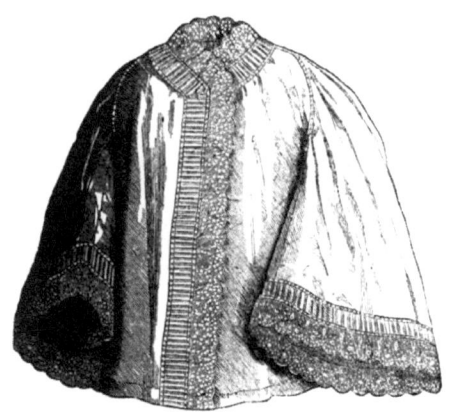

THE "ALICE" NIGHT DRESS

We give two excellent designs for the short night-dresses, so useful in case of illness, and by many preferred to be worn altogether in the summer season. The Alice is of white cambric; the sleeve set in a point on the shoulder; the trimming and plaiting of cambric, with a flounce of fine *broderie Anglais* set on without fullness.

THE "ELSIE" NIGHT DRESS

Of striped dimity; the ruffles are all made *in revers*, or to turn back from the neck, front, and wrist. They are also of corded dimity, and the scallop is done with red cotton; fastened with pearl or gold studs.

NOVELTIES FOR JANUARY

Fig 1 - Garrote collar and neck-tie for morning or home dress, suited in fact, for all plain toilets at home and abroad, and extremely serviceable in traveling. The collar is of plain linen, the habit shirt of cambric, the neck-tie of plain black, blue, or crimson silk, the ends lightly embroidered or plain as fancy may dictate. They are very fashionable at this moment, particularly for young ladies.

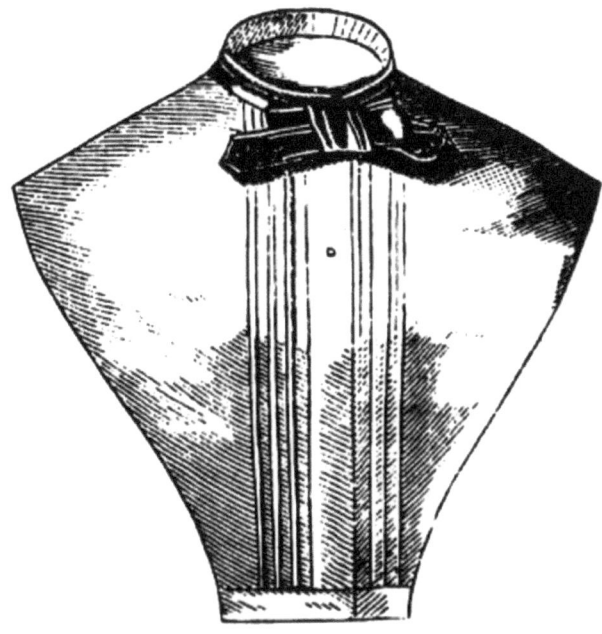

Fig. 2 - Another style of habit-shirt, a frill of embroidered muslin set on with an inserting of embroidered cambric. The frill should be nearly plain.

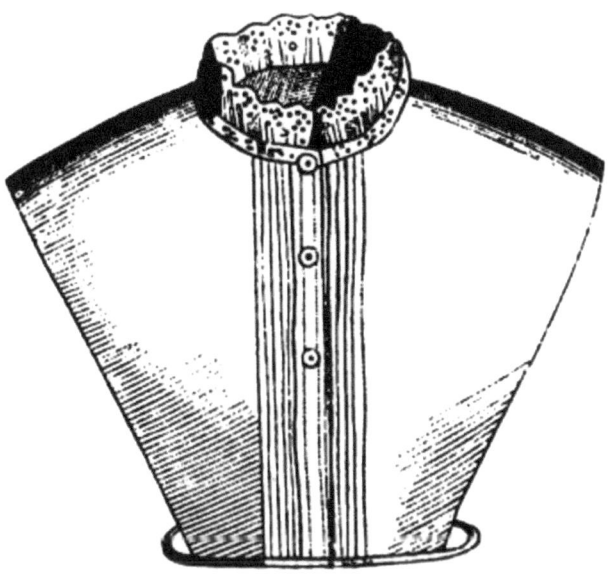

Fig. 3 & 4 - A real novelty in the way of undersleeves; to be worn with a short dress sleeve, or with a Greek sleeve that is entirely open to the cap on the forearm. For evening dress, they should be made of tulle and Valenciennes inserting. For the day, of Muslin and Swiss embroidery. *Fig. 4* is the most desirable but both are more novel than graceful.

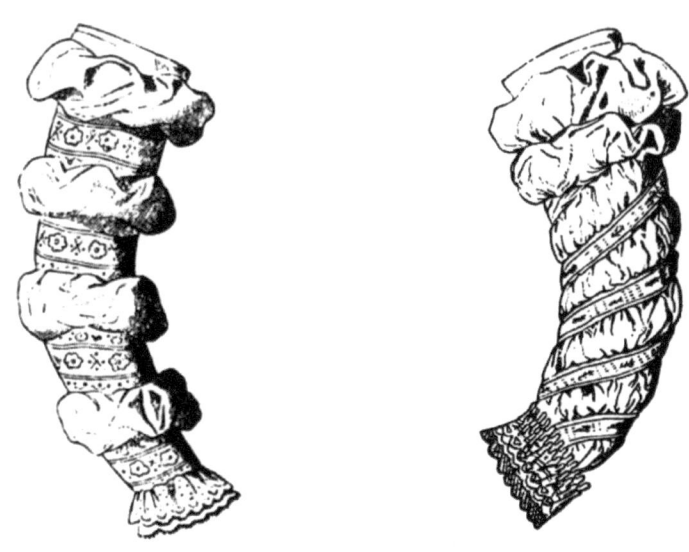

A POINTED YOKE CHEMISE, TRIMMED WITH PLAITS AND BRODERIE ANGLAISE

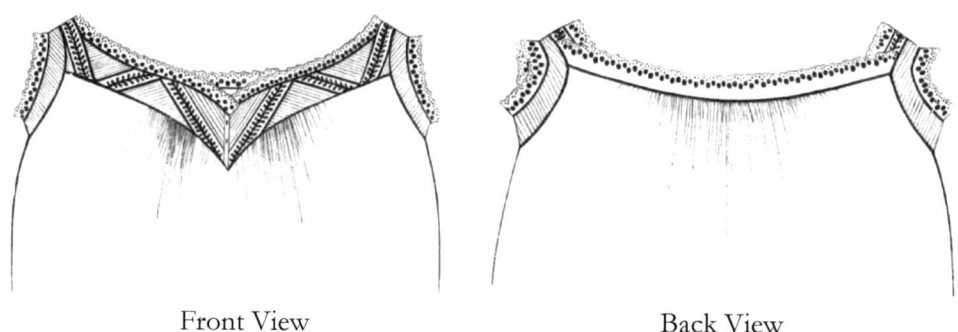

Front View   Back View

Fig. 5 - Cordon and flat bows for the hair, of black velvet and gold colored ribbon. It is a good and becoming headdress

Fig. 6 - Dress cap with roses and gold lace

Fig. 8 - Chenille net for the hair with a bunch of aquatic grasses and thin blossoms in gold

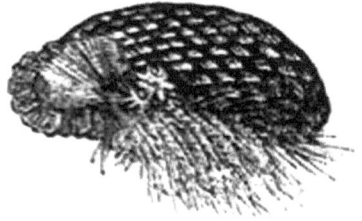

Fig. 7 - Black velvet net for the hair, with four heavy tassels in Gold

CARRIAGE SHOE

This shoe is made of black or any dark colored velvet, richly embroidered, and bound with satin ribbon. The sole is of stout wash leather, wadded and lined with satin. It is a warm and handsome carriage shoe.

TURKISH LOUNGING CAP

Materials – Rich crimson cloth, black velvet, Albert braid of both colors, gold thread, gold braid, and a tassel made in passementerie to combine all these colors. The ground of the cap is in cloth, the lower part only (which is applique) being in black velvet. The center of the crown is in the same material.

In the engraving, those parts that are in velvet are represented in black.
The broad white lines indicate gold braid, which is used to cover the edge of the velvet where it joins the cloth, as well as to form certain scrolls. The double lines on the cloth are in black Albert and gold thread. On the velvet, they are crimson Albert and gold thread, sewed down in the usual manner.

This sort of work especially commends itself from being so easily and rapidly executed; and in the opinion of many it is far richer and more effective for this purpose than either crochet or anything else. It is extremely warm and light, and, if small pieces are added for ears, it forms a delightful travelling cap.

To make it up, procure some black silk and common bed ticking, also a little black silk cord. Cut out the black silk lining the full size; but that of ticking about an inch narrower in the head-piece, so that it may not reach the edge where the velvet and cloth give already sufficient thickness. Gather the silk head-piece into the round for the crown, so as to make the lining separate from the cap; but work the ticking and cloth together. Tack the lining in round the crown, and down the joining at the side; turn in the edges round the head, and sew round the black silk cord, and the tassel in the center of the crown.

CRAFTING & NEEDLE WORKS

THE CHINTZ WORK BASKET

This basket is made of bright colored furniture chintz. As will be seen by the picture, its construction is very simple, being made of pasteboard, cut any size the maker may fancy and the shape of those in the engraving. These are covered neatly with chintz and sewed together. The little box to the left is for buttons; it is made of pasteboard cut to fit accurately into the basket with a cover of tin, covered in chintz. The advantage of tin is that it will not curl as a pasteboard one would. There is a little stuffed cushion fitted into the button box for pins. The little bag is of chintz and intended for a thimble. The two little bags on the right of the button box are for spools of cotton. A needle book comes next, having a cover of pasteboard sewed over the flannel. The bag to the right is made of chintz, very full, gathered in at the bottom, and confined at the top by a ribbon; this is for tape and the many little trimmings to be found in a ladies work basket. At the side opposite the needle book, there is a bag of chintz for the scissors, and a strip sewed down tightly and fastened at proper distances for papers of needles, and bodkins. The handle is a strip of tin covered with chintz, fastened at the sides by bows of ribbon.

BOURSE IMPERATRICE

Materials – Broad gold braid, gold thread No. 0, two dozen rings nearly one fourth inch in diameter, a skein of purse silk of any color that may be desired, and passementerie tassels, bars and cord composed of the same color, with gold.

The star in the center of this purse is the part first done. Bend the end of the gold braid down an inch, draw an end of the silk through the double braid an eighth of an inch from the fold, and wind it round the braid for rather more than half an inch; fasten off the silk. There will be an end of braid uncovered with silk.

Leave it in both thicknesses of braid, and again fold down an inch. Treat this the same. Do this ten times, which will make up twenty inches of braid. Arrange the piece in the form of a star, as seen in the engraving, and sew the center firmly, to keep all the points in their true position. Do another star exactly like this for the opposite side. Now cover all the rings with crochet, sew them together as in the engraving and work a gold rosette in the center of each. Tack them down on a piece of toile *ciré* with the star in the center, and unite them by button hole bars, carrying a line also round the star just above where the silk is wound round, to form a wheel.

All the points of the wheel must also be connected with the bars and rings. Both sides being done precisely alike may be united at the sides. A flat ornament in passementerie (termed a macaroon) is sewed in the center of each star, and the trimmings, tassel, and bars are added

A NEEDLE BOOK AND PIN CUSHION COMBINED

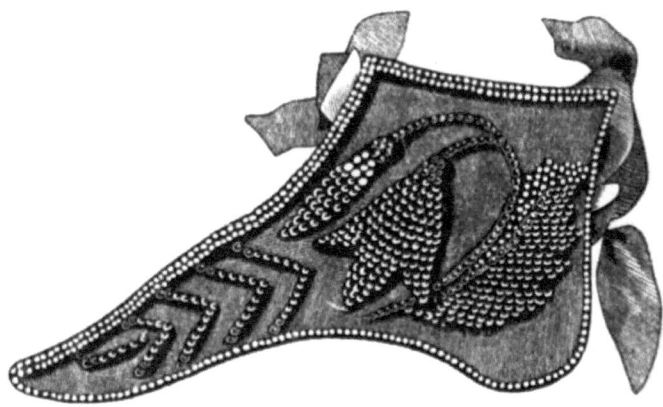

Materials – Two nails of violet-colored silk, some white chalk beads, some crystal, also some gold, a little larger than seed beads, a small piece of fine flannel for the needles and pins, and some ribbon for tying.

First cut the exact shape in tissue paper, then cut four pieces the same in card-board, also four pieces of flannel somewhat less in size, and four pieces of silk, two larger and two a little smaller, for the lining.

For the Pincushion – Cut four thicknesses of flannel, cover two pieces of card-board, tack the flannel on to one piece of the former, and to the second piece sew on a small piece of the silk, about half an inch in width, but tapering towards the end represented as the heel, now sew this on the first covered piece, sew the two pieces of card-board up at the back of the heel, round the ankle and instep.

For the Needle-book – Cover two pieces of card-board and line them with some silk, then snip the edges of the flannel and sew them to the instep part of the pattern. Now sew the two portions of the design together at the part which represents the instep.

Sew on the beads, as shown in the engraving; only observe that underneath the flowers and leaves is a piece of white calico to throw up the white of the beads. A small pair of scissors may be inserted between the needle-book and cushion.

LOUNGER'S CUSHION OR PILLOW

Materials – One and a half ounce bright scarlet eight-thread Berlin wool, a little more than half an ounce each of black and white ditto.

The cushion or sofa pillow is made in the new crochet stitch. The crochet hook, we must observe, may be made by anyone with a penknife, from a cedar-wood knitting needle, No. 3, by simply cutting a hook at the end. No crochet hook that is sold will perfectly answer the purpose, as the stem must be long, and of the same dimensions throughout, with a knob at the end.

Make a chain of any length required, and work back on it, bringing the wool in a loop through each stitch, which you then slip on the hook, thus taking up all the stitches. Second row (in which, having all the stitches on the needle, you proceed to take them off). Bring the thread through the first stitch; and afterwards through two stitches together, namely, the one just made and the one beyond, until only one is left on the needle. This forms the first stitch of the next row, which is similar to the first, except that, instead of a chain stitch, you take up an upright bar of wool, which seems to be, not on the tip, but at the side of the work. Work backwards and forwards until you have done enough, observing always to fasten on the new color so as to do the last stitch of the taking off row with it.

For this cushion, with the black wool, make a chain of sixty stitches* and do two rows. Join on white, and do two rows, black two rows*; repeat four times within the stars. Make a cushion or small bolster the same size, allowing a little for stretching; fill it with horsehair; cover it with black sarsenet or calico. Join up the crochet, and cover the cushion; draw up the ends.

For the Cord – With the scarlet wool and a coarse bone hook, make five chain, close into a round, and work round and round in single crochet until sufficient is done. Leave a bit of wool at each end to sew the cord on with.

For the Tassels – Get a friend to hold her hands apart so that a thread wound round them will be twenty one inches long. Wind round this thirty strands of scarlet, twelve of black, and the same of white wool. Tie these strands tightly twice, leaving three quarters of an inch between. Then divide the space equally, and tie in the middle.

Divide each space, and tie again in the middle, and subdivide in the same way, allowing a little larger space on each side of the two first ties, and making thirty four spaces altogether, two of which are larger than the rest. Cut in the center of each space, and there will be beautiful mossy balls, which only want a little trimming. Take a rug-needle threaded with scarlet wool, making a knot in the end. Thread on eight of the small balls; allow eight inches of wool for them; make a knot, and cut it off.

Do the same with the remainder of the thirty-two. Sew on the cord at each end of the cushion. Then take a bit of scarlet wool and the rug-needle, fasten on, slip the needle through one of the two large balls and under the center of two strands of wool with balls on them, then back through the ball, and fasten off, leaving a handsome tassel of sixteen balls in lengths of four, with a large ball connecting the whole. Do the others in the same way

This sachet is made in the form of an envelope and is intended to contain a lady's night-dress, etc. Either on a short excursion or to lie on the pillow during the day, forming an elegant ornament on the bed. It is to be worked in square crochet from the engraving, beginning with three squares, and so increasing to the proper width.

The back is plain square crochet, with the border running round.

The edging is worked separately, and sewn on after the sachet is made up. The lining should be of a color to match the hangings of the bed, and of a material to wash with the work.

KNITTED BABY SHOE AND SOCK

These are knitted on steel needles, in Berlin wool of two colors. The shoe in one color, and the sock in white form the prettiest contrast; pink and white, maize and white, or blue and white, are all suitable.

The shoe is in plain knitting, and ought to be worked in tight and even; the sock is in the cable and hem-stitch pattern, the top being completed by two rows of netting, the first row being on a larger mesh than the second, one stitch of the netting in every stitch of the knitting.

A narrow ribbon, the color of the shoe, is interlaced round the ankle, which ties in the front with a bow, and keeps it from slipping off the foot. The row of netting on the fine mesh ought to be in the colored wool.

"TOP OF STOOL"
COLOR PLATE

BRUSSELS EMBROIDERY ON NET

We present to our subscribers a new style of ornamental embroidery, which is especially pretty for many purposes. It is worked on a clear Brussels net, not too fine. The diamonds, which appear crossed, are darned with a fine, soft cotton. These can be worked with the greatest regularity by counting the threads of the net, and keeping them exactly the same size. Leaving one hole of the net between each short length of the darning, as will be seen in our illustration, gives it a much lighter appearance. The alternate diamonds are filled in with a sprig, embroidered in satin stitch, which shows to great advantage on the light net ground.

A COLLAR AND CUFF IN IMITATION OF HONITON LACE

A design which can be worked so as to produce a very close imitation of the Honiton lace-work. The sprigs as they are made upon the pillow are all separate, being afterwards arranged and sewn together according to the individual taste.

In our design the parts touch each other with very few exceptions. It is to be worked on either clear thin French cambric or a Swiss muslin. The design must be traced in *perfectionné* cotton, and sewn over with a very fine one. The centers of every flower are filled up with lace stitches of various kinds, adding greatly to the beauty of the effect. The veins of all the leaves must be carefully and distinctly indicated; in every case a clear and sharp outline is essential.

When the whole of the needle-work has been completed, the superfluous parts must be cut out, and the result will be an elegant collar, closely resembling those formed of the Honiton sprigs.

BRAIDING FOR AN INFANT'S CLOAK

JESSAMINE PATTERN EMBROIDERY ON TAPEWORK

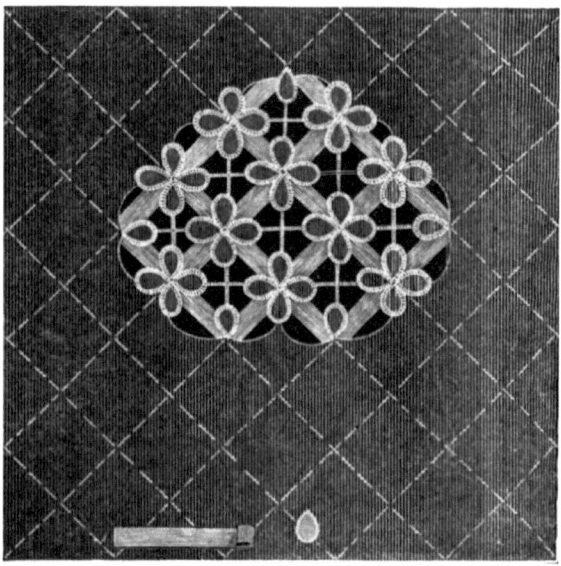

Materials – Cotton, No. 6; embroidery cotton No. 12; a piece of cambric muslin of the requisite size; and tape three eighths of an inch wide, of that kind, which at some shops is called "twilled tape", "India tape", "Chinese tape;" but it is of the kind that will not curl or get hard in the washing, and is rather coarse looking than otherwise.

This is useful for sofa pillows, anti-macassars, for insertion for petticoats, for a deep border for a child's dress, or a deep border round eiderdown quilts.

First measure with an inch measure, along the top and bottom of the cambric, spaces an inch and a half wide; mark these with a hard pencil. These must exactly correspond on each side; now crease it across in diagonal lines, and run a white cotton through the creases, now crease the cambric across the reverse way, and also run in a cotton (if the cambric is a long piece, only a small portion need be done at a time.) Now on these lines of cotton, loosely but firmly run the tape – loosely, because these threads, as well as those of the dividing lines, have to be ultimately taken out; and firmly, that the tape might not slip. Now turn the work on the side where the tape does not appear, trace off the leaf from the engraving, gum it on some stiff card; when dry, cut out the shape. Lay it on the work, at the point where the lines cross each other, and run a hard pencil round. Make four of these leaves in the same way, then, with No. 30 cotton lightly sew the No. 6 cotton round, but not so as to flatten it. Make several of these stars in the same way; then overcast them very thickly with embroidery cotton.

Make the cross bars, one bar going quite across with two threads of embroidery cotton, then overcast with button-hole stitch; the second bar, make also entirely across, but in overcasting, when at the center, catch the first bar with one firm stitch, then finish. The cambric under the bars and on the tape has now to be cut out with sharp scissors

EMBROIDERY DESIGNS

EMBROIDERY FOR AN INFANTS CLOAK

BRAIDING FOR A BOYS BLOUSE

CORNER FOR A POCKET HANKERCHIEF

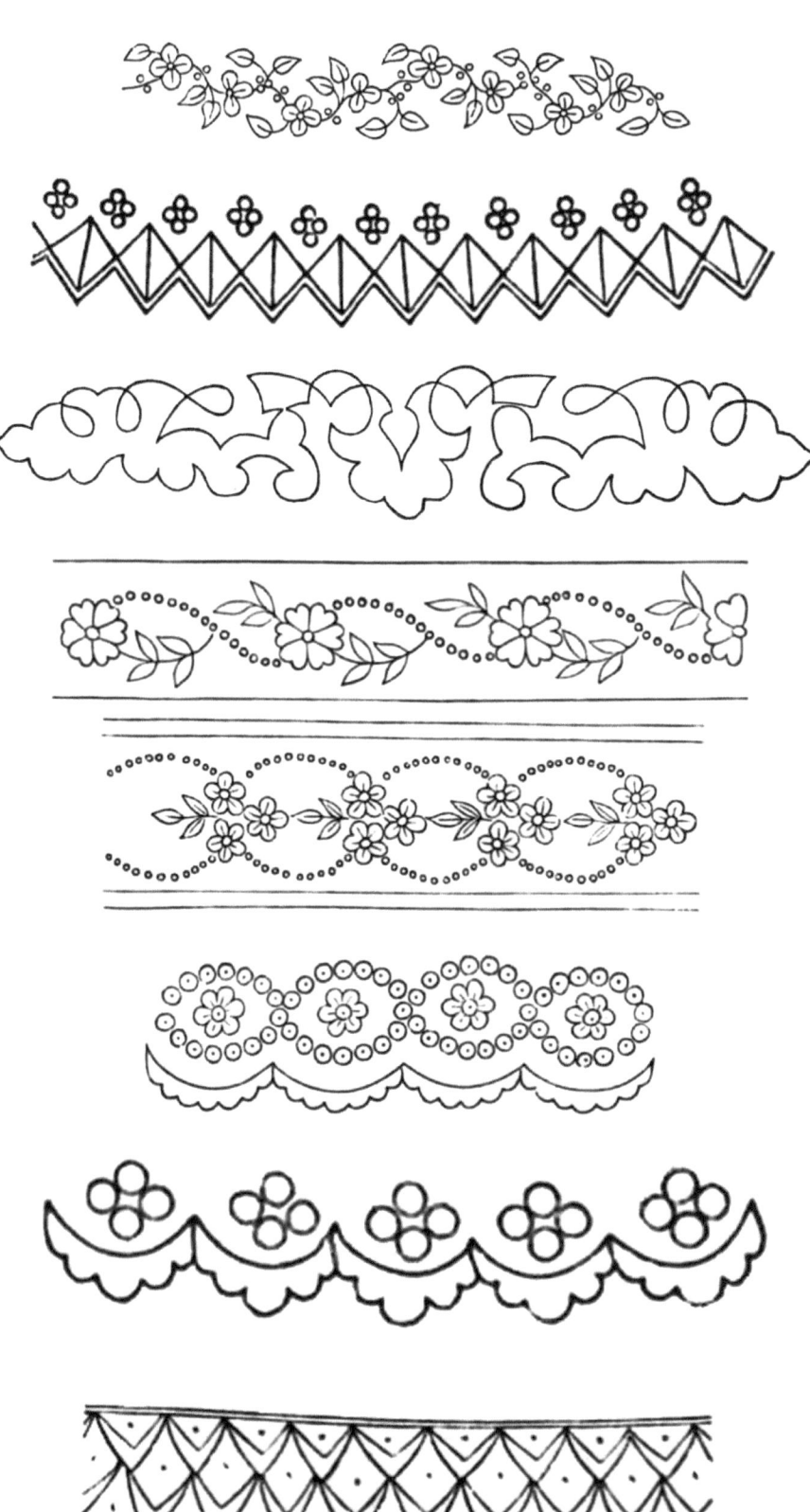

CHAPTER 2
FEBRUARY 1861

DESCRIPTION OF FASHION-PLATE FOR FEBRUARY 1861

Fig. 1 – Dinner-dress, also suited to a small evening party. Dress of Slate colored *poult-de-soie*, the skirt single and ornamented by a rich Greek pattern of *applique* in black velvet, edged by a narrow gold cord and extremely narrow ruche of black silk ribbon; three puffs of black satin to correspond cover the hem of the skirt. The waist is in broad fan-shaped plaits, moderately low. The scarf ceinture, or girdle, a marked feature of the winter dress, has an application of velvet, and is edged with the ribbon ruche. The sleeves are quite new, and in excellent taste. The velvet torsade which crosses the hair is relieved by lappets of the same and blossoms of the yellow jessamine, which relieve its somber style. Pearl necklace.

Fig. 2 – Evening-dress for a very young lady. Robe of embroidered muslin, with double skirt; the lower one has five narrow flounces; the upper has a rich pattern of embroidery to correspond with the flounces. The waist and sleeves are of muslin, drawn in longitudinal puffs, with insertings of embroidery. Corsage cut square on the shoulders. *Ciche peigne* and sash of the same ribbon – a rich taffeta plaid, with a Greek fringe woven in one. Nothing could be more simple or charming for a young lady just coming out.

Fig. 3 – Dinner-dress of taffeta *rose des Alps*, made quite plain; its chief point being the new sleeve, which is tasteful as well as quite new. It is a modification of the Francis First; the fullness being quite at the back of the arm, and caught into puffs by bands of ribbed velvet ribbon, several shades darker than the dress, edged with narrow guipure lace. Headdress composed of loops of ribbon (black and gold), with two full blown roses to the right, the lower one set in black blonde.

Fig. 4 – Dress of delicate brocaded silk, a single rose on a grey ground. Garibaldi coat, fitting rather closely to the figure, trimmed with folds of reps silk; buttons of the same. Bonnet of *rose des Alps*, in velvet: the curtain having an edge of blonde. A half wreath of grapes to correspond with the shade of velvet, alternating with tufts of leaves, falls to the right. A single cluster of grapes crosses the forehead and forms the garniture of the blonde cap, with leaves from the wreath bending under the brim.

Fig. 5 – Bridal morning-dress, elaborate and tasteful; material a rich corded silk, maize shot with black. The waist fits neatly to the figure, with bretelles of satin ribbon *plissé* or fluted; the front of the skirt turns back in a gradual slope, the trimming being continued from the bretelles. The corsage is closed, and the skirt ornamented by bows of gold-colored satin ribbon. The sleeves are a graceful flowing shape, and a small, round pelerine is trimmed to correspond. Hair dressed low, with a black and gold net. Small, upright ruff of embroidered muslin; loose sleeves of the same. Underskirt of plain cambric, with ruffles finished by needle worked points.

Child's Dress – Renfrew jacket and full skirt of ribbed cloth, a new shade of tan color; the jacket has pretty *pattés* of braid, and is trimmed by bias folds of silk, a contrasting shade. Black velvet cap

THE ZOUAVE
(A Negligée Toilet)

From the establishment of G. Brodie, 51 Canal Street, New York
Drawn by L.T. Voigt, from actual articles of costume

We vary our report for this month, and give an indoor costume instead of the pardessus to which we have hitherto confined our illustration. The season for the latter has so far advanced that no further novelties are desirable. Instead, therefore, of them, we present this graceful undress for home wear.

We need only explain that the ornamental design is wrought in gold braid upon a black cloth ground.

This embroidery is much improved by a bright green silk cord, or braid, accompanying the gold, as the harmonizing effect of this color relieves the garish crudity of the metal. The sleeves are also cross-laced with cording to match, completed by tassels.

Velvets, instead of cloth, make extremely beautiful and becoming articles of this description, and any favorite color may be employed.

CHITCHAT UPON NEW YORK AND PHILADELPHIA FASHIONS FOR FEBRUARY

By reference to our ample fashion-plate, which has unusual fidelity to existing modes as well as unusual grace to recommend it, the new Francis the First sleeve, a prominent novelty, will be perfectly understood. The puff at the back is a pointed gore, coming into the sleeve proper just above the elbow, being set in with a slight fullness. The rich velvet and lace bands make it a desirable sleeve, for a handsome material, where a tight one is to be avoided, and something fresher than the pagoda is desired.

The original Francis First is still worn more or less, the last improvement being a band with ends or lappets fastened by a button at the bottom, that is, the under part of the sleeve. Tight sleeves are chiefly made up for walking-dresses, in heavy materials, and then are lightened by puffs and jockeys at the top and often deep-pointed cuff at the wrist. In flowing or pagoda sleeves there is great variety, being principally found in the arrangement of the rimming. The back seam or back part of the sleeve is frequently trimmed richly, or the *fiat*, by which is meant the front, if it were a coat sleeve for instance. In bishop sleeves there is generally a loose cuff, allowing a small undersleeve or frill of lace pointed and prettily trimmed. Elderly ladies find a tight cuff, pointed on top, a very comfortable fashion. The fullness at the top may be plaited and confined by buttons, or simply gathered. We have before us a bishop sleeve, with a very deep close-pointed cuff reaching half-way to the elbow, with a corresponding jockey or cap above the puff. Another good sleeve is a pagoda shape, quite short on the forearm. The *fiat* has a trimming of two ruches, placed parallel with each other so as to enclose a plain bias of silk the width of a ribbon. The dress itself is of violet silk, the ruches are of two shades of violet ribbon, box-plaited in the middle; and at intervals, in the strip thus enclosed, are rosettes of violet-colored silk and black lace. The corsage and skirt have trimmings to correspond, the plain spaces being considerably wider, allowing treble rows of rosettes placed in diamonds. In some of the gored dresses – we mean where each separate breadth of a plain skirt is gored – on edge of each breadth is trimmed and made to lap over the next. It is a pretty style for some materials. Skirts gored in this way insure a good slope, and are generally becoming; but few people like to waste the material, and prevent all future repairs by turnings upside down, where economy is a consideration, as we are glad to suppose it is with most of our readers.

We have just opened a pretty design for a dress of plain silk; the skirt full, the breadths gored without overlapping, and trimmed at the bottom by five narrow flounces, *fluted*, not plaited or gathered on, the upper part only being attached to the dress with a small heading. Between each flounce there is a space of about half an inch; the dress is of black silk, the flounces and headings being bound with white silk. The corsage is plain, and ornamented by a row of buttons, quite large, black with white centers. The sleeves are demi-wide at the lower part, and finished by turned-up cuffs or revers. These are cut with large scallops, and bordered by a narrow fluted frill of black silk edged with white. A similar frill extends up the back seam to the shoulder. The ceinture, or broad sash, is of black ribbon edged with white, the bow quite on one side.

One deep flounce or *plissé* of the same silk as the dress is also worn. If a *plissé*, it should be about fourteen inches deep, headed by one row of wide black velvet ribbon, and several widths of narrow. A wide velvet is placed above the hem of the flounce, which is an inch deep, and corresponding rows of smaller ones.

Another skirt – the dress being violet silk – has three narrow flounces or ruffles around the bottom of the skirt, headed by a *bouillonné* of the same. The corsage is low and made high for ordinary wear by a small round pelerine, coming just on the shoulder, buttoned up in front, trimmed with a puff (*bouillonné*) and two frills. The sleeves are demi-wide, puff at the top; at the bottom the same trimming that is on the pelerine. Black velvet waist ribbon, bow, and long ends.

Shirts having plastrons or a plain piece set on the front, variously ornamented, or side trimmings of lace, ruches, or passementerie, are frequently seen; also plain skirts, with *patées* (straps) of passementerie, mixed with jet or tassels, and most elegant of all, flat bows of guipure lace, are perhaps the favorite style of the larger part of the community the present season. The trimming on the corsage, sleeve, and skirt should always correspond.

The rich *armure* (striped) silks, and those watered in stripes, certainly need very little decoration beyond a white silk facing to the sleeve, with the satin ruche, either white or the predomination color of the dress, placed inside. Fancy buttons are in great demand, lozenge shaped and oval as well as round; and the flat ornaments of passementerie were never surpassed in variety and richness. The fancy for black, corded or turned up with white, which the French artistes give us in consideration of Eugenie's becoming court mourning, first for her sister, the Duchess of Alba, and then for the Empress of Russia, is a marked feature of the season in cloaks, bonnets, and, as we have seen, in dresses. We may come to like it, but the contrast is too startling for immediate use!

The Garibaldi wraps manufactured by Brodie are an improvement upon the design we give, inasmuch as the sleeves are more flowing and buttons are plentiful. It is the favorite garment of the season. The *pardessus circassini* is new. It is made of the same fancy tints in ribbed cloth, dark brown being the best shade. It laps completely from left to right, from the top to the bottom, in an oblique direction, fastened by a row of buttons. The sleeves are extremely full; have three flat plaits on the shoulder, each plat having four lozenge shaped buttons. All the edges of this garment are timed by a border of a new rough wooly or furry texture called *Astracan de laine*.

Bonnets of quilting remain in great favor. There is a novelty which we can scarcely give by description. For instance, a bonnet of dark green velvet, lined with a paler green satin; on each side the lining turns over the edge of the brim in a point, making a revers of the satin on the velvet, which is edged with very fine gold cord. The cape of velvet has the satin lining forming a pointed revers in the same way. These revers, both on the brim and curtain, are fastened by small gold buttons.

Among the best bonnets of the season, one composed of black velvet, is trimmed with ruches and puffs of blonde, a bouquet of damask roses without leaves and a long black ostrich feather, passing along the right side, is disposed much in the same way as on the round hats. A bonnet of black quilted silk has been trimmed with fuchsia color velvet, white blonde, and black lace, and an Agrafe of jet. We may mention another bonnet, composed of velvet of the beautiful tint of the Parma violet. This bonnet is trimmed with passementerie, tassels and ruches of blonde. There is no trimming on the curtain. Several bonnets intended for *negligée* costume are composed a combination of silk and velvet. When feathers are employed in trimming bonnets destined for plain costume, they should be small and in tufts. For bonnets worn in a superior style of outdoor dress, one long feather often forms part of the trimming; frequently it is fixed on the top of the bonnet, and then passes down the side and across the top of the curtain. Some of the prettiest morning caps we have recently seen are of a round form; they are composed on insertion and guipure, and are trimmed with a frill of guipure and bows of ribbon. Morning caps are sometimes lined with silks of different colors, as lilac, blue, etc.

THE MEDORA THE GARIBALDI THE IMOGEN

THE PROMENADE DRESS

Coat of black silk, having at the bottom, a ruffle of purple silk, over which falls a rich lace. The bishop sleeves and small cape are trimmed to correspond. The Zouave suit for a little boy is made of poplin, braided.

THE EUPHEMIA

This dress is of Marguerite colored silk, trimmed with quilled ribbon. The front width of the dress is gored, and the sleeve is a loose coat sleeve, with gauntlet cuff.

CHILDRENS FASHIONS

Dress of Striped Poplin: Two skirts, trimmed with quilled ribbon. The corsage has on it a *Sevigné* cape.

Dress of French Merino: To be embroidered with silk.

INFANTS CHRISTENING ROBE

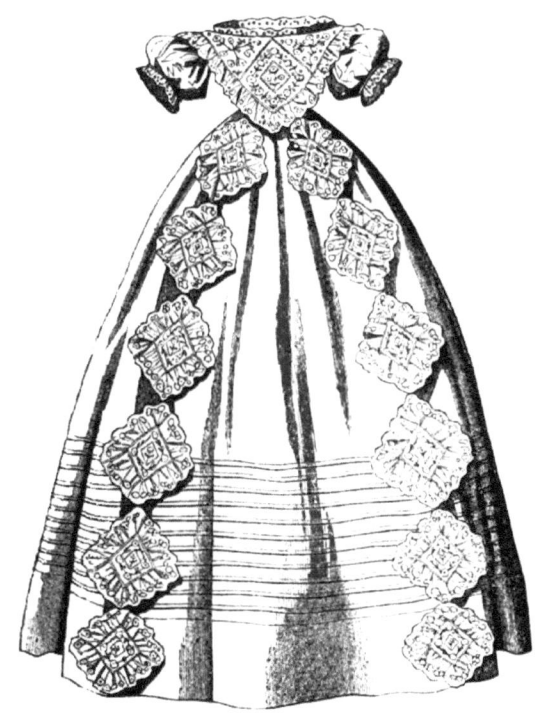

Made of fine French cambric, and trimmed with rosettes made of flouncing.

DRESS FOR A LITTLE BOY
To be made of pearl colored poplin, and braided with Magenta colored cord.

PARTY DRESS FOR A LITTLE GIRL
Made of Solferino silk, braided with gold and trimmed with drop buttons

INFANTS SHORT DRESS
Made of linen cambric, with embroidered side stripes trimmed with flouncing. The waist is made of tucks and inserting.

DRESS FOR A LITTLE GIRL
To be made of rose color or blue French merino, embroidered

A BLACK SILK APRON FOR A CHILD

Trimmed with two ruffles of narrow ribbon, with three rows of narrow velvet above it

A NEW STYLE OF BIB

Made of Marseilles, with rows of machine stitching on it. It buttons round the neck, and is fastened round the waist with a band.

Hoops and Farthingales
Philadelphia February 1861

The merry dames of Elizabeth's court, in a wild spirit of fun, adopted the fashion of hideously deforming farthingales, to ridicule the enormous trunk-hose worn by gentleman of that period, determined, if not successful in shaming away the absurdity altogether, at least to have a preposterous contrivance of their own. The idea was full of women's wit. But, Alas! They were caught in their own snare; precious stones were profusely displayed on the bodices and skirts of brocade gowns, and vanity soon discovered that the stiff whalebone framework under the upper skirt formed an excellent showcase for family jewels. The passion for display, thus gratified, the farthingale at once became the darling of court costume, and in its original shape continued in feminine favor till the reign of Queen Anne, when it underwent the modification lately revived for us – the hoop.

In vein did the Spectator lash and ridicule by turns, the "unnatural disguisement;" in vain did grossest caricatures appear, and wits exhaust their invention in lampoons and current epigrams; in vain even the publication of a grave pamphlet, entitled "The enormous abomination of the Hoop-petticoat, as the fashion now is;" the mode, for once immutable, stands on the

Lady of the reign of George III

page of folly an enduring monument to feminine persistency.

Encouraged by the prolonged and undisputed sway of the farthingale, the hoop maintained an absolute supremacy through the three succeeding reigns, though often undergoing changes which only served to make it more and more ridiculous. The most ludicrous of these alterations were the triangular shaped hoops, which, according to the Spectator, gave a lady all the appearance of being in a go-cart. And the "pocket-hoops," which looked like nothing so much as panniers on the sides of a donkey — we mean the quadruped. In a print, bearing the date 1780 we find this absurdity ridiculed in the figure of a girl so attired placed beside a pannier-laden ass. A droll incident is related by Bulwer about the wife of an English ambassador to Constantinople, in the time of James I. The lady, attended by her serving woman, all attired in enormous farthingales, waited upon the sultana, who received them with every show of respect and hospitality. Soon, however, the woman's curiosity got the better of her courtesy, and she gravely asked if it were possible that such could be the shape peculiar to the women of England. The English lady, in reply, hastened to assure her that the forms in no wise differed from those of the women of other countries, and carefully demonstrated to her highness the construction of their dress, which alone bestowed the appearance so puzzling to her. There could scarcely be a more wholesome satire upon the absurd fashion than is conveyed in the simple recital of this well-authenticated anecdote.

A French paper gives an amusing anecdote of a lady who went to a cathedral to "confess" in a hooped petticoat; of course it was necessary to enter the tiny confessional and prostrate herself before the iron grating between her and the priest. In vain did she make vigorous efforts at the door to compress her unyielding dress; it stoutly refused, swelling like an air bed in all sorts of ludicrous tumors at every new endeavor, until, scarlet with confusion, the lady turned and hastily made her escape, unshriven, with a few additional sins of impatience, anger and wounded vanity to enumerate on her return.

The monstrous appearance of the ladies' hoops, when viewed from behind, may be seen from the following cut copied from one of Rigaud's views (1740).

The exceedingly small cap, at this time fashionable, and the close upturned hair beneath it, give an extraordinary meanness to the head, particularly when the liberality of gown and petticoat is taken into consideration. The lady to the left wears a black hood with an ample fringed cape, which envelopes her shoulders, and reposes on the summit of the hoop. The gentleman wears a small wig and bag; the skirts of his coat are turned back, and were sometimes of a color different from the rest of the stuff of which it was made, as were the cuffs and lapels.

What a curious picture of the "hoop" times do we gain from a play of an early period! "Five hours ago," says one of the characters, "I set a dozen maids to attire a boy like a nice gentlewoman; but there is such doing with their looking-glasses; pinning, unpinning; setting, unsetting; formings and conformings; painting of blue veins and cheeks; such a stir with sticks, combs, cascanets, dressings, purls, fall squares, busks, bodices, scarfs, necklaces, carcanets, rabatoes, borders, tires, fans, palisades, puffs, ruffs, cuffs, muffs, pusles, fustles, partlets, frizlets, bandlets, fillets, corslets, pendulets, amulets, annulets, bracelets, and so many *lets* (stops or hindrances), that she is scarce dressed to the girdle. And now there is such calling for farthingales, kirtles, busk-points, shoe-ties, and the like, that seven peddlers' shops – nay, all Stourbridge Fair will scarcely furnish her. A ship is sooner rigged by far than a gentlewoman made ready."

"For the abolition of hoops at court we are indebted to the taste of George IV.," says *Planché* in his "History of British Costume." Pity it is that they should be revived under a female sovereign; or, if not revived, their place supplied by a contrivance which, if lighter, produces the same preposterous effect. We allude of course to Crinoline, against which we are quite inclined to join in a crusade, as our readers may probably have already gathered.

We commend to their serious attention the following forcible remarks upon the absurdity, not to say worse, of inflated skirts, from a daily paper: - "We have no pretensions to erudition in the specific nomenclature of the various structures of horsehair, basket-work, watch-spring, whale-bone, iron bars, buckram, wire gauze, and osier-plaiting now used by ladies for the purpose of distending their skirts to a preternatural degree of amplitude. It will be sufficient, we trust, to apply the generic term 'crinoline' to all the preposterous fabrics which convert that human form once called 'divine,' and idealized in the Venus de Medici's, into the similitude now of a Chinese tombola, now of a gigantic washing-bowl, now of a great bell covered with variegated silk, now of the receiver of a colossal air-pump. The hideous fashion of crinoline, then, dates its second efflorescence – for, in the shape of hoops and panniers, it flourished with rank luxuriance a century since – from the time of the union of the Countess Eugenie de Montijo with that exemplary public and private character who in 1852 gloried in being a parvenu, and is now hail-fellow-well-met with the *Monsieur mon frère* of the Emperor Alexander. From the adoption of crinoline at the Tuileries resulted certainly in its establishment in the other courts and cities of Europe. It spread like the plague. The trade winds bore it with wide waving wings to the West Indies. The Gulf Stream has naturalized it on the remote shores of the Spanish Main. The primeval female settlers in New York, in the days when it was a Dutch colony, were remarkable for wearing a round dozen of linsey woolsy petti-coats; but the large skirted belles of Broadway and Fifth Avenue now put, with a single under garment, their great-great-grandmothers to shame. Crinoline is an indispensable adjunct of the gala costume of colored persons at 'dignity balls;' and if its pestiferous influence continues to extend itself, we may look for the assumption of this unsightly fashion by Zulu Kaffirs and by the tattooed tirewomen of Queen Pomare."

The extent to which people may be led to disfigure themselves by a blind compliance with the fashion of the day was never more strikingly displayed than in the custom of dotting the face with black patches of different patterns. It might easily be supposed that the annexed sketch is a caricature, but such is not the case; it is a correct likeness of a lady in the time of Charles the First, with her face in full dress. Patching was much admired during the reign of that sovereign and for several succeeding years. Some authors think that the fashion came originally from Arabia.

No sooner was it brought to England and France than it became an absolute furor. In the former country, old and young, the maiden of sixteen and the gray-haired grandmamma, covered their faces with these black spots shaped like suns, moons, stars, hearts, crosses, and lozenges, and some even, as in the instance before us, carried the mode to the extravagant extent of shaping the patches to represent a carriage and horses.

NOVELTIES FOR FEBRUARY

Night-caps for a bridal wardrobe; the most tasteful, and at the same time becoming and serviceable styles that we have given in years

Fig. 1 - Is particularly comfortable; it is cut one piece, and the crown receives the full twist or braid of hair. The frill is put on in a new way, and, together with the band and bow, is of the same material as the cap, fine linen lawn. The frill is scalloped in needle-work; the band and strings have a narrow rolled hem.

Fig. 2 - Is of the same material, the crown coming into the cape, and the band looped instead of tied; the strings are broad, and all the trimming has a needle-work finish

Fig. 3 - Dress cap of white over black blonde; trimming, blonde, full blown rose, buds, and foliage, with a large bow of black velvet ribbon at the opposite side

Fig. 4 – Fichu of black and white lace for evening dress; it is trimmed between the rows of lace by narrow black velvet, and a rosette of the same, with long loops, fastens it at the waist

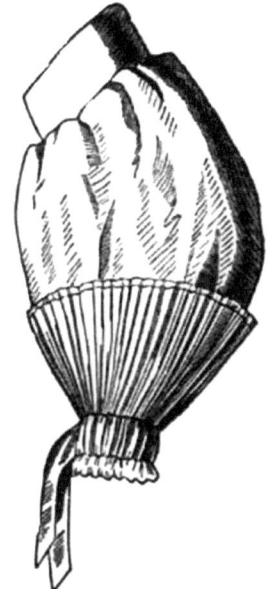

Figs. 5 and 6 – Undersleeves for morning wear, of Tarleton, French muslin, or crape; they set close to the wrist with frills of the same materials

A MUSLIN NIGHT DRESS
With yoke and trimmings of heavy *piqué*

NIGHT DRESS WITH PLAITED YOKE

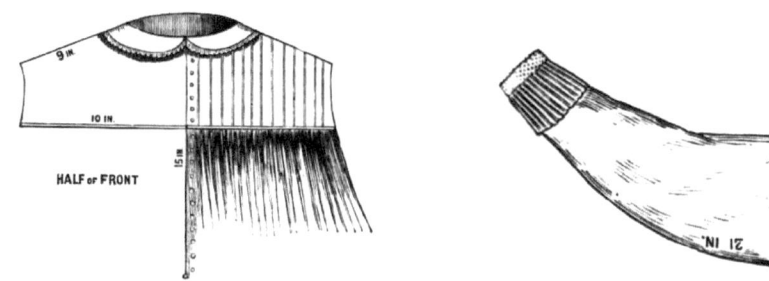

The yoke is not cut off, but plaited on the whole piece, and cut into shape afterwards, the plaits being confined by a narrow band stitched on both edges

CHEMISE PATTERNS

CRAFTING & NEEDLE WORKS

BAG TO BE BRAIDED ON VELVET OR CASHMERE

Gold braid on velvet or cerise on black cashmere are both pretty. To those that are unacquainted with the method, of transferring the designs to velvet, or any dark material, it would be as well to say that the pattern should be drawn on thick paper, and then carefully pricked. Then the pattern should be laid over the material to be worked, and some powdered starch or whitening rubbed over it; on removing the pattern, the design will be traced in white spots, which are then to be followed out with a camel's hair pencil and white lead.

THE CINDERELLA SLIPPER

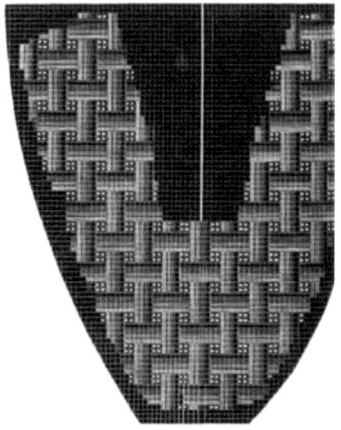

Materials: Two skeins, each of four shades, of scarlet wool, the darkest to be the color of a dark clove pink, the next of a military scarlet, the next two shades lighter, and the next two shades lighter again; one bunch of No. 6 steel beads; one quarter yard of Penelope canvas, that which measures twelve double threads to the inch; four wool needles; and one reel of No. 30 cotton.

This pretty slipper is adapted for a child four years old, but may be made either larger or smaller. Its glittering appearance, which sparkles with every movement of the foot, has an exquisite effect. As a morning slipper for young ladies, it cannot fail to please; for fancy fairs, it would also prove a very saleable article.

First pencil from the engraving the outline of the slipper in thin writing or other paper; then cut it exactly in the pencil marks; pin or tack it on the canvas; then, with needle and black cotton, tack an outline on the canvas outside the paper all round, but observe to have only 16 stitches across the instep; fasten the cotton off securely, and run a black thread through the center between the 16 stitches.

Now, with the darkest wool, cross-stitch over this outline of cotton. Then commence to work the slipper thus; Begin first stripe close to the line of instep, but two stitches of the canvas from the center thread of black, and having the heel of the slipper at the right hand; with the lightest shade on the 2nd row of canvas from the center work 8 cross-stitches; then slip the needle under four threads of canvas, and work 8 more stitches; slip 4; work any that may be left in same row. Take the 3 next shades, and work exactly the same. Thus there will be two rows of wool stitches on each the dividing line of black thread.

2nd stripe — Miss 2 rows of canvas; miss 4; work 8; miss 4; work 8; miss 4; work the remainder with the remaining three shades exactly the same.

3rd stripe — Miss 2 rows of the canvas; work 8; miss 4; work 8; miss 4; work 8; miss the remainder, and finish the stripe towards the heel in similar manner.

It will be scarcely necessary to give any further directions for this pattern, which latter must be worked entirely over the slipper before proceeding to work the bars across, which are worked exactly in the same way; but, instead of slipping the needle under the canvas, the needle will be slipped under the 4 worked rows; but observe that all the stitches are crossed in the same direction. The intersection of these bars will cause 4 stitches of canvas to be left between each bar (see engraving), and these 4 stitches are filled up with steel beads, thus: Take No. 30 cotton, doubled, and fine needle; fasten the cotton into back of slipper; thread two beads; cross these over the stitch of canvas the same way as the wool stitches are crossed; then 2 more over next stitch, and the same over the other 2 stitches of canvas. Thus there are 8 beads in each 4 stitches of canvas; but, as the beads would wear off round the sole, and round the edge of the slipper where the binding comes, fill these squares in with steel colored twist or silk used double. The slipper should be trimmed with a rosette of scarlet or cerise color satin ribbon, of a tint not to obscure the brightness of the wool.

INDIAN CANOE WORK-BASKET
For Carrying on The arm, With A Little Piece of Work or Knitting

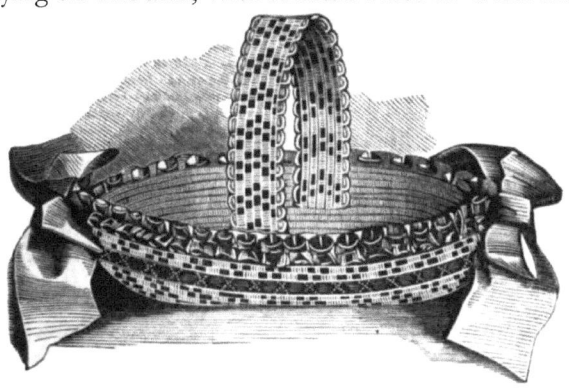

Materials: One ball of crochet cord, gray or drab; one knot of colored satin cord; satin ribbon, and a coarse crochet hook.

Make a chain loosely, nine inches long and work on it one row of sc. Then hold on the cord, and work over it, 4 stitches, 2 ch, miss 2, 1 stitch over cord; 2 ch, miss 2, repeat to the end. At the finish of the row, cut off the crochet cord, but not the satin, which bend back along the next row, and work in the same way; only the last of the four stitches must come on the second chain stitch after the four of the previous round.

The third row the same.

The fourth you again bend back the satin cord, and do the same stitches, making the fourth crochet stitch come over the third of the last row.

In the fifth row, the satin cord is, as in the third, ready to work over; do the same as the fourth. After these five, cut off the cord nearly close.

Do one row of sc without the satin cord. Then the open row, thus: 1 long tc stitch, 1 diamond open hem: repeat to the end. Then a row of sc.

Now resume the satin cord; repeat the five rows with it, and the three without, until five cord stripes are done. Do one row of sc, and then a row round; that is, on the foundation chain as well, to close the two sides for the top of the basket.

With a needle and crochet cord, join up and fasten the threads at the two ends.

Run a narrow ribbon through the open rows under the diamonds, and over the straight bars.

Make the handle exactly like one stripe, with the satin cord; with a simple scallop edge on each side, thus: *1 sc on each ch, 1 sc over sc. Inserting the hook in the row beneath it. * repeat to the end. The handle should be about eleven inches long, and sewed inside the basket, which may be lined with silk, or not, according to the taste of the worker. The ends of the basket are drawn, so as to be rounded. Quill some ribbon, and set it on round the top, with a bow of broader ribbon at each end.

The diamond open-hem is worked thus: begin with the thread three times round the work, as for long treble crochet: do half the stitch, having drawn it twice through. Pass the thread twice more round, miss two, and work an ordinary long tc stitch, only draw the hook through at the third movement; 2 ch, put the thread at the third movement; 2 ch, put the thread once over the hook, and do a dc stitch where the two bars join. A perfect cross or X is thus made.

THE RAILWAY STOCKING
To be worked in cotton thread or worsted

When on the leg   When first knit   When done and stretched

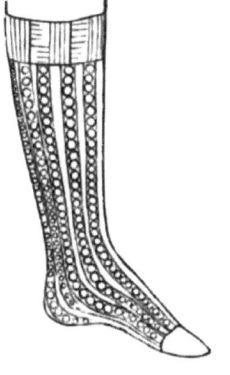  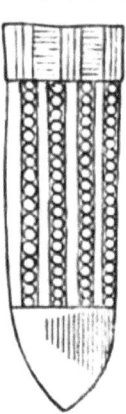

Cast on the needles as many stitches as would be required for an ordinary stocking for a child. Knit it once around, then rib it until an inch long, then bind off. Take up the stitches and commence knitting straight around plain stocking stitch until you have a finger and a half done; then knit once around, dropping every other stitch off the needle; then stretch out the stocking, and the stitches will run down until it reaches the ribbed piece, and so farther, forming a beautiful open worked stocking. Having kept the remaining stitches on the needles, finish off the toe by knitting straight around, narrowing every time on each needle. It will shape itself on the leg and still be sufficiently long, as it only requires two fingers in length for a lady's stocking

KNITTING BASKET

Perhaps there are few kinds of work which require a basket expressly arranged for their own reception so much as knitting, on account of the almost fatal injury which it sustains when needles are drawn out and loops are dropped. The central opening is in bright blue Berlin wool, as well as the small part within the loop at each end. The ground within the diamonds is in maize-color. Both of these are much improved by being worked in floss silk. The ground on the exterior of the design is shaded crimsons, dark medium, and light. It requires three pieces of this form to make the basket; the two sides must be worked alike, but the third, which is the bottom of the basket, only requires to be worked in the stripes of the shaded ground. All three must be stitched on card-board of the same shape and size, neatly lined with silk or German velvet, and sewn together on the outside, the stitches being concealed by a row of beads. After this the handle must be attached, which may be of double wire, twisted round with a little cotton-wool, and then with ribbon and beads. All this being done, a silk cord must be taken, the end fastened down close to the handle, and the cord wound round and round, each twist touching, but not over-wrapping the last, until about an inch and a half of the end of the basket is enclosed, this being an important point for the safety of the needles.

A NORWEGIAN MORNING OR BONNET-CAP IN SHETLAND WOOL

Materials: Half an ounce each of cerise and white Shetland wool; two steel knitting plus, No. 12; crochet hook, No. 2.

Cast on 240 stitches. K (or knit) two plain rows *; now knit one stitch; take two together; knit 115 stitches; take two together, and take two together again; now K the remainder, taking two together before the last stitch. The next row back is plain; now repeat from * till there are 18 ribs of knitting in which there are 36 rows alternately decreased and plain. Take the white wool – knit three rows in the same way, which is one rib and one row, decreasing as before: K one stitch; take two together; wind with wool twice over the pins; take two together, wind twice over the pin again till there are 41 holes; then take two together twice; make 41 holes again; take two together; K 1; now knit three rows plain, again decreasing as before.

Now with cerise wool, knit six ribs or twelve rows, decreasing as before. Then with white the same as the first white stripe. Then continue with white and cerise alternately till there are four white and four cerise stripes irrespective of the first deep border. Now, with cerise, knit 16 rows, decreasing as before. This finishes with one stitch. For the border stitches, with 1 ch between each L; in one loop of the knitting 3 ch; 2 more L as before in an equal space to the 3 ch; this is along the front only. 2d row, 9 L with 1 ch between each u the 1 ch; 1 ch de between next 2 L; 1 ch 9 L with 1 ch between each u next; 1 ch repeat.

along the front, with cerise, make 2 L This last row is worked with the knitting at the back within the row of L stitches. Run cerise ribbon in the alternate holes of the white rows, and the same in the alternate L stitches of the border.

THE KNITTED WINTER SPENSER

Materials: Seven skeins of dark fleecy four-thread; one skein each of grey fleecy, four shades; No 8 pins; No. 1 Penelope crochet hook.

Stitch Brioche, thread forward, slip 1, knit 2 together, the same backwards and forwards.
Cast on 141 stitches, knit 2 plain rows.
Knit 40 rows.
Knit 4 ribs besides the outside half rib.
Increase, do this by picking up two of the back stitches with the right hand needle, placing them on the left, wool forward, slip 1, knit 39 ribs, increase as before, knit 4 ribs.
Knit 10 rows
Knit 5 ribs, increase, knit 39 ribs, increase, knit 5 ribs
Knit 10 rows.
Knit 6 ribs, increase, knit 39 ribs, Increase, knit 6 ribs.
Knit 10 rows.
Knit 7 ribs, increase, knit 7 ribs, cast off 2 ribs, knit 21 ribs, cast off 2 ribs, knit 7 ribs, increase, knit 7 ribs.
Pass off the fronts on to a thread, knit 44 rows for the back, increase a rib on each side nearest the shoulder.
Knit 10 rows.
Decrease by casting off 1 rib 8 times – that is, 1 rib at the beginning of each row; there will be 8 ribs, and 7 ribs on the top of the neck.
Knit a plain row, cast off.
Take up the front, knit 7 ribs, increase, knit 7 ribs.
Knit 10 rows.
Knit 8 ribs, increase, knit 7 ribs.
Knit 30 rows.
Increase a rib the side nearest the shoulder.
Knit 10 rows.
Cast off three ribs, and then decrease every row equally till to a point.

For the Sleeves
Increase a rib, knit 60 rows, decrease a rib, knit 22 rows, cast off.

Cast on 81 stitches, knit 22 rows. Work 4 rows of long stitches in crochet all round with the four shades of gray fleecy.

KNITTED CUFF IN BRIOCHE

Materials: Six skeins of colored four-thread Berlin wool; one skein of black Shetland wool; No. 15 pins; No. 2 Penelope crochet hook.

Cast on 57 stitches, knit two plain rows, knit 70 rows, knit two plain rows, cast off. Sew up the cuff. On the side that was cast off make 5 chain, de into 2d loop, 5 chain, de into every second loop. With Shetland de under the 5 chain, 5 chain, de under next five, 2 chain, twist the wool twice over the hook, 7 long under next 5, 2 chain, repeat.

Do under the 2 chain, 5 chain, de under the 2 chain, 5 chain, de under the 5 chain, 5 chain, repeat. Five-chain, de under the 5 chain, repeat.

WINTER CUFFS IN DOUBLE KNITTING

Materials: White four-thread Berlin wool, and four skeins of scarlet; two bone or wooden pins of such a size that a string put tightly round shall measure half an inch.

Double knitting is one of the best stitches that can be used for comforters, cuffs and chest-protectors, also for babies' cot-covers, being very light, soft, and elastic, and not liable to get hard in the washing, and of course, being double, the warmth is very great.

For a Lady's Cuff — Cast on in scarlet wool 56 stitches and for a gentleman's 66 (the number of stitches must always be even). Knit 4 plain rows, then join on the white, and *; knit 1; bring the wool in front (but not over the pin). Slip 1, pass the wool back. Repeat from *. Each row is precisely the same. Observe that the last stitch of each row is always slipped, and also that the back-loop in each row is the one which is always slipped.

EMBROIDERY PATTERN FOR A PIANO STOOL

To be worked in cloth or velvet, with chenille or wool, or else on canvas, and the ground filled up with some dark color which will throw out the figures well. The Footstool in this number is to be worked the same way.

A CRAPED NECK-TIE

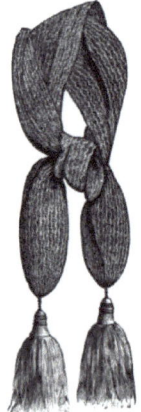

Materials: Cotton, No. 60; a pair of bone knitting pins, No 12; two lumps of sugar dissolved in half a pint of hot water, and let remain till cold; two chenille tassels.

This is one of the prettiest articles for a neck-tie that can be made; having, when finished, all the appearance of soft white crape, and may be adopted either in mourning or out, by adding either black, colored, or white tassels. Cast on the pin 460 stitches, and knit in plain garter-stitch till it is five nails wide; then cast off, but not too tight; then sew a strip of calico on to each side, but only so that it can be easily untacked. If the work is at all soiled, wash it with white curd soap and water; then rinse it perfectly, and squeeze it in a cloth very dry; after that dip it in the sugar and water, squeeze it slightly, and lay it out on a doubled sheet to dry; afterwards take off the calico, sew it up, and add tassels. The washing and rinsing in sugar and water will always give it the appearance of being new.

EMBROIDERY DESIGNS

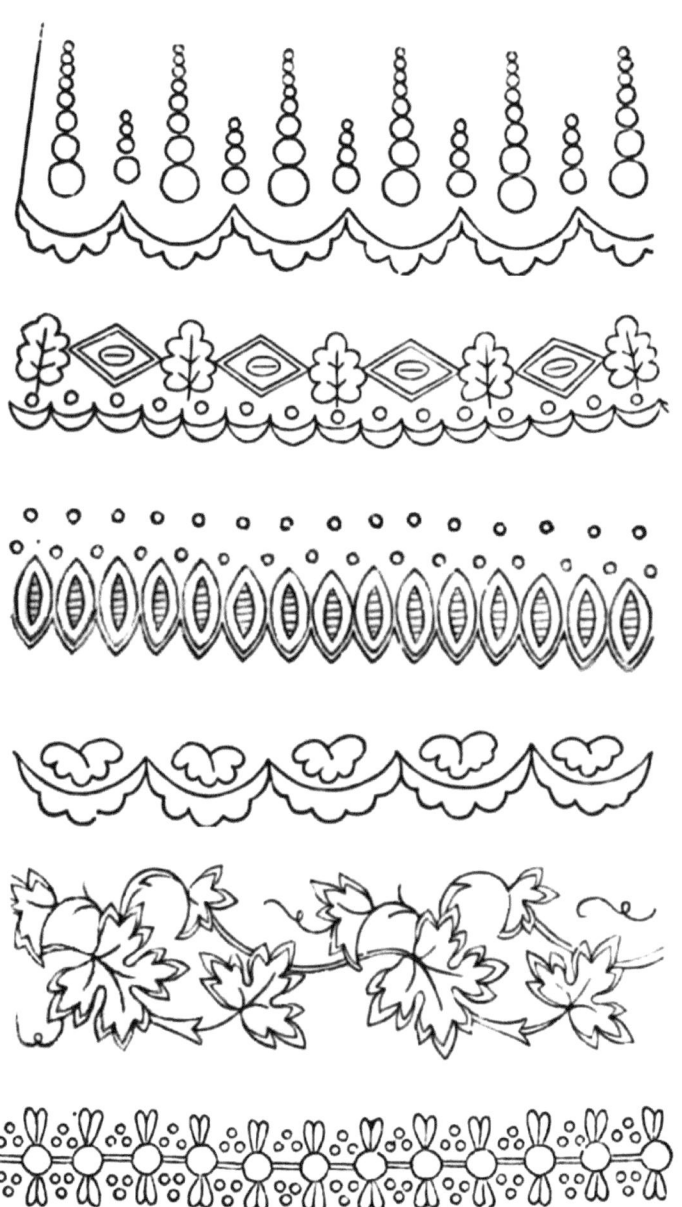

CHAPTER 3
MARCH 1861

DESCRIPTION OF FASHION-PLATE FOR MARCH 1861

Fig. 1 – Dinner dress of pearl colored *poult de soie*, trimmed with lilac silk and quillings of narrow ribbon. The overskirt is gored, of one piece with the body slashed at the side, and caught together by bands of lilac silk, and finished with three tassels. The underskirt is full and not gored. The cap is trimmed with ribbon and flowers to match the dress.

Fig. 2 – Child's dress of Solferino silk, flounced up to the waist; low neck and short sleeves. Garibaldi coat of light silk, finished with pinked ruffles. Hat of white straw, trimmed with black velvet and a long white ostrich plume.

Fig. 3 – Black *moiré* walking dress, with deep puffing on the skirt. The body is composed of velvet and *moiré*, the lower part, both back and front, being of velvet, trimmed with puffings. Sleeves flowing, and trimmed with *moiré* puffings. Straw bonnet, bound with gold color, and trimmed with a gold colored net, with cord and tassels; strings and cape of Solferino ribbon.

Fig. 4 – Rich promenade dress of green silk, with black velvet stripes made perfectly plain. Bonnet of white silk covered with black lace, with a bunch of black flowers, having gold centers at the side, a black and white ruche inside; gold color strings.

Fig. 5 – Dress of tan-colored silk, trimmed with flounces of the same, and bands of Marguerite silk edged with black lace, having at intervals *pattés* of black gimp; body trimmed *en bretelle*; sleeves puffed, and quite small at the wrist. Ceinture or girdle of wide tan colored ribbon, with lace inserted at the ends, and trimmed with fringe. The headdress is a net of Marguerite chenille, with two large tassels at the side.

Fig. 6 – Evening-dress of white muslin, puffed half way up the skirt, and a short tunic of rows of puffs and inserting edged with lace. Plain corsage, pointed behind and before, and laced up the back.

The bertha is formed of folds of illusion in the *Sevigné* style, and trimmed with a fall of *point applique* lace. The under-sleeve is of muslin puffed, and quite short; over this is a demi-angel sleeve of illusion, edged with lace. Coiffure of green velvet, with gold pendants.

CHITCHAT UPON NEW YORK AND PHILADELPHIA FASHIONS, FOR MARCH

The season is unusually late in opening, owing to the financial embarrassments of midwinter, the time when most of our large importing houses are usually beginning to receive their goods. Large orders for expensive novelties were countermanded, others were delayed, and we are now seeing the effect of these things.

There is one department of dress goods in which, it is sadly true, there is always a certain demand. Death does not delay his work for any commercial crisis; and perhaps the earliest orders that reached Philadelphia were intended for the *Masion de Deuil of Besson & Son*, 981 Chestnut Street. This well-known house keeps steadily on its way; and since their removal to the elegantly neat place of business now occupied by them, its excellent light, so necessary in the selection of black goods, proves that theirs are always reliable. A "good black" is always the first thing to be considered in the choice of mourning. If it be rusty or gray, no matter how costly the material, the effect is shabby. For deep black, the material most in vogue for summer wear will be *barége grenadine*, a less costly article than the real grenadine; for though of much the same tissue, it is of mixed wool and silk, while the other is all silk. It will range from 50 cents to $1 a yard in price. Real grenadine, always in vogue, may be had, according to quality, from 75 cents to $1.50. A very serviceable article, that will be in general wear the present season for house dresses in plain black, is the old favorite Balzarine, which is afforded as low as 18 cents a yard. There are also Tomatan's and crape *bariges* from 31 to 62$^{1/2}$ cents. There is a disposition towards making up English crape over black silk – the dress and mantle alike – for best wear. It is truly elegant, but expensive, though certainly the most suitable material together with grenadine, for evening wear.

We have now come to second mourning goods, in which there are both novelty and variety; and though they are "only calicos," we must admire it in passing, the neat and varied designs of Hoyle's prints, in purple, mauve, and gray, upon a black or white ground.

Barége Anglais is still expected to be the popular fabric for street dress in the summer heats, both in and out of mourning – large importations have been made. At *Bessen's* we find some entirely new designs in black and purple, gray and white, white and lilac, etc., distinguished by the dotted, striped, and *chinée* grounds, and a set figure *printed* upon the material; as for instance, a mauve pansy without leaves, on a black ground.

In foulards, this point of set figures is still more noticeable; as, for instance, a purple pansy, or a white Marguerite on a black ground.

Where there are two colors combined the figure is called *Cammaieny*; when it is woven to stand out like embroidery, it is known as *brochée* or Jacquard.

In travelling dress goods, which are also serviceable for general spring wear, as well as the foulards, there is the Syria poplin, the India *glacée*, gray Valencias at 62$^{1/2}$ cents, and black and white Cruvellis at 37$^{1/2}$ cents, a large variety. These will be worn much the same by people in or out of mourning.

In first mourning, black crape collars and cuffs on grenadine or crape sleeves will still continue to be worn. The English fashion of adding a gold thread to the *appliqué* pattern in crape, may find favor in New York, and at the South, but scarcely in neat, plain Philadelphia, where mourning usually *is mourning*, and not a mass of crape bows, bugles, and tinsel. There is the usual variety of white Tarleton collars and cuffs in folds and piping; but the novelty of the season is a laced *appliqué*, the figure being traced in a satin stitch with embroidery silk, which gives it a pretty effect. The lapel style is still in favor, though many prefer the round collar, with a small point behind, coming straight across in front to meet the brooch, extremely narrow and very neat.

In the foulards for ordinary wear, the same styles are shown in colors upon a mode or dark, plain ground. Pansies, clusters of berries, fruit, as the cherry, the plum are among the newest designs; following the Jacquard figures on the silks, and rep goods of the past winter. These same designs will also be reproduced upon the *barége Anglais*, the Valencias, and other thin wool, or silk and wool tissues. So of the light spring silks – but of these next month.

The shape of bonnets is much less of a poke than last year; flatter on top, and more open at the ears. A drawn lining for straws of crape, silk, or satin, with the edge projecting a little to form a tiny fluff of the material, when seen from the outside. The tendency is to discard blonde ruches altogether for bands, rolls, and plaitings of ribbon, plain blonde, and flowers. There is a great variety of braids, mixtures of gray and brown *orin* prevailing, and some delicately-fine Dunstables and split French straws; chip is also seen with rice straw. Leghorns are the only straw bonnets seen on the street, as yet.

Puffed sleeves, whether in a straight graduation from the shoulder to the wrist, or two above the elbow terminating in a tight sleeve below, will be worn for the plainer materials, early silks, etc.; the black velvet point, or bodice-girdle as it might be described, is suitable for the same materials. It is a very favorite style, nearly superseding the broad scarf-girdles.

Madame Demorest, at 473 Broadway, has a dressmaking department in the charge of an unusually obliging and competent lady; a great convenience to her numerous customers in patterns and crinoline. Wedding or travelling outfits, mourning orders, etc. receive prompt attention. We have seen a traveling outfit undertaken in the two days' notice, and thoroughly well executed, arranged from the ever fresh and artistic styles of the *Moniteur, La Mode*, and other reliable Parisian authorities.

Cotton Balmoral petticoats, in the same neat, light colors that have distinguished those in wool, silk, and wool, etc. the past winter, will be found a most serviceable article for spring wear, or for travelling through the season. They are much lighter, and of course cooler than those our readers are generally familiar with. They are much lighter, and of course cooler than those our readers are generally familiar with. They are also suitable as an underskirt for equestrians. We close with some sensible suggestions as to costume, from a contemporary we should be glad to credit, with the good sense of the advice to ladies who ride, very suitable for this season of the year. In our next we shall have fuller descriptions of bonnets by Mrs. Scofield and others, Brodie's Spring wraps, etc. etc. As to riding dress –

"To begin at the top, the present style of round brimmed straw or beaver Spanish hats (not wide brimmed flats), so fashionable for young ladies' travelling headgear, is an admirable riding-hat. It would be best to leave off the lace and head-frill usually worn, as this might dash about the eyes and obstruct the sight in case of a flurry. Plumes could be added with charming effect. Dress the hair low back, and if gathered in a net, according to the present style, so much the better. It is always annoying to have their hair get loose and go flying about while on a lively ride, unless it is dressed on purpose to float at will. The underclothes have much to do with the grace of a riding costume. Hoops and all other devices for making the dress stand out must be positively dispensed with; and all starch goods, either for underskirts or outside habit. It does not alarm us nor shock us to see the flutter of a white petticoat or an embroidered skirt, but when such things make a show on the field, it is a sure sign that the lady is not dressed right.

"A sleeved chemise of light flannel stuff, a single short petticoat of the same, trousers to match the outside habit, rather full and gathered at the ankle in an elastic band, and buttoned about the side at the waist, is a bill of under-costume that sits well and tells no tales, while the horse is showing his best paces. Gaiters or morocco boots with heels, and long stockings, of course, will complete the footgear.

"The habit may be of soft cloth, merino, or velvet, according to the taste and convenience of the wearer, but never of any stiff or starchy material that will flap about and float up to expose the under garments. Besides, all grace is marred by the action of a habit that will balloon about, and fill and flap like a foresail. Let the habit come well up and plain about the throat, the sleeves close at the wrist, the skirt no more than half a yard longer than a walking-dress, and if for riding upon a low horse, one-third of a yard extra is long enough.

"It is neither safe nor elegant to see an over long skirt flapping about the horse's legs, or dragging up dirt or mud. The jacket may be made separate from the skirt if desired, but there the habit is made whole there is less danger of its getting out of fix, and when once buttoned up in front, the lady may feel safe that she is dressed, and not likely to be surprised by having her garments parting company just at a time when she needs her hands to take care of her horse. A few bars and buttons upon the bosom of the jacket, and a narrow linen collar are about all that are desirable in the way of further ornament. Add to the above a pair of gauntlets."

SPRING FASHIONS MARCH 1861

Fig. 1 – A Magenta colored silk, with tunic skirt, trimmed with one flounce. The skirt does not meet in front, in order to show the front breadths of the lower skirt, which are trimmed *en tablier*, with three flounces each, five inches in width, and headed with a quilling of black velvet, having a gold braid sewed in the center of it. The Waist is trimmed with a bertha of one flounce, and the belt is black and gold, with a heavy gold clasp. Bonnet of pansy colored silk, trimmed with mauve satin buttons and god cord.

Fig. 2 - Dress of Marguerite silk, made perfectly plain. Mantle of rich thread lace, trimmed at the bottom with a looped fringe, and finished at the neck with a very *recherché* hood. Bonnet of straw, trimmed with light green velvet, lace and Narcissus, with black hearts. The inside trimming is a thick roll of green velvet, a small bunch of flowers on the right side, and short tabs.

Fig. 3 – A brown spring silk, with six flounces bound with brown velvet. Mantle of same material as the dress, trimmed with a wide puffing, Flounces, bows, and velvet. Bonnet of plain silk, drawn and trimmed with ruchings of illusion.

Fig. 4 – Dress of rich mauve silk, with black velvet stripes. Circassian pardessus of black reps silk, trimmed with wide black velvet, having on each edge a thick cording of white silk. Bonnet of white velvet, lined with Solferino silk, and trimmed with flowers of the same tint.

THE MONACEDA

From the establishment of G. Brodie, 51 Canal Street, New York
Drawn by L.T. Voigt, from actual articles of costume

We commence in this issue to present the styles which await the favor of our friends. There is in this mode, an elegance and simplicity that will render it a great favorite. The material is in black silk, with a passementerie of great beauty.

SHORT HAIR FOR LADIES

"I know, Mr. Godey, to an absolute certainty, from both *reason* and *experience*, that short hair would be a great comfort and convenience, and a *real blessing* to woman-kind everywhere. Any intelligent lady or gentleman must admit that it is a great tax upon us to have so much hair to be done up and arranged every day, and sometimes oftener, for a common lifetime – amounting to many thousand times – just to suit a foolish fashion, and because our mothers and grandmothers did before us. Men have not submitted and will not submit to this inconvenience, yet women have to.

Long hair, to the sick and afflicted women everywhere over the world, is absolutely a burden, and to all others it is a great and useless inconvenience. And where is the "glory" of all "its fair length," so much talked about, when done up in a knot on the back of the head? It is nonsense to talk of its *length* as its chief element of beauty when that quality is forever concealed from human gaze, as it is in the done-up style, which makes it to all intents and purposes even shorter than the men's.

Where then is its beauty? Are these knots of hair on the back of our heads so very handsome? This round, knotted, imprisoned mass which gives us a conception of anything else except the length of a lady's hair? Must we sacrifice the health of the hair, its freedom, its flowing nature, the comfort of the wearer, the natural shape of the head, and all things else, for the sake of the *length* of hair, which, after all we do not get to see in the done-up style; not even as much as in the flowing short style.

Let me briefly show in contrast the points of difference between short hair and done-up hair. When the hair is cut to a convenient length in the neck we have the freedom of the hair, its health, the comfort of the wearer, it's downward flowing nature, which poets so much admire, and which is the natural condition of the hair, and we have the natural shape of the head, always beautiful; the undergrowth of hair behind at the junction of the head and neck, is all concealed; besides, the hair, when cut evenly around in the neck, forms a most beautiful silken border, and the color of the hair in contrast with the whiteness of the neck forms one of the most brilliant, beautiful, and angelic contrasts in the world. Then we have a greater show of the length of the hair.

Now, contrast all these points of beauty with the entire lack of the same in done-up hair, and then let anyone decide which style is the most beautiful. And how grandly flowing hair for women corresponds with, and how symbolical of her own gentle, flowing nature! Now, Mr. Godey, I submit the points I have made in favor of the convenience, comfort, and beauty of short hair for woman – which are but a few things that can be said in its favor – whether the blessings that would flow from it would not justify considerable effort on our part to change public sentiment in its favor? I have every reason to believe, from those whom I have talked with, that there are thousands in our land who would adopt short hair at once were they not over-awed by adverse public opinion. But they think, like thousands of others, that they might almost 'as well be out of the world as out of the fashion.'

Mr. Godey, I know you have the interest and welfare of woman-kind at heart, and now will you aid me a little with your advice, counsel, and instructions in my efforts to change public sentiment in favor of the benefits, comforts, and blessings that short hair would give to woman-kind everywhere? Please answer soon, if it suits your convenience and pleasure, and instruct me how I can best deal with this subject to insure success."

SPRING BONNETS

Fig. 1 – A Neapolitan braid, gray and white, trimmed with Solferino and gray ribbon drawn into rosettes on one side, with straw centers, which give them much the appearance of poppies; a long loop of ribbon and two straw tassels complete the trimming of the left side, and on the other side the ribbon is drawn down perfectly plain. The cape and front of the bonnet are finished with a puffing of Solferino crape. The inside trimming consist of a band and tabs of illusion.

Fig. 2 – An English chip bonnet, with pansy colored velvet cape. On the right side of the bonnet are two bows of pansy ribbon worked with gold stars, and on the other a large bunch of scarlet flowers. The inside trimming is of ribbon and flowers.

Fig. 3 – Fine split straw, with dark crown, trimmed with a sapphire blue ribbon, and a white ribbon. On the right side of the bonnet is a large waterlily, with buds and leaves. The inside trimming is a roll of sapphire blue velvet, black tabs, and a small lily on one side.

Fig. 4 – A Tuscan braid, trimmed on one side with white ribbon bound with black velvet, and black lace rosettes with jet centers; and on the left side are handsome jet tassels fixed by medallions of white gimp. The inside trimming is a puffing of white illusion, and large black rosettes, with jet pendants. This is a beautiful style of bonnet for light mourning.

NOVELTIES FOR MARCH
"Juvenile Fashions"

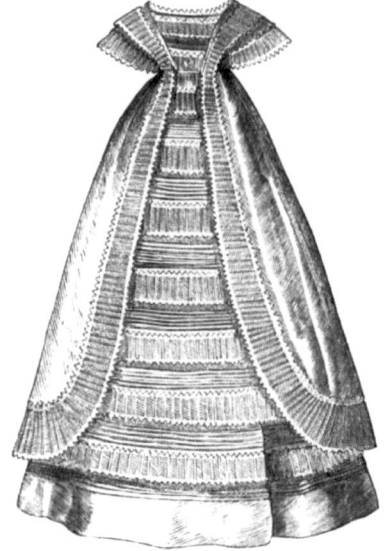

Fig. 1 - Christening robe, en tablier (apron fashion); the front breadth is trimmed across with alternate groups of fine tucks, and a quilled or fluted cambric ruffle, with a needle worked scallop. The tunic has a trimming of the same, and forms revers each side of the waist. Sleeves to correspond. Many prefer inserting to alternate with the tucks, as it is less trouble in ironing.

Fig. 2 - Embroidered cambric dress for a child approaching short clothes; the sleeves are in a puff; the round yoke is covered by an embroidered bertha.

Fig. 3 - Dress of Chambray cambric, any pretty solid color. The skirt has two groups of plain bands, set on with a colored cord, the same color but a darker shade, and these bands have needle-worked scallops of the same. Straight waist, in flat plaits

Fig. 4 – Poplin dress with a peasant chemisette of cambric; the dress trimmed with a ribbon ruche.

Fig. 5 – A very serviceable apron, in fine bird's-eye, with worked cambric ruffles or simple edging.

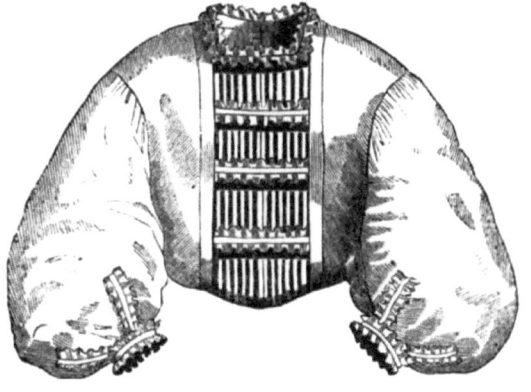

Fig. 6 – Shirt for Zouave jacket; square neck, trimmed with fluted ruffle. The bosom is formed of plaits and small ruffles fluted.

Fig. 7 - Bertha made of thin muslin, and trimmed with puffs, with rows of black velvet between them. The lower part of the bertha is cut in waves, edged with a worked ruffle, and on each wave is a black velvet rosette.

Fig. 8 - Gauntlet cuff for top of glove; made of black silk, with velvet inserted, and braided with gold braid.

Fig. 9 – Neck-tie of green silk; the part going under the collar is cut to fit the neck; the ends are embroidered with gold braid, and trimmed with black lace.

Fig. 10 – Tie of cherry silk, cut the same as *Fig. 9*; ends embroidered with gold braid, and spotted with gold beads

Fig. 11 – Neck-tie of velvet, with embroidered ends.

THE GARIBALDI SUIT

PLAIN MORNING SLIP FOR AN INFANT

To Be Made of Brilliant
Child's Gaiter, to be made of cloth or velvet

Childs Legging, for cloth or velvet

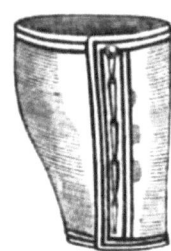

CHILD'S GARIBALDI
Made of velvet cloth, bound and trimmed with a bright colored silk

CRAFTING & NEEDLE WORKS

WHAT-NOT BRAIDED IN A NEW STYLE

Materials: A piece of fine green cloth, stamped according to the engraving, for the back and front of the What-not; one piece of gold colored Russia silk braid, one piece of crimson purse silk, four yards cord (gold and green), and four tassels to match.

There are two novelties in this pretty what-not: one is the shape, which is extremely elegant; the other is the mode of braiding, which is done, not by taking the stitches through the soutache, but across it at regular distances, with silk of a contrasting color. It is thus possible to harmonize three colors in the same article; and indeed, the work quite loses the appearances of ordinary braiding. The ends of the braid must be drawn through to the wrong side of the cloth as usual.

It is afterwards to be made up, over stout cardboard, and lined with crimson or gold colored silk. There is a plain piece at each end, the back and front being about two inches apart. The lining should be set on in plaits here and there. The bottom has a layer of wadding under the silk, and the edges are finished with silk cord. One pair of tassels hangs from the cord by which it is suspended; the other two are placed at the corners in front.

The colors selected should be such as will suit the room. Brown cloth with gold colored braid will always look well, whether crossed with green, crimson, scarlet, or blue. This style of braiding may be employed for any other purpose with excellent effect.

A NETTED D'OYLEY

Materials: Cotton, No. 12; steel mesh, No. 12

Beginning with one stitch, and increase every row till you have forty-six stitches. Net one row without any increase, and then reverse it, and decrease it by taking two together at the end of the row. Before daring the pattern, let the square be washed and stiffened.

For the Border: With a flat mesh the following size:

Net three into every one; then, with a smaller round mesh, net two rows all round. They should be darned with knitting cotton, No. 20, and care taken to fill the holes well in, as they wash much better.

CHEESE DOYLEY IN CROCHET

Materials: No. 12, 16, or 20 Crochet Cotton

This neat pattern of D'Oyley is to be worked in ordinary square crochet, and forms a neat and appropriate ornament for the table, besides at the same time performing a very acceptable duty as a protector of cheese from the myriad of flies, which often times swarm upon the festive board.

DANCING DOLLS

To the young beginner this is a very easy pattern to commence and practice upon. If our young pupils have any difficulty in cutting out by the eye, without drawing, they can procure a sheet of tracing paper; by placing this upon the object and going over the outline with a soft black lead pencil, then reversing the tracing and placing the pencil lines upon the paper you wish to cut out, and going over the back of the same lines with a sharp-pointed pencil, the outline of the pattern will be clearly marked out. But it is much better to attempt and cut out the subject without drawing at all, as practicing both the eye and the hand at the same time.

Take a piece of thin writing paper, and fold it four or five times; double the same again and cut out the half, *Fig. 2*. When opened out they will make *Fig. 3*; and by cutting out two sets of four or five each, and fixing the hands together with a little gum, they can be made to form the circle as in *Fig.* 1

Fig. 2

Fig. 3

BRAIDED SLIPPER PATTERN

Materials: Velvet or cloth, with gold, silver, or Russia silk braid.

This design, though simple, will be found very effective. The slipper may be marked either in the French style (the fronts and sides separate), or joined at the heel.

It would be extremely pretty worked in chain-stitch, with shaded silk, and with an outline of gold thread

KNITTED ARTIFICIAL FLOWERS
(White Garden Lillie)

6 petals, 6 stamens, 1 pistol, are required to form each flower; 2 knitting needles, No. 19, and a skein of superfine white Shetland wool.

Cast on four stitches.
1st row – slip one, purl two, knit one
2nd row – make one, purl one, knit two, purl one
3rd row – make one, knit one, purl two, knit two
4th row – make one, purl two, knit two, purl two
5th row – make one, knit two, purl two, knit two, purl one
6th row – make one, knit one, purl two, knit two, purl two, knit one
7th row – make one, purl one, knit two, purl two alternately at the end of the row
8th row – make one, knit two, purl two alternately to the end of the row
9th row – make one, purl two, knit two to end of row; knit last stitch plain
10th – make one, purl two, knit two to end of row; purl the last stitch
11th – make one, knit one, knit and purl two alternately to the end of row

You will now have 14 inches, making 7 ribs; continue these 7 ribs until you have knitted a length of 3 inches from the beginning of the work. Break off the wool, leaving a bit long enough to thread a rug needle; with this needle take up 7 stitches, which you must fasten off; then the other 7, and fasten in the same way, which completes one petal. Take a piece of fine wire sufficiently long to leave a small bit at the end for a stalk, and sew it neatly round the edge of the petal with white wood, which will make it in form.

Pistil – Cut a length of wire of about eight inches, fold a bit of green Berlin wool in six, and split in two another bit of the same wool, place this lengthwise with the other wool, and place the wire across the wool, fold the wire down, and twist it as tightly as possible, thus inclosing the wool; turn down the shortest end of the split wool, and twist the longest round it and the wire, so as to cover them evenly; fasten the wool with a slip-knot at the end of the stem. Cut off a part of the green wool at the top, so as to leave merely a neat little tuft of wool at the end of the wire.

Stamens are made in the same way as the pistil, merely using yellow Berlin wool instead of green, and covering the stem with white instead of green. Place one stamen with every petal, twisting the wires of both together. The pistil is to be placed in the center of the flowers when made up. Sew the petals together, leaving them open about an inch at the top, as neatly as possible, and draw them close at the bottom, twisting the stems together.

Buds – Several buds are required; the large ones are of a very pale shade of green, the smaller ones of rather deeper color. They look best in double knitting, and should be done in different sized from twelve to twenty stitches. Knit about an inch of these different widths, and open them like a little bag. Take a piece of coarse wire, double some common wool about the thickness of your finger, put it across the wire, which must be folded down and twisted very tight; put this wool into the little bag, and gather the stitches of the bud at the top, catching the wire with your needle to fasten it. This will form the shape of the bud; fasten the stitches also at the bottom, and cover the stem with green wool split in two.

Leaves – Different shades and sizes are required. Begin them all at the top, casting on four stitches; they look best in double knitting, without putting the wool twice round the needle; increase one stitch every second or third row, till you have eight stitches for the smallest, and sixteen for the largest size. Continue to knit without increase, till the leaf is the required length. The longest must be placed at the bottom of the stem when making up.

To finish a leaf, pull your needle out and thread a rug needle with the wool, and pass it through the stitches so as to form a little bag, into which you must insert a bit of double wire: catch this at the top or sides to fix it and it will keep the leaf in shape. Draw the wool tight on while the stitches are threaded, and twist the wool at bottom round the little stem.

The next operation consists in mounting the branch. Begin at the top with the smallest bud, round the stem of which some green wire must be twisted. Fix it at the top of a piece of bonnet wire, the length required for the long stem; continue to twist the wool round, and thus fasten the second bud, and the rest in the same way, at very small intervals. The flowers are fastened in a similar manner, according to taste, adding the leaves as needed.

Six buds, three flowers, and eight or ten leaves, form a beautiful ranch.

Although the petals of the lily can be made up with the wool as it is, they look much better if, after being knitted, they are washed with a little blue in the water, and quickly dried, before the wire is put round them.

LUTE PINCUSSION

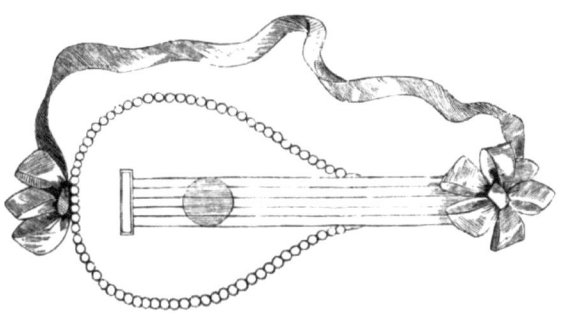

This little article is made in the following simple way: Cut two pieces of cardboard to the shape given, cover them with colored satin or velvet, lay a small spot of black velvet on the one intended for the front, and fasten it down with a few stitches in silk. Then take some fine gold thread, and make the long stitches to represent the strings of the lute; sew the two pieces together, attach a bow to the end, stitch a row of pins all around, and the little article will be completed.

QUILTING DESIGNS

EMBROIDERY DESIGNS

COLLAR IN EMBROIDERY

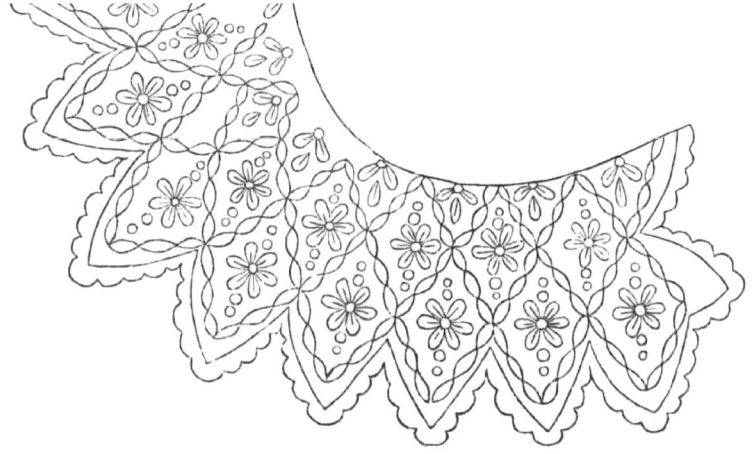

BRAIDING PATTERN

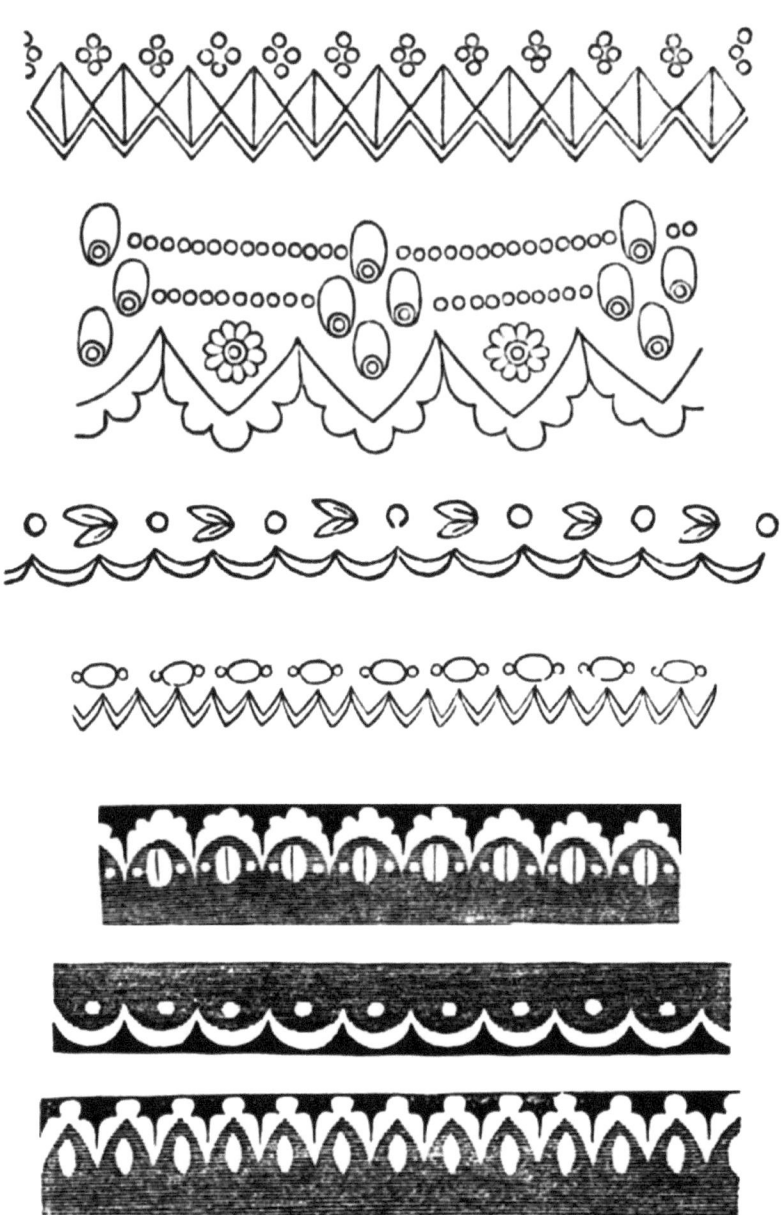

IMPERIAL BASQUINE FOR A LADY

This garment, for winter, is made of stout cloth or velvet; for summer, thin cloth or silk. When made of cloth it has a pretty binding or narrow velvet turned over the edge; when silk, it is trimmed with guipure and has velvet buttons.

The skirt of the side piece of the back laps over on the skirt of the back, so as to form a plait like that seen in men's coats. At regular intervals, large buttons like the trimming fasten the two skirts together. The sides remain open, but require a trimming similar to that of the back.

In front, the skirt laps over on the side-piece and offers the same repetition of trimming as the skirt of the back.

No. 1 – (Back) Half a yard in length and width to be added to the pattern
No. 2 – (Side Piece of Back) Add 10 inches in length and 12 in breadth
No. 3 – (Front) Add 17 inches in length, and 23 inches in width. It is fastened by large buttons
No. 4 – (Side-Piece of Front) Add 8 inches in length, and 26 inches in width
No. 5 – (Under-Side of Sleeve)
No. 6 – (Upper-Side of Sleeve) It is to be trimmed like the shirt.

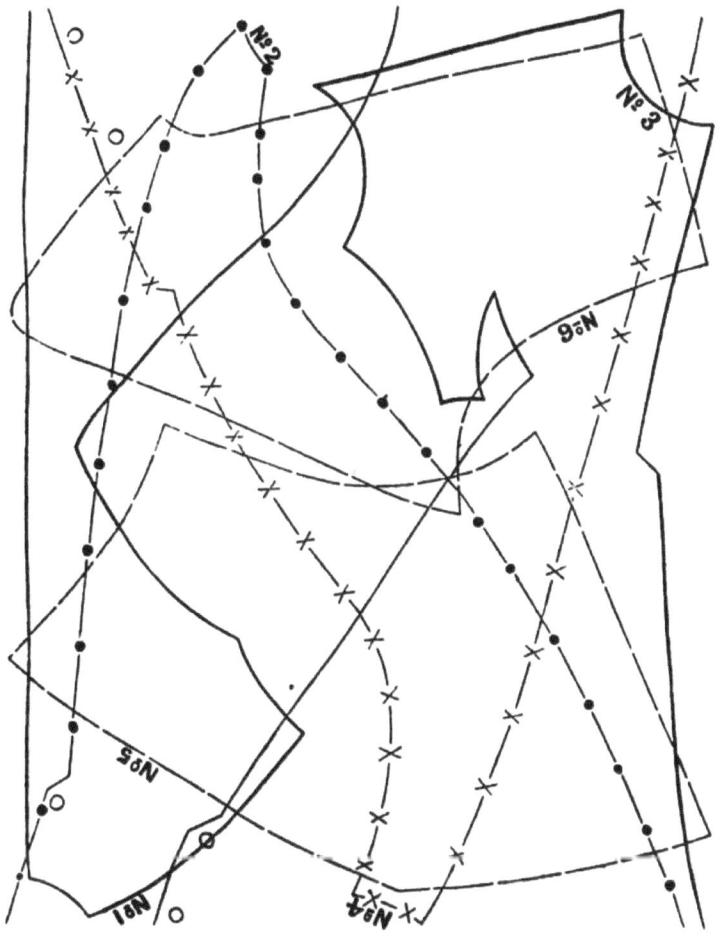

IMPERIAL BASQUINE PATTERN PIECES

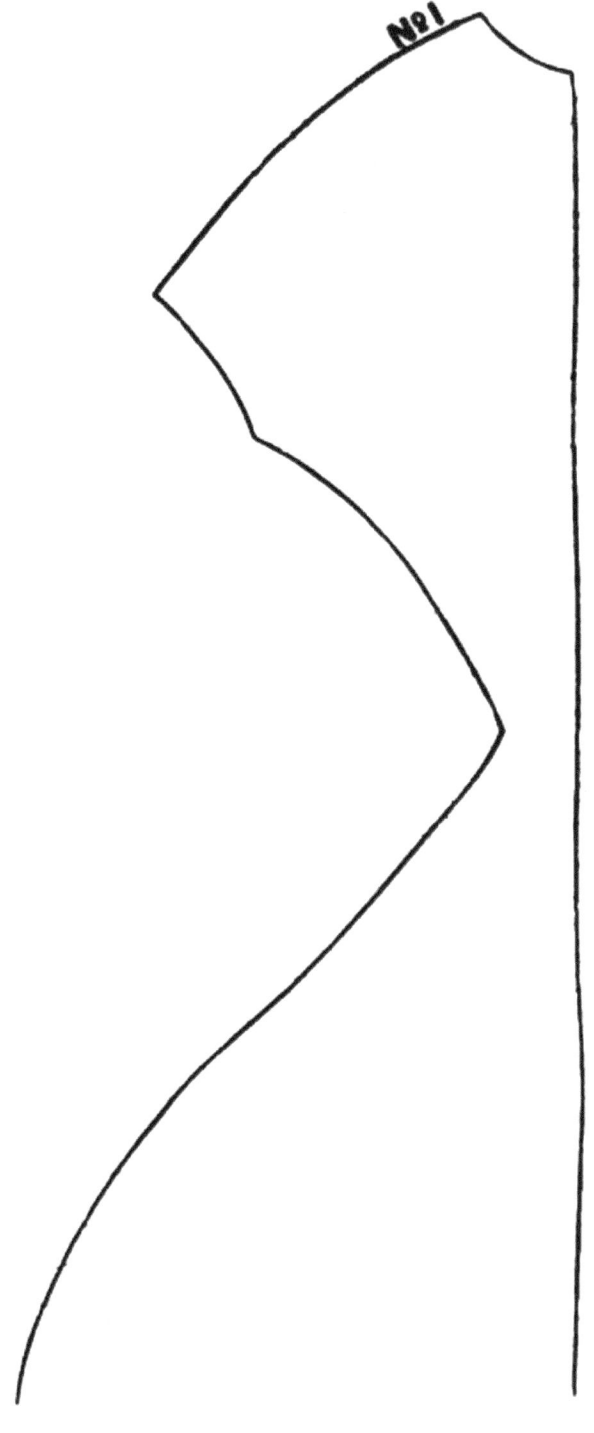

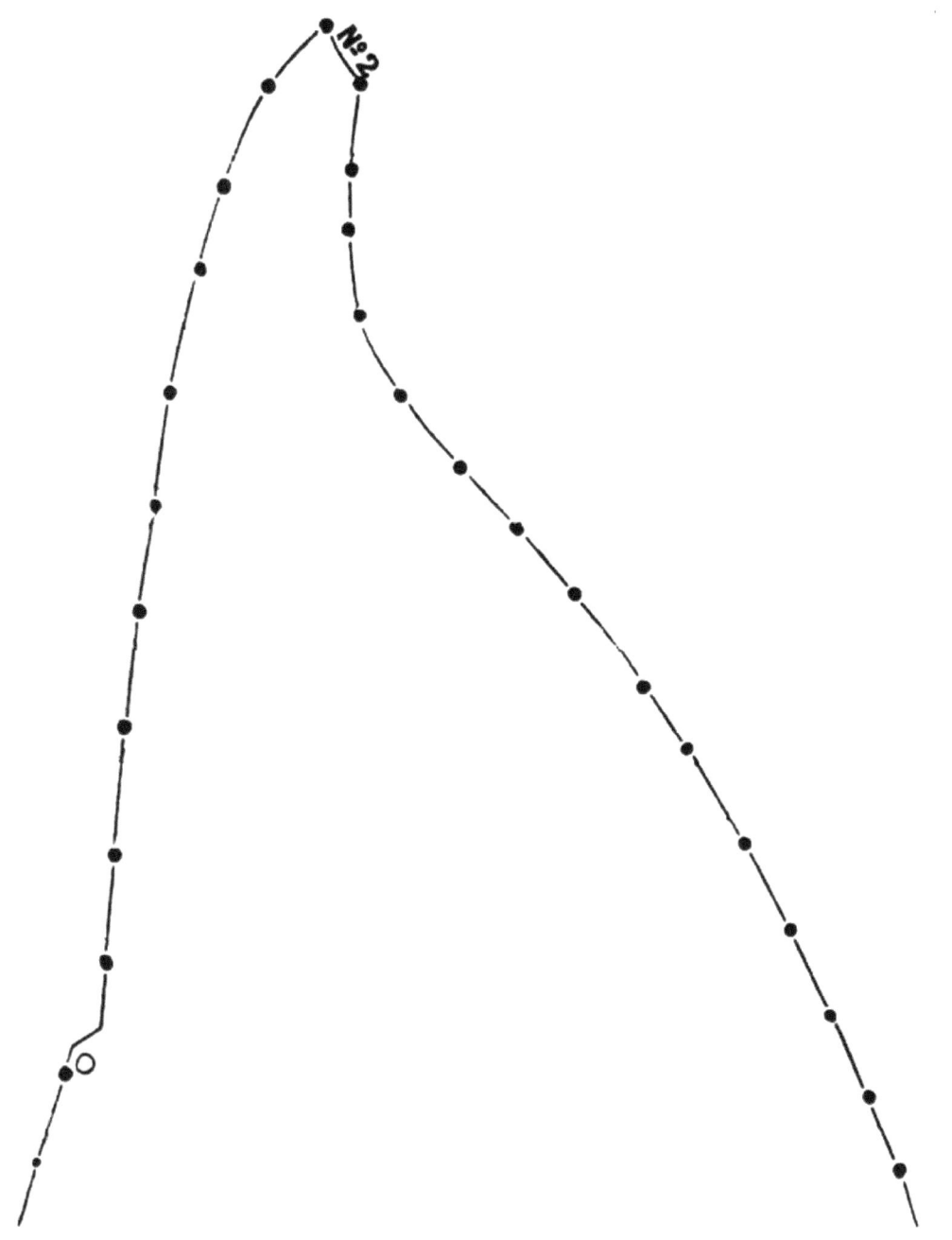

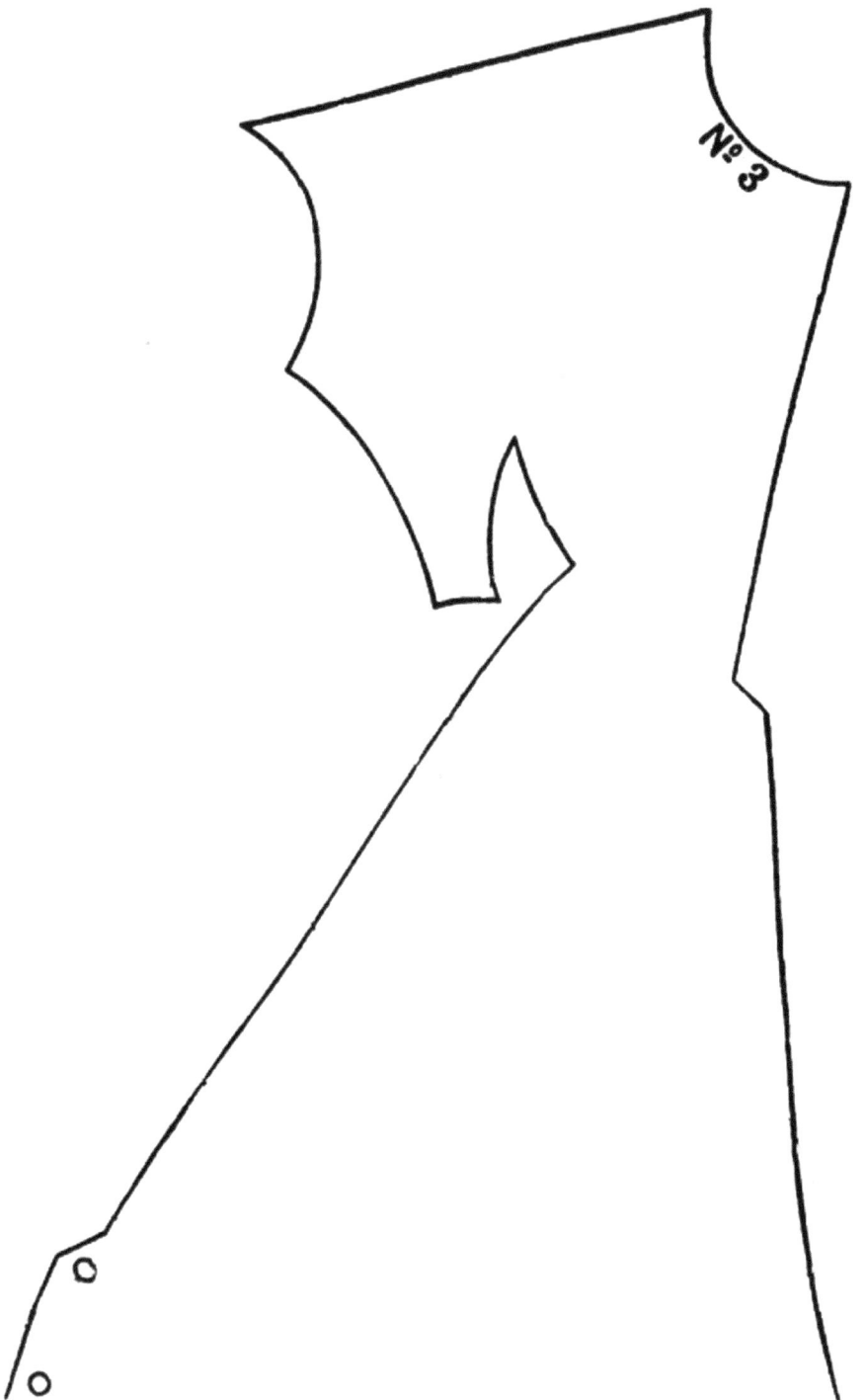

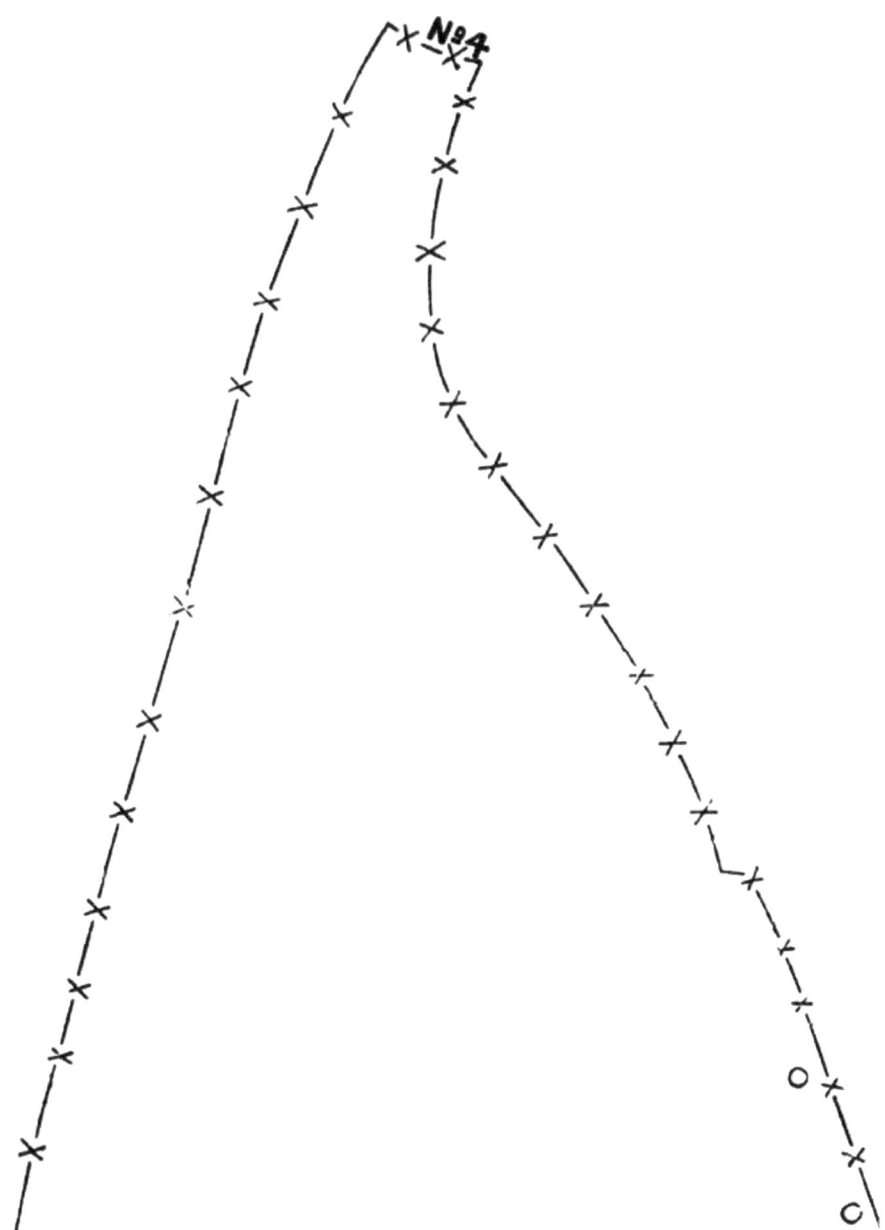

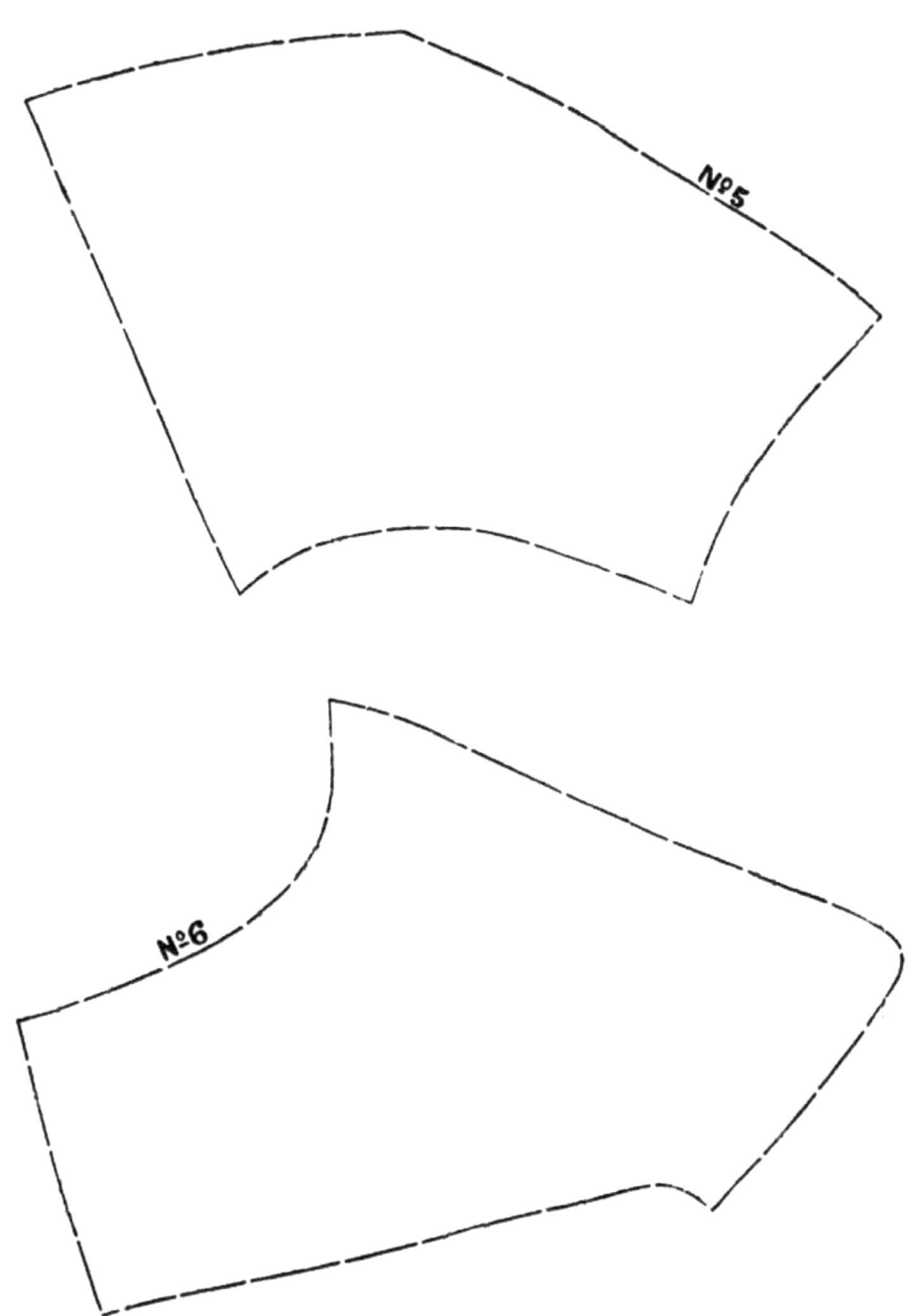

CHAPTER 4
APRIL 1861

DESCRIPTION OF FASHION-PLATE FOR APRIL 1861

Fig. 1 – Child's walking-dress of blue cashmere, with small round pelerine. The dress is braided with very narrow black velvet, and has long ends of the cashmere, braided, fastened to a belt falling at the back.

Fig. 2 – infant's robe, elegantly embroidered *en tablier*: trimmed with blue rosettes; wide sash of blue ribbon, and cap trimmed to match.

Fig. 3 – Nurses' dress of brown de laine, with narrow frill at the neck.

Fig. 4 – Dress of lavender-colored silk, with nine graduated flounces bound with lavender silk, relieved with black velvet stripes; sash bound with the same; body plain, trimmed with folds of the material, crossing from right to left in front; angel sleeves, trimmed with a puffing of the silk, and caught together with narrow bands. Straw-colored gloves, with two buttons, and worked with lavender-color. Bonnet of rice straw, trimmed with fuchsia-colored ribbon and Marguerites of the same color.

Fig. 5 – A wine colored silk, with three flounces bound with black velvet and a puffing at the bottom of the skirt; then three flounces graduated in their width, and a puffing put on in festoons, each festoon being caught up with a large ribbon bow and ends; body trimmed *en berthé*, with two ruffles and a puffing; sleeves loose, and trimmed to match the skirt. Ribbon sash, with bow and ends. Gloves worked with wine color, to match the dress. Frill of lace round the neck.

Fig. 6 – Green silk dress, having the front breadth gored, and nine very small ruffles at the bottom of the skirt; a row of buttons down the front of the dress; body plain; sleeves with caps, and trimmed at the bottom with box plaits and ruching. Point lace collar and sleeves. Leghorn bonnet, trimmed with bunches of cherries; the bonnet ribbon has also cherries worked on it. Gloves worked with green.

CHITCHAT UPON NEW YORK AND PHILADELPHIA FASHIONS, FOR APRIL

At this season, when everyone is wearing straw bonnets and everybody buying them, the expense of Leghorns and the so-called Tuscans, our English or French straws, is often a matter of wonder and questioning. We are sure our readers will be interested in an account of their manufacture, before we go on to chat of their shapes and styles. Leghorns come as perhaps our readers know, in the shape of a flat, round mat, and from it are cut and pressed into any prevailing shape.

"It is chiefly in the neighborhood of Florence, Pisa, the district of Sienna, and in the upper part of the valley of the Arno, that the best mats are made for straw hats. In these countries, whole families, old and young, may be seen occupied at this kind of work; and it is certain that this branch of industry brings in a very large sum annually to the country. The cost of the raw material is inconsiderable; but the value of the work is so great that the women of the Valley of the Arno commit their domestic affairs to people from the mountains, that they may be able to devote all their time to the lucrative manufacture of straw plait. The following is the information which the author of this notice has obtained relative to this kind of industry. The straw used in working these mats is grown in districts mountainous and sterile. It is produced from a kind of wheat, of which the grain is very small. This straw, though slender, has much consistency, and the upper part of the stalk being perfectly hollow, is easily dried. It is pulled out of the earth before the grain begins to form. After being freed from the soil which adheres to the root, it is formed into small sheaves to be winnowed; the part above the last joint of the stem is then plucked off, which is from four to six inches long, the ear remaining attached to it. This being done, it is bleached alternately by the dew and the sunshine. Rain is very injurious to it, and destroys much of its whiteness. When a sudden shower comes on, everyone is in motion gathering up the straw. The lower parts of the straw are treated in the same manner, and employed in forming mats of an inferior quality The upper parts, torn off just to the knot, are sorted according to their degree of fineness. This sampling is made with much care, and usually affords straw of three different prices. A quantity of straw worth three quarters of paoli ($4^{1/2}$ d.), after having undergone this process, is sold for ten paoli (4s. 7d.). The tress is formed of seven or nine straws, which are begun at the lower end, and are consumed, in plaiting, to within an inch and a half of the upper extremity, including the ear. All the ends of the straws that have been consumed are left out, so that the ears shall be on the other side of the tress. As fast as it is worked it is rolled on a cylinder of wood. When it is finished, the projecting ends and ears are cut off; it is then passed with force between the hand and a piece of wood, cut with a sharp edge to press and polish it. The tresses thus prepared, are used so that a complete hat shall be formed of one piece. They are sewed together with raw silk. The diameter of the hat is in general the same; the only difference consists in the degree of fineness, and consequently, the number of turns which the tress has made in completing the hat. These hats have from twenty to eighty such turns, the number regulating the price, which varies from 20 paoli (9s. 2d.)

to 100 piastres (upwards of £20). Those of the first quality have no fixed price. A hat which sells for 100 piastres affords a profit of 40 to the merchant; the straw and silk costing 20 piastres, and the labor 40 piastres. The workers gain about three or five paoli (1s. 4d. or 2s. 3d.) per day. Several mercantile houses at Florence and Leghorn buy these hats on the spots where they are worked. There is one of these houses which annually export them to the value of 400,000 florins (£3,500). French speculators have tried to cultivate this sort of straw, but they have not been able to obtain so fine a quality as that of Tuscany."

Many of the Leghorns this season are simply and gracefully trimmed with a plume of feathers on one side, and in the inside is a roll of velvet, with a small feather or bouquet of flowers. Tabs are not so much worn this spring; they are replaced by the roll or bandeau of velvet, and the full inside lining described in the last chat, but this style is not generally so becoming as the soft lace tabs. Clusters of cherries make a pretty trimming, as shown in Fig. 6 of our fashion late.

For travelling bonnets we notice at Mrs. Scofield's many of plain-colored silks trimmed with silk, forming a great contrast. The shapes are not as drooping over the face as they have been during the past winter, but stand high from the head, and are of medium size. English spit straws and thin lace straws will be much worn, the fronts being bound with a wide ribbon, violet, apple green, Havané, and lilac being the favorite colors.

Hats, no so universally worn by ladies at watering places, and also much liked for travelling, are of great variety this season; they are trimmed with pheasants' and other game birds' feathers; the graceful Coque plume is also much worn. We see a number of turban shaped hats for children, handsomely trimmed with plumes.

For walking dresses, plain silks or small stripes are much in vogue; the skirts are much timed up the front with fan shaped ornaments of silk edged with lace, *pattés* of velvet and lace, etc. etc.; *bouillonnés* and ruches are much in favor; also, small flounces at the bottom of the skirt; many are seed on in waves. We notice a very *recherché* dress of wine colored silk with five small flounces at the bottom of the skirt, then a row of bows placed *d volonté*, then five more small flounces; the body is plain, with a point; sleeves loose, and trimmed with flounces and bows to match the skirt.

Pierrot buttons and bows up the seams of every breadth, and three rows on the body, and velvet *pattés* are the principal styles for the *Redingote* or *L'Impératrice* dress which still continues to be worn, and which our readers know is the gored dress, body and skirt in one piece, and for a slight figure this style is exceedingly becoming. The sleeves are round and cut with an elbow, slit up slanting and trimmed with a row of buttons from the elbow to the hand. Corsages *d plastron* are very becoming to some figures — the plastron is generally of velvet, or else of silk of some color to contrast well with the dress, richly worked with jet beads. Many of the skirts have pockets on the outside shaped and trimmed like the plastron on the body. Green, wine, and violet are the favorite colors for spring silks. Most of the bodies are made round so as to display the elegant gilt belts, buckles, clasps, and the pointed velvet waistbands now so much in vogue, more so than the ceinture or sash, which, however, is always pretty. Favorite patterns for *Chambéry* printed muslins, *barége Anglais*, foulards, etc. etc., are bunches of flowers or fruits, and small figures scattered over them. The foulards are generally of a dark ground, and as they are of a texture not easily rumpled, we particularly recommend them to our lady friends.

We have seen some black silk dresses with *bouillonnés* of apple green or violet silk, edged with a ruche of black guipure, inserted between every breadth of the skirt, which had a charming effect.

Some dresses are made with the skirt perfectly plain in front, the plaits commencing about two inches on either side of the center.

Shawls of the same material as the dresses, whether of *barége*, grenadine, or muslin are to be much worn.

The Zouave jacket, with Greek vest, or full embroidered muslin shirt falling about two inches over the skirt still continues a favorite both for ladies and children, and is made of both thick and thin materials.

Steel-colored silk jupes or underskirts quilted and trimmed with black velvet are among the novelties for street wear this spring.

Brodie's travelling and street wraps are of great variety in style; the loose sack and *bournous* with fancy hoods, however, we think the favorites. They are generally made of bright striped materials, such as Magenta and white, Solferino and gray, *chinée*, with several different colored, bright stripes, etc., but we have seen some very pretty plain goods, in different shades of gray, gray and *chinée*, gray and blue, or green. The novelty of the season, however, is the bright tartan striped materials; these brilliant stripes, sobered down by gray or *chinée*, have a charming effect, and make a very stylish cloak. Of dress mantles and bonnets we will speak in our next month's chat.

SPRING FASHIONS

THE ANDALUSIAN

From the establishment of G. Brodie, 51 Canal Street, New York.
Drawn by L.T. Voigt from actual articles of costume.

We take pleasure in offering this beautiful style to our lady friends for a spring garment. There are certain peculiarities to which we call attention. For those who prefer the pelisse of a marked style, the border is not of the same color as that of the body of the garment, but is of white purple, etc.; the black lace which edges it, lies over this lighter color, thus showing its pattern, etc., much more strongly than if falling over a black ground. A line of this lighter colored silk is left also uncovered, as a heading or relief to the lace.

Fig. 1 – A gored dress of wine colored silk, buttoned up in front, with a lapel on the right side of the body formed of velvet, edged with a quilled ribbon; this trimming extends down the skirt on the left side until within about a quarter of a yard of the bottom, when it turns sharply to the right and meets the velvet trimming which is placed about two inches from the bottom of the skirt; the sleeves are full coat sleeves, with cap drawn into a loose gauntlet cuff; small *appliqué* lace collar and sleeves to match.

From the establishment of A.T. Stewart, Broadway, New York

Fig. 2 - A cashmere *robe de chamber* of a light oak color with a very deep border of rich flowers on a darker oak ground. A small cape is on the body, which is full, and fastened at the throat and waist, but a little open in the middle to show a worked chemisette; sleeves and collar of embroidered muslin.

MORNING ROBE

From the establishment of A.T. Stewart, Broadway, New York

Fig. 3 – Morning robe of Marie Louise blue; the border is very rich, being of silk and wool; a portion of the front breadth is white, with rich bordering crossing it; body plain; gold colored silk cord and tassel. Linen collar and sleeves, finished with a narrow ruffle.

Fig. 4 – Green silk dress, buttoned over like a coat; lapels to turn over, edged with a ruche; straight waist, with sash; sleeves full, with gauntlet cuff.

Boys Dress - Light cloth; jacket, vest, and pants being of the same material, and the first two bound with black velvet.

Girl's dress – A straw hat with plume; black silk coat trimmed with black velvet.

PATTERN FOR NIGHT-DRESS

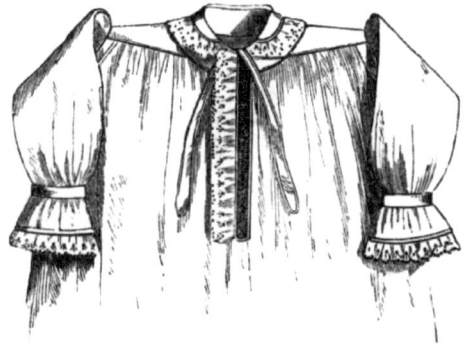 

This Night-dress, as will be seen by the illustration, is easily made, and is a pattern that wears very well – the neck and shoulder pieces all being made of double material. Four and a half yards of long-cloth, fourteen inches of insertion, two and a half yards of embroidery, with a single row down the front, and three and a quarter yards with a double row, will be required to make one garment. Divide the long-cloth into three pieces, all of the same size, and tear one width in half; the two and a half widths are for the body, and the half width for the sleeves, collar, neck piece, shoulder pieces, etc.; so by carefully cutting out, there should be no more calico required, and not a piece should be wasted.

After having sewn the seams and hemmed the bottom, measure the half of the front, and tear it down twelve inches; this is for the opening. Hem this opening on each side, and gather the top of the Night-dress, both back and front; cord the shoulder pieces, and put these on to a portion of the top of the Night-dress, the remainder belonging to the neck piece. The garment is now ready for the sleeves. These are gathered three inches from the bottom, and a band felled over large enough for the hand to slip through. The bottom of the sleeve is finished off with embroidery, and the top gathered in to the armhole; a narrow binder, one inch wide, is then felled down on the wrong side. Our illustration clearly shows where the binder should go, and the shape of the armhole.

After making and trimming the collar, fasten it on to the neck-piece, and stitch this (the neck-piece) on to the gathers and shoulder pieces, the letters C to C showing exactly how far the gathers extend. Line both the shoulder and neck pieces on the wrong side by felling down some long-cloth cut out in the same shape, and finish off the hem down the front with insertion and embroidery, put on with a cording.

This Night dress may be made much handsomer by letting in extra rows of insertion down the front, on each side of the opening, and by putting a band of insertion on the sleeves, instead of one made of long-cloth. A double row of work up the front – that is to say, placed on each side of the insertion – would be an improvement; but these little matters must, of course, be left to the taste and judgment of the worker.

CHILDREN'S FASHIONS

ZOUVE JACKET FOR A
LITTLE GIRL

THE VICTOR COAT

MINNIE APRON

High neck and long sleeves, adapted for a child from five to seven years, pretty in pink or blue chambre, trimmed with white braid. Requires two and a half to three yards of material, and pearl or thread buttons.

AQUILA APRON
(Back view)

Waist is plain with a single box plait in front, ornamented with buttons; skirt cut circular, and has a polka joined in at the waist; long sleeves gathered at the wrist with a plain cuff; high neck and buttons at the back; will admit of considerable trimming.

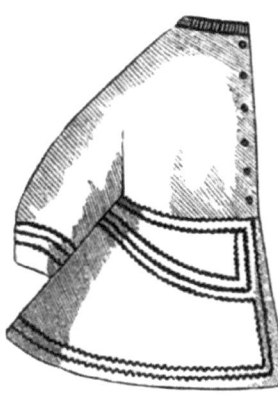

LULU APRON
(Front & Back View)

Low neck with a polka cut in connection with the waist, which has a pretty effect over the circular skirt; shoulders finished with a bow of ribbons. Requires two yards of silk.

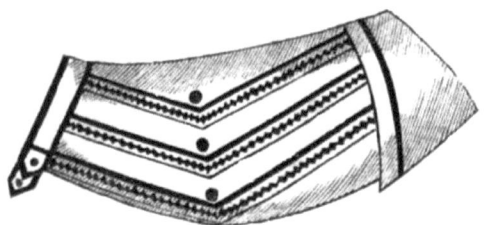

ARIADNE SLEEVE
A small bishop sleeve, with pointed cap and three waves thrown back from the front; waist slightly gathered into a loose pendent band.

BRETELLE
The "Paysanne" bretelle, made of velvet, edged with narrow guipure lace, and strapped with ribbon, being made in black velvet, and separate from the dress, may be made with any color.

CRISTELLA SLEEVE
Flowing sleeve with points turned back from the front, and finished with tassels and braid gimp.

Godey's Arm Chair

The wedding dress of the Princess of Polignac, who married the rich banker's son, M. Mires, in Paris, is described by Le Follet. It was of *moiré*, quite plain in the skirt, but with long train, high body, buttoned in front with fine pearls; an English lace collar, fastened at the throat by a diamond brooch; the bouquet of orange blossom, fastened at the waist; the coiffure with a diadem of white lilac and roses; the hair fastened behind under a rich comb of diamonds; an immense veil of English lace thrown over the head and falling nearly to the bottom of the dress, completed this *distingué* toilet. The second bridesmaid had on a dress of white silk, trimmed round the skirt with three rows of pinked silk ruching, the third row carried up to the waist. The bouquet of orange flowers placed in the bow of the sash, which was also trimmed with ruches. A diadem wreath of white roses and lilies of the valley, over which was thrown the large, square veil of plain tulle, simply hemmed. The third bridesmaid, who was young and beautiful, wore a dress at once simple and elegant. It was composed of white tarlatine, very fine and thin, covered with pink flounces of the same. A high, full body, with a ruche round the throat. A wide scarf of white silk, with fringed ends round the waist, fastened in a bow at the side, in which was placed the orange flower bouquet. A diadem wreath of white moss rosebuds in the hair, over which a large veil, also of tarlatine, reaching nearly to the feet.

ELGIN SACK

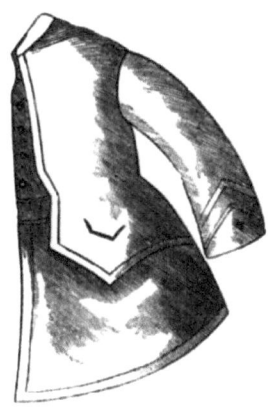

Boy's sack, with jacket front and plain back, especially designed for home wear, and may be trimmed in any style that fancy may dictate. For a child of six years, it requires about four yards of single width material.

INFANTS BIB
To be made of *piqué*, embroidered with floss thread, and fastened at the back with buttons.

NOVELTIES FOR APRIL

Fig. 1 & 2 – Caps suitable for breakfast and home wear. The bow in *Fig. 1* consists of Solferino velvet ribbon. *Fig. 2* has a coronal of embroidered cambric, with loops of gold colored satin ribbon.

Fig. 3 - A delicate wreath in white velvet leaves with plumy, feathery pendants. It is intended to surround the hair, and fall on the neck. This is a graceful style of mounting for any kind of leaves – a floral ornament now greatly used.

Fig. 4 - A quiet and ladylike headdress suited for a dinner or small evening party. Black velvet, jet sides, a fall of black lace, to the right, a bow of black velvet ribbon with flowing ends, to the left, a full blown rose with trailing foliage.

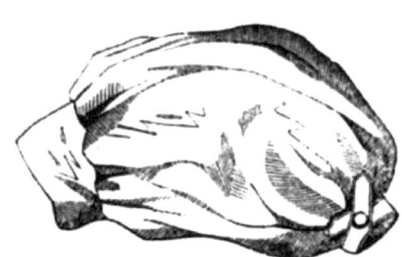

Fig. 5 & 6 – Plain linen collars and sleeves in this style will continue to be worn during the spring for walking-dress, and in summer for traveling. The variation consists in the feather stitch edge as in *Fig. 6*; or the cord, as in *fig. 5*.

Fig. 7 – Lace cape of an excellent shape, suitable for evening wear. The tulle foundation is slightly puffed between the transverse rows of lace, which may be of Valenciennes, or any neat point; a double fall of broader lace edges the fichu.

SPRING BONNETS

Fig. 1 – Represents a Paillasson straw of very thick plait, richly trimmed on the outside with roses, corn flowers, grasses and loops of straw. The inside trimming is a ruche and bouquet of flowers on one side, and over the top and on the other side is simply a roll of green ribbon, to suit the strings and cape of bonnet.

Fig. 2 – A bonnet of rice straw, trimmed with white ribbon and black velvet, with wheat-ears on one side. The inside trimming is field flowers and blonde lace.

FANCY BELT

To be made of black or any fancy colored silk, black velvet and gold braid, with a handsome gold buckle.

HEADDRESSES

Fig. 1 – Coiffure of pieces of black velvet, trimmed with either black or white lace, and formed into a wreath, caught in front and at the back by pendants of black and gold bugles.

Fig. 2 – Net formed of narrow black velvet, fastened with jet beads, and trimmed with loops of black ribbon worked with jet beads; a velvet bow with jet buckle finishes this wreath with loops in the center.

SAVING PURSE

This purse is for money in reserve, to be kept in some safe place. Cut a piece of cardboard as wide as the top of the purse, leave the lid to wrap over, and a diamond point at each end of the bottom. Lay a strip of silk over each end, simply giving them the required folds to form the shape. Then lay a piece of fancy ribbon over the central part, if possible, making the fastening fall in the middle of the pattern, and adding a pretty button with a loop. Place a small silk tassel, on each side at the ends of the silk and strings.

TOILET MAT
To be worked with white and pink crochet cotton.

CRAFTING & NEEDLEWORKS

EMBROIDDERED OVERLAPPING COLLARS AND CUFFS

In this neat and beautifully designed collar we present our readers with a novelty which we think will meet with general favor. It can be made of lined cambric, muslin, or any other kind of fabric to suit the taste of those who work it. The square figures in the design, near the points of the collar and cuffs, are to be worked in a button hole, which when they are overlapped, can be fastened with a stud at the neck or sleeve buttons at the wrists. The points of the cuff up to the sleeve button hole can be lined with silk of any color to suit the taste or dress of the wearer.

TEAPOT INKSTAND

Take a common glass inkstand, cover it with black velvet, attach a wire handle and spout, covered also with black velvet; cut a circular top in cardboard large enough to project beyond the opening of the inkstand; fasten this on to the top of a cork, about three-quarters of an inch thick, by means of an ornamental pin, the head of which forms the lid of the teapot. Cover the whole with beadwork, according to our design, and fasten it down upon the mat.

TURBAN BAG

Take a paper pill box, cut it down one-third, lay over its bottom a small piece of cotton-wool, cover this with a small piece of satin, or gold spotted crape. Make a small bag to fit the round, sew it round the rim, put on the folds of the turban, add a silk tassel to the top of the crown, and fill the bag with sweetmeats.

INFANTS EMBROIDERED SHOE

Materials — White French merino or cashmere; and white, purple or green silk and brown satin.

We give the two parts of which the entire shoe is composed, and the design may be may be worked entirely in white silk or in the appropriate colors. If the latter, the veining of the leaves must be in the darker shade of green than the leaf itself. The upper petals of the flowers are worked in French knots; the scrolls in *point de chainette*, the calyx of the buds in pale green; the buds in purple silk.

To make-up these shoes, quilt some finest of twill muslin, with flannels for the lining; binding this lining and outer part together with a piping-cord, covered with white silk. The soles of these very small shoes are usually also made of merino, quilted; but they may, if preferred, cork soles, bound with white ribbon.

LAMP MAT IN CROCHET

The center is of white, the star in black; then alternate rows of deep crimson and orange. The border is formed by making balls of worsted of three shades of green, and sewing them on in regular order, the lightest being outside.

DESIGN IN BERLIN WOOL-WORK FOR MATS, SLIPPERS, ETC.

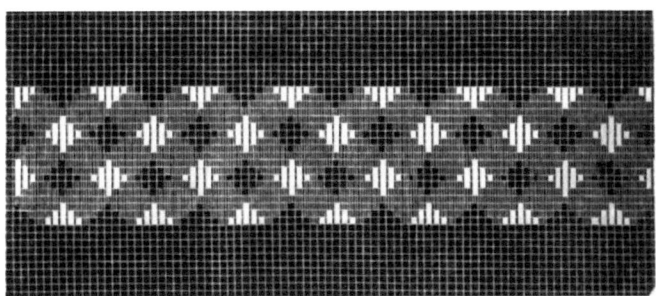

Simple patterns in Berlin wool-work, producing lively and pleasing effects, are amongst those supplies for the work table which every lady finds most useful for various purposes, enabling her with perfect ease to make many pretty articles, which, if great arrangement were necessary, would never be undertaken. The little design which we have now given is one of these, being perfectly easy of execution, and especially pretty when completed. Wools of three different colors are all that are required, worked in the following manner: The lines which form the sides of the diamonds are in a brilliant green, inclining to a blue; when they appear to cross, the small square becomes a very dark green, approaching to a black, the ground or under diamonds being white. Another pretty arrangement of colors is to take a ruby for the sides of the diamonds, a black for the crossings, and a white for the ground; or a blue may be substituted for the ruby with equally good effect. This little design will be found well suited for cushions, mats, slippers, and many other articles, and it may be worked on either fine or coarse canvas, according to the article for which it may be required.

TAPER STAND

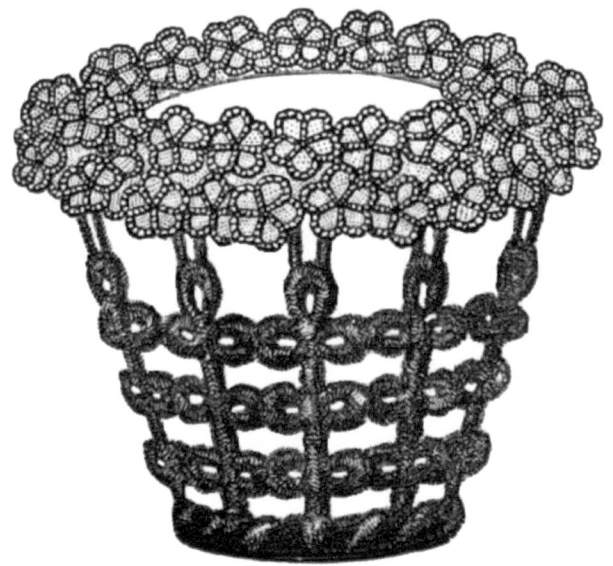

Materials – Transparent glass beads – white; green chenille, three shades; oak brown chenille; green silk; gold beads; and wire covered with silk, the darkest shade of green.

The taper-stand given in our engraving makes a beautiful and appropriate present to give a gentleman. The border is made of rosettes of beads, and an explanation of one will suffice for all.

Take the wire and string upon it one gold bead, then seven of the transparent beads, then cross the wire to form a petal; put on seven more transparent beads, then one gold one, and again cross the wire for the second petal. Make three more petals like the first two, and then join all by passing the wire through the center of them to form the stalk. Maker forty-four of these rosettes or flowers, and join them by twisting the stalks, as you see in the engraving. Make the stalks turn down, and twist them to form a strong wire at the lower edge of the border of rosettes. Cover this neatly with green silk, cut bias.

The body of the stand is made of similar petals of wore covered with chenille of alternate green and brown, the brown solid, and the green of the second shade. Unite the border, by bars of the lightest green chenille over wire, and form the base by twisting the darkest green chenille and the brown together.

Cover a round card with green silk, and stitch the base finely to it. This makes the bottom of the stand.

FANCY TIDY

QUILTING DESIGN

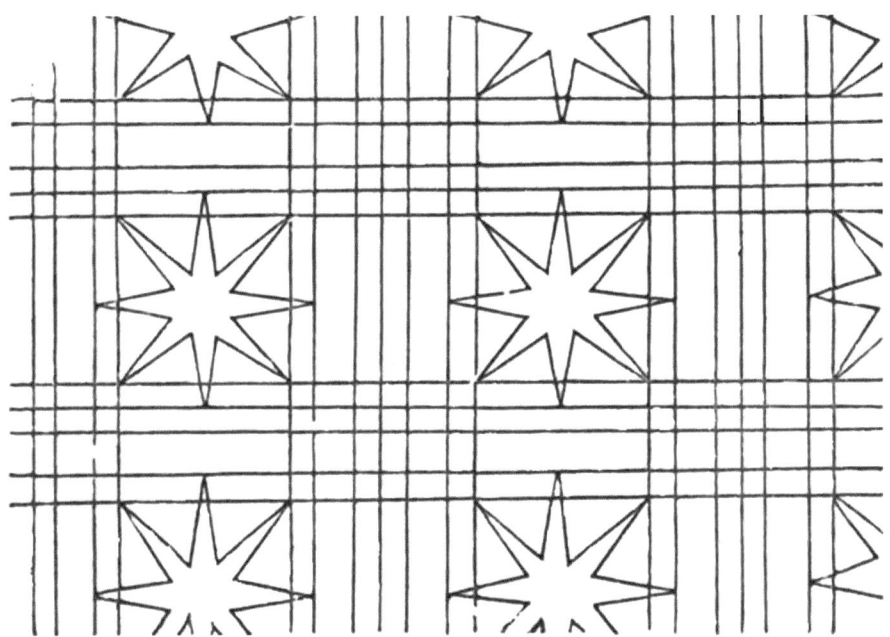

PATTERN FOR A LADIES WRAPPER

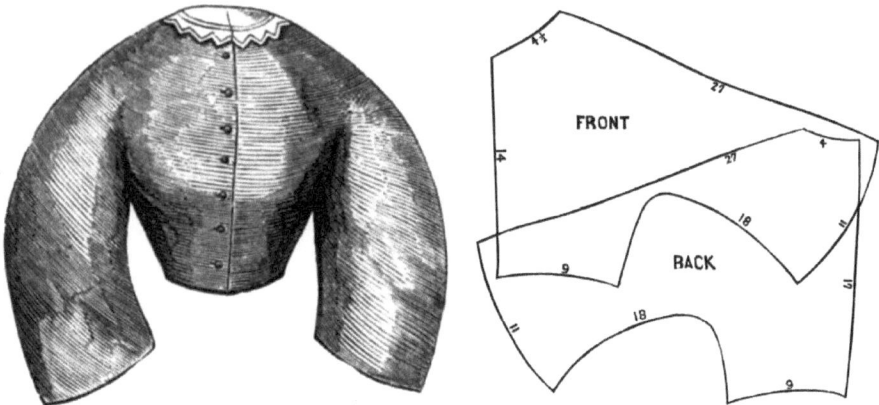

This wrapper pattern possesses peculiar advantages in its simplicity and adaptation to any figure – the back and front being exactly alike, and the only alteration necessary being in the size of the neck. It can be made of any material, perfectly plain, or very richly trimmed. It does not require the aid of the dressmaker, as any lady can make and trim a dress for herself. Cashmere trimmed with velvet, lawn with ruffles, or white material with flouncing, look equally well. Plain chintz, with puffs of the same. The connecting seam is on the shoulder, the waist should have a string run in the hem to make it fit smoothly.

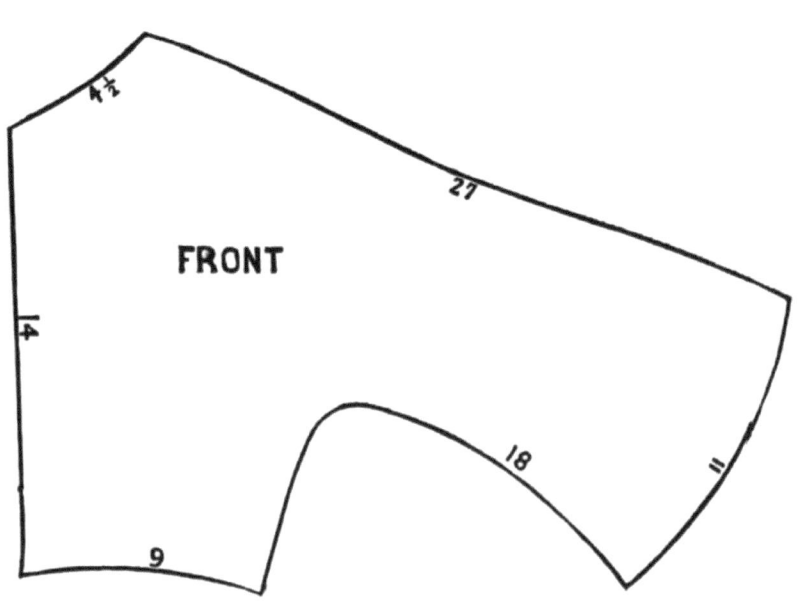

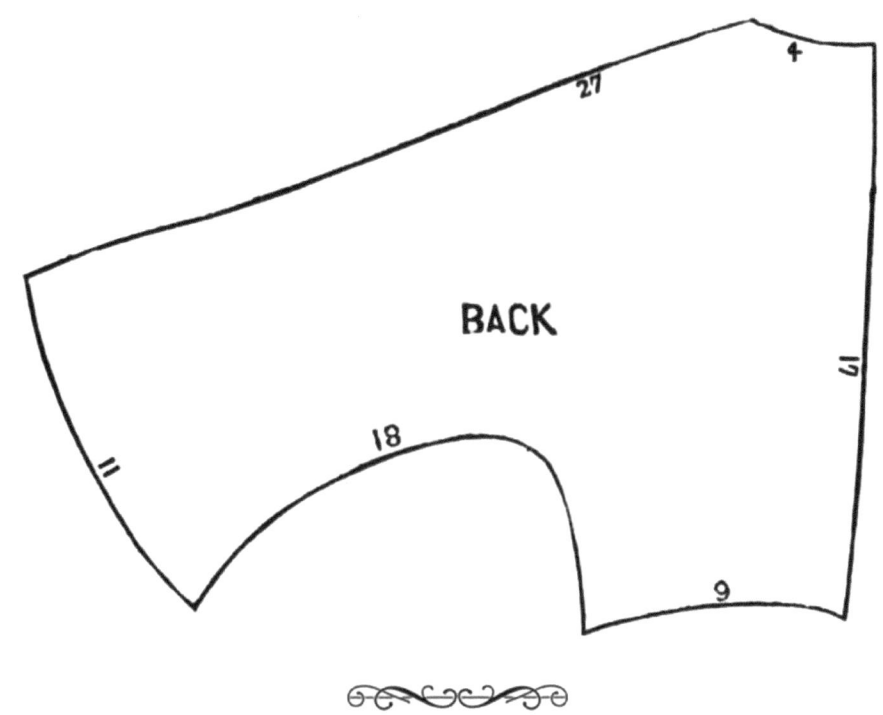

EMBROIDERY DESIGNS

BORDER IN BRODERIE ANGLAIS
AND BUTTONHOLE STITCH

CHAPTER 5
MAY 1861

GODEY'S FASHIONS FOR MAY 1861.
"HOW DO YOU LIKE MY NEW HORSE"

Fig. 1 – Brown spring silk, gored, the body and skirt being in one piece. The front breadth is cut out in squares, and has the appearance of being buttoned over on either side; it is, however, only cut on one side; the squares are edged with black thread lace; the buttons are silk, with velvet centers. This trimming is also on the side breadths, but only extends half way up the skirt. The sleeves are cut with an elbow, and trimmed to suit the skirt. English split straw hat, with plume and demi veil of black lace.

Fig. 2 – Dress suitable for a watering place, or evening company. It is of white *glacé* silk, made infant waist, with a semi-loose sleeve, drawn lengthwise into puffs, and trimmed with box plaited blue ribbon. The skirt is trimmed with *bouillonnés* or puffs, about half a yard in depth, separated by rows of blue ribbon, box plaited. The gloves have two buttons at the wrist and scalloped tops. A large bow, with ends of very wide blue ribbon is placed at the back of the waist.

Fig. 3 – Green cloth habit of the new shade, made with a plaited jockey at the back, and having small pockets in front. A standing linen collar, with black velvet necktie. Coat sleeve, with gauntlet cuff. Leghorn Spanish hat, trimmed with black velvet and white ostrich plumes. The side saddle has three horns, which is a great protection to the fair equestrienne.

Fig. 4 – Rich purple silk, with plain round waist with velvet belt. The skirt is made three quarters of a yard longer than usual, and is drawn up at intervals to the proper length, forming puffs, with pointed pieces of purple velvet put on to cover the seams. This is one of the newest trimmings, and is very stylish. The sleeves are done in the same manner. Black straw hat, with peacock plumes.

CHITCHAT UPON NEW YORK AND PHILADELPHIA FASHIONS FOR MAY

The fine May weather has brought out all the spring novelties, and the streets are gay with pretty bonnets, dresses, and mantles. The prevailing colors for bonnets seem to be black and white, violet, light green, and Magenta, though we see some of pink, blue, and mallow. Bunches of fruit and aquatic plants are extensively employed as ornaments, but light feathers are in very good taste, and there is quite a novel arrangement of them: for instance, a bonnet of embroidered white tulle had a border of violet velvet edged with black lace; a tulle crown covered with small very light feathers, white and violet; a tulle curtain bordered with velvet, and as a bandeau point and blonde lace; the strings were one white and the other violet, edged with black lace. Many of the bonnets for young ladies have long illusion veils, either hemmed or edged with blonde caught on top of the bonnet with a large bunch of flowers, and tied under the chin; they are very light and youthful looking. Some of the prettiest bonnets are of white crape trimmed with flowers, lace or velvet scarfs; one we noticed decorated on the front by a very full blonde ruche in the middle of which was a compact row of red daisies. The bandeau was composed of a row of daisies placed on a velvet band. Another bonnet trimmed outside with a double point of cherry velvet, inside with bunches of black berries and cherry velvet. Black continues to be worn.

We saw a pretty bonnet the other day, which, without being very novel, was still rich and quiet. It was composed of fine black hair embroidered with buttercups in silken straw. The ribbon with which it was timed was a black ground embroidered also with silken straw; the flowers were entirely black, with jet centers. Chips will be much worn, and as they are so beautiful of themselves they require but little trimming, a spray of flowers on one side being quite sufficient. All kinds of mixed straws will be worn, as well as black, white, and gray. The small, close bonnets called Capelines, sometimes adopted in the county by those who do not like the jaunty little straw hats so much in vogue, are this summer being made of worked muslin lined with colored silk or gauze, and the colors usually selected for this purpose are mallow, pink, blue, lilac, and cerise; they are trimmed with ruches of tulle and ribbon. Other capelines, of a less gay and elegant style, are composed of jaconets, silk, *piqué*, etc.

From bonnets we next pass to caps; and for ladies who wear caps our fashionable milliner has brought out some very light and pretty ones. A very graceful one formed a net, made of gold thread at the back, and was finished on one side with a bow of black lace and on the other with a delicate pink rose. There are many other styles, and some particularly pretty breakfast caps; we can, however, give them but a passing notice.

Nets for the hair are by no means laid aside; they are still very much worn in morning dress, and also in evening *negligée*. Those made of colored chenille or velvet are very becoming; they are usually finished with tassels or rosettes.

Among Brodie's large assortment of silk wraps we noticed some which were extremely stylish; they were mostly of the paletot shape, with thick cods down each seam, and richly ornamented by crochet and bead *patés*, though there are many mantles and circles with over seams, also corded down each seam. Many were corded with white and trimmed with black and white braid, much resembling stitching, and black and white buttons ornamenting the seams. Some had only pointed collars, others square or pointed capes, corded and richly trimmed with lace or made entirely of lace. Other wraps were edged with purple and various colors, with pelerine capes, the ends extending down in front to the end of the wrap, with a narrow black lace falling over this colored silk, which had a very pretty effect. Crochet trimmings, lace tassels, and fancy hoods arranged in a hundred different ways almost bewilder one by their style and beauty.

The most fastidious cannot fail to find an elegant and varied style of dress goods to meet their wants and taste at the establishment of Messrs. A. T. Stewart & Co., New York. We saw so many and such beautiful goods that we cannot pretend to do them justice. However, to begin with the less expensive, the chintzes, they are unusually gay and delicate, being generally of white grounds with small figures and bouquets of flowers in the gayest chintz colors thrown over them. The chintz lawns pleased us much; they are rather thicker than a lawn, with a cord through them, and a raised dot of white on a pink, blue, or lilac ground. Most of the muslins were white grounds, with pin dots and single flowers scattered over them Three new colors have come out this year in muslins – a new red, purple, and green; and a great recommendation in the eyes of housekeepers is that they are all fast colors. There is a new material, called silk muslin, much resembling grenadine, the exception being that grenadine is all silk, and the other silk and cotton. In this style of goods were five and seven flounced robes. The beautiful organdies, so delicate in texture, had, like the muslins, white grounds with pin dots and stripes and bouquets of the most exquisite flowers, or else a mottled gray ground, more delicate than a *chiné*, with very peculiar figures in gay chintz colors. We saw a few seven and five flounced robes, but the novelty of the season is the Chevron dress of which we give a cut in the front of the book. This dress has diagonal stripes of *rose de chiné*, about an inch and a half in width, meeting in the center of the breadth, and between these stripes are bouquets of roses with their foliage, which has a charming effect. We have had this design in silk, but this is the first appearance of diagonal stipes on muslin. Very few flounced dresses, or rather robe dresses, will be worn through we saw a few in organdy and *barége* Anglais. This latter material can be had in the plain *chiné* from 12 1/2 to 37 1/2 cents, but the newest styles have embroidered figures over them, which add greatly to their beauty. The summer or Manchester poplins have a cord through them, and are worked with spots in gay-colored silk, of much the same style as many of the silks, and much resembling them in appearance.

Mozambique is another new material; this is thicker than *barége Anglais*, and very suitable for travelling dresses. It can be had in plain chintz, plaids, cheques, stripes, or plain grounds with embroidered figures in gay colors; this last style is exceedingly pretty. The grenadine *barége* is of the same style as the Mozambique's – a black or delicate gray ground with embroidered spots or figures worked in silk. Pekin cloth, thicker than the last mentioned material, is also very nice for traveling dresses.

The rich silks are generally of a *chiné* ground, with large dashed figures, or else a solid ground with very rich embroidered figures or sprays of flowers thrown over them *d volante*. These silks are $4.50 a yard, but the same designs are carried out in less expensive goods. The light summer silks are cheques or stripes, with dashed figures; there are also many solid grounds with a thread of white crossing them.

For ladies and children the turban style of hat will be the rage. They can be had of white, black, gray or mixed straw. Another style is somewhat of the mushroom shape, but has the brim set up about an inch on the crown, and instead of slanting gradually off goes off in a curve, and rolls under at the edge of the brim; these also are to be had of all colors, and will be trimmed with | peacocks' and game birds' feathers.

THE CHEVRON ORGANDY DRESS

From a design furnished by A.D. Letson, Esq.,
of the House of A.T. Stewart & Co., New York

THE SARAGOSSA

From the establishment of G. Brodie, 51 Canal Street, New York
Drawn by L.T. Voigt from actual articles of costume

This beautiful novelty is constructed of two colors of silk – a light hue, and black taffeta; purple is much esteemed for the lighter tint. This is ornamented with exquisite designs of passementerie. The character of the garment requires no elucidation beyond the engraving.

DESCRIPTION OF DRESSES WORN AT THE LATE DRAWING-ROOM RECEPTION OF HER MAJESTY QUEEN VICTORIA

Viscountess Somerton – Costume *dé cour*, composed of a train of the richest white taffetas d'Italie, lined with silk, very tastefully trimmed with tulle and ribbons; corsage to correspond, with Brussels point lace, and bouquet of roses *du roi*; skirts of white tulle over white glacé covered with magnificent flounces of Brussels point lace and roses *du roi*. Coiffure of ostrich feathers, lappets and diamonds.

Lady MacDonald – Train of rich white glacé, trimmed with bouillons of mauve tulle and blonde; petticoat composed of alternate rows of mauve and white tulle and tunic en point over a slip of white glacé. Headdress, plumes, flowers, and lappets; ornaments, diamonds.

Lady Churchill – Costume *dé cour*, composed of a train of the richest white Terry velvet, lined with blue glacé trimmed with turquoise blue Lyons velvet and French blonde; corsage drape, ornamented with blonde and diamonds; skirt of white tulle de Lyons over white satin, covered with French blonde. Headdress, ostrich feathers, diamonds, and lappets.

Lady Carington – Train of mauve Terry velvet, lined with white glacé, and trimmed with black laced; a double skirt of white glace, trimmed with black lace and mauve crape, and bouquets of fern leaves. Headdress, feathers and lace lappets; ornaments, diamonds.

Lady Templemore – Dress of black glacé, with bouillonné skirts of black sparkling tulle; tunique of handsome black lace looped with bunches of black grass; corsage to correspond; train of superb black moiré antique, with bouillons of sparkling tulle, *parsémé* with grass. Headdress, black feathers and long tulle veil; ornaments, jet.

Lady Overstone – Train of black satin, lined with white glacé and trimmed with black lace; petticoat of white crape over glacé, with flounces of black lace, and trimmed with satin ribbon and tulle. Headdress, feathers and lace lappets; ornaments, diamonds.

Lady Wodehouse – Train of the richest Gothic *moiré* of a novel design, vert d'Azoff, lined with silk, and very elegantly trimmed with Brussels point lace, tulle, and ribbon; corsage to correspond, with lace and bouquet of violet and silver daisies; skirts of vert d'Azoff tulle over taffetas d'Italie, covered with flounces of Brussels point lace and trimmings of tulle. Coiffure of ostrich feathers, and wreaths of violets and silver daisies, Brussels lace lappets parure of diamonds.

Lady Naas – Train of white glacé, trimmed with bouillons of tulle and blue ruches; petticoat composed of alternate rows of blue and white tulle, over a white glacé slip. Headdress, plumes, flowers, and lappets; ornaments, diamonds, and turquoise.

Lady Jane Peel – Train of lilac moiré, lined with white glacé, trimmed with Brussels lace, edged with lilac chenille; corsage and sleeves trimmed with lilac tulle, Brussels lace, and diamonds; petticoat, double skirt of white glacé; upper skirt trimmed with two flounces of Brussels lace, and plaiting open at the side, with bouillons of tulle and bows of ribbon. Headdress diamonds, feathers, and Brussels lace; ornaments diamonds.

Among the principal novelties for this season are the little photographs, called from their smallness, "visiting cards," which may be had very cheap, and which enable an individual to bestow a likeness of himself, at small cost, on his entire circle.

SPRING BONNET

Neapolitan braid bonnet, with an apple green ribbon laid over the front; strings and cape of the same, and a bunch of blue chrysanthemums on one side. In the inside is a lilac velvet roll, with a bunch of leaves on one side, and on the other is a puffing of illusion with velvet bow

WHITE MUSLIN MANTLE

To be trimmed with small fluted ruffles and one deep flounce

INFANTS PIQUE COAT
Trimmed With Flouncing

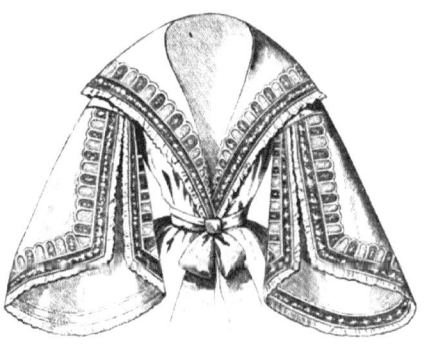

MORNING ROBE

White *piqué*, made surplice, with cape rounded in the back and pointed in front, trimmed with flouncing.

GENTELMAN'S SHIRT

NOVELTIES FOR MAY

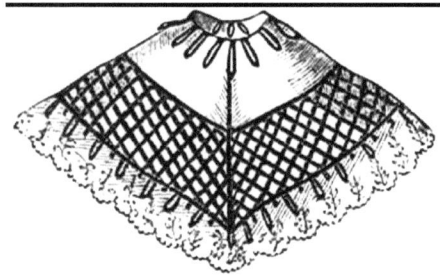

BIRTHA CAPE OR FICHU

Fig. 1 - For wearing in the evening, or with a low backed dress in summer. The foundation is Brussels net; the loops and lozenge trimming of narrow velvet ribbon; plain fall, of any neat point.

Fig. 2 – Collar and habit shirt, suitable for mourning; the folds may be of clear muslin or Tarleton; the needle worked edge of black, as is also the knot of ribbon, which forms a pretty variation to the lappet shape of the collar.

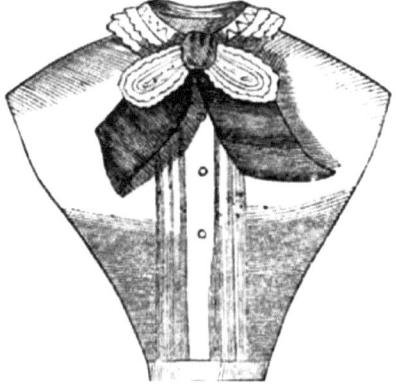

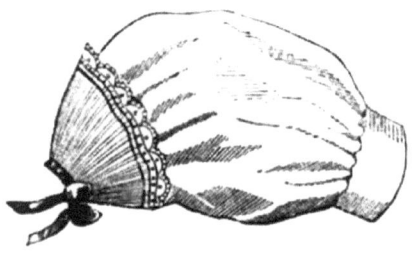

Fig. 3 – Undersleeve of clear muslin, with a deep frill, *en revers* at the wrist, fastened by an elastic band, with a medium velvet ribbon.

Fig. 4 – The tongue shaped cuff or lappet *en revers* (turned back), is much worn by those who prefer a close sleeve; the star shaped ornaments, if in mourning, should be of crepe; in black velvet, otherwise.

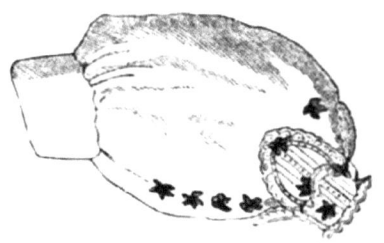

Figs. 5 & 6 – Caps for morning wear. The round cowl shape of *Fig. 5* is perhaps the most desirable.

Fig. 5

Fig. 6

Fig. 7 – A white chip hat with a very light white feather on one side; cape trimmed with violet velvet and white blonde strings of white ribbon; full ruche of white blonde, with a bouquet on the right side

Fig. 7

Fig. 8 – Coiffure for a young lady

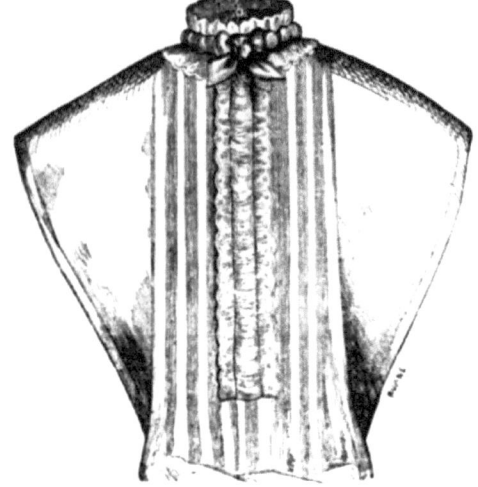

Fig. 9 – Zouave chemisette

A very simple style of short night-dress, easily made, and very comfortable

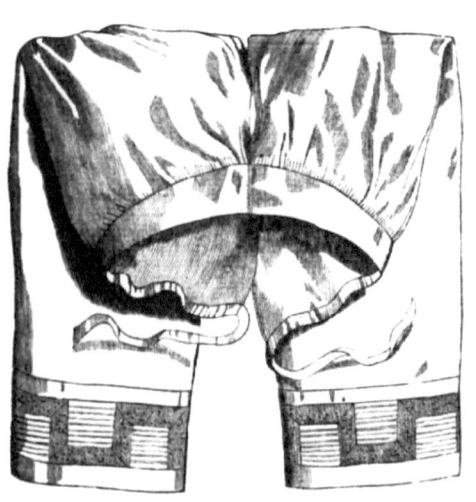

A new style of drawers, very comfortable and easily made

CRAFTING & NEEDLEWORKS

BUTTERFLY PEN WIPER

The body of the butterfly is of velvet stuffed with cotton, and entirely covered with gold beads. The eyes are red, and the horns stiff gold cord, with a bead on the ends. The wings can be made of cloth or velvet, the latter, however, is much the richest, and two or more colors should be used; they are to be embroidered with silk, fancy beads, and bugles. Pieces of cloth or flannel are cut the same size of the wings and sewed underneath to wipe the pens on. The size of the engraving is the proper size for the pen wiper.

BUTTERFLY SLIPPER

To be braided on velvet or cloth, with gold and fancy colored braids.

DESIGN FOR PATCHWORK

Our page compels us to reduce the size of the pattern; but, by a little attention, sections may easily be cut of any dimensions desired. Take a piece of clean stout white paper, and fold it in all the parallel sloping lines seen in our engraving. These may be at any distance from the other; only regular and equal. It will be seen that a line drawn exactly between every pair of parallels will take in the points. Draw these lines with a pencil; to distinguish them from those caused by the folding, and the proper forms can be readily obtained. Cut them out, and from them others in cardboard, if for a large piece of work, and you have all your sections ready, without the possibility of a misfit. The two eight pointed figures are differently arranged. A may be filled up in eight pieces, while B should be composed of nine – a star of eight points to the center, and eight diamonds round it. Or, if on a sufficiently large scale, the inner star may be of eight pieces, two very distinct shades of the eight pieces. Two very distinct shades of the same color will look better for A than many different tints. B may have a dark center and bright points, or vice versa. The intermediate figure, C should be of such neutral tints or dark shades as may throw up the brilliant hues of which the star should be composed.

We have said that this design may be applied to another purpose. Worked on canvas, in wools, the outlines done in black, it would be both rich looking and easily worked. Elderly people and children can often do a piece where they can count threads, where a painted pattern would puzzle them. No. 14 or 16 canvas, and eight thread wool should be used. Orange, claret, blue (if good), and brilliant greens look well in such a pattern.

TOILET MAT

Take white crochet cotton, No. 8, tie a small ring, and in it work 18 long crochet stitches.

2d row – Two long stitches between every stitch.

3d – Three long stitches in every bunch of two stitches.

4th – Three long stitches between the first and second stitch of every bunch.

5th – Four long stitches between the first and second stitch of every bunch, and so on increasing one stitch every row, until you have the mat the size you desire. The one in the engraving is increased to ten stitches in every bunch. The last two rows are done in colors.

KNITTED ARTIFICIAL FLOWERS, FUCHSIA

If knitted in good size China silk, it does well to ornament caps or bonnets.

Calyx – Four calyxes are required for each flower; cast on eight stitches with crimson *split wool*.

1st row – Knit plain
2d – Purl
3d – Knit plain
4th – Purl
5th – Make one, knit two; repeat to the end of row
6th – Purl
7th – Knit plain
8th – Purl
9th – Knit plain
10th – Purl
11th – Knit plain
12th – Purl
13th – Make one, knit three; repeat to the end of the row
14th – Purl
15th – Make one, knit four; repeat
16th – Purl
17th – Make one, knit five to the end of row
18th – Knit six stitches, turn back and purl the same (leaving the rest of the stitches on the needle). Continue knitting and purling the six stitches until you have six small rows; then decrease one stitch, knit four; next row, decrease one, purl three, knit a row plain; then decrease one, purl two; lastly slip one, knit two together, turn the slipped stitch over, fasten the wool by putting it through the last stitch. This completes one division of the calyx. Break off the wool, leaving about a yard on the work, in order to carry down the wool to the stitches, which are still on the needle Then with the same wool, knit six more stitches, which must be done especially as the first, forming the second division, and with the same wool knit the third and fourth, which finishes the calyx. Sew a bit of fine wire (with the same split wool) round the end of each division, and the ends of the wire must be sown two by two on the inside of the flower before it is sown up.

Corolla - is small in the Fuchsia, and less apparent than the calyx. The color of the wool must be either purple or dark puce.

Cast on eight stitches

1st row – Knit plain

2d – Purl

3d – Make one, knit two; repeat throughout the row

4th – Purl

5th – Knit plain

6th – Purl

7th – Make one, knit three; throughout the row

8th – Purl

9th – Knit plain

10th – Purl

11th – Knit four stitches, turn back, decrease one, purl two, and finish by slipping one, knitting two together, turning the slipped stitch over, and putting the wool through the loop; bring the wool down the edge in the same way as for the calyx, and knit the second, third, and fourth divisions like the first. Sew a bit of wire round the edge, following the sinuosity of the work, and sew the two edges together.

Pistil and Stamen - can be made like the lily, but very much finer and smaller; but a simpler and easier method is, to stiffen some pale green, or white sewing cotton, with gum, and cut eight pieces of it of about five or six inches long, for the stamen, and one bit rather longer for the pistil; tie them together, and dip the longest in gum, and then in some green powder, or wool cut as fine as powder, and the rest, first in gum, and then immediately in yellow powder, or wool cut as fine, which will answer quite as well for the purpose. Mount your flower, by placing the stamens and pistil inside the corolla, and that to within the calyx, sufficiently low to show the corolla slightly; sew the open side of the calyx, and twist all the stalks together, covering the little stem with green wool.

Buds – Cast on four stitches, knit one row plain, purl one row.

3d row – Make one stitch, knit one throughout the row

4th – Purl

5th – Knit plain

6th – Purl

7th – Make one, knit two throughout the row

8th – Purl

9th – Knit plain

10th – Purl

Then gather all the stitches with a rug needle, make a little ball of red wool, put a bit of wire across it, fold over, and twist the wire quite tight, cover the little ball with the piece just knitted, sew the opening neatly, and gather up the stitches at the stem, which must be covered with crimson wool.

Leaf – Cast on three stitches, knit, and purl alternate rows, increasing one stitch at the beginning of each row until the leaf is of the breadth desired (about seven stitches for the smallest, and fourteen or sixteen stitches for the larges); then knit and purl four rows without increase, and begin to decrease in every row, until you have but three stitches left, which knit as one, and fasten off. Sew a fine wire round the leaves, leaving a small bit at the end as a stalk, and also a fine wire doubled, at the back of the leaf, in the center, which will keep it in shape.

Several shades and sizes of leaves are required, as also several buds and flowers, to form a handsome branch.

SMALL RETICULE OR PURSE, IN APPLICATION

Materials – A piece of cinnamon brown cloth, on which the design is laid in black velvet and blue cloth. Red braid, gold braid, and gold thread, passementerie tassel, and slides, and cord to match.

This article consists of four pieces, on all of which the design is repeated; they are sewed together down the sides, and meet in a point. The black velvet is represented as black in the engraving; the lighter pattern is in blue cloth. Both are edged throughout with gold braid, laid on so as to conceal the part where the *appliqué* and ground join. The braided patterns on the velvet and the blue cloth are done in red braid, edged with gold thread.

To make it, have four pieces of wash-leather, cut the same shape as the sides of the bag, and join them up, join up the bag also, put the lining in, and fasten it lightly down the seams. Turn in the edges at the top; sew them together, finish with a cord and small rings, covered with crochet, through which the strings are run.

Any other combination of colors may be used, care being taken that they harmonize sufficiently well.

CROCHET TIDY
TO BE WORKED IN SQUARE CROCHET

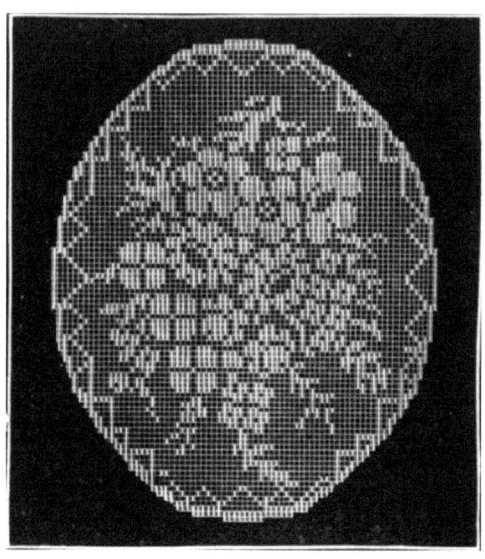

Count the number of squares in the extreme width and multiply by three, with the addition of one for the length of chain; and then select a cotton which will bring the tidy to the size you require. In an oval tidy, you do not commence on a chain of the full length, but on one that will make the number of squares at the side. In this tidy, as there are twelve squares, thirty-seven chain must be made. Break off. In the next row, as there are six squares extra on each side, make a chain of eighteen, then work on the chain for the twelve close squares; then finish with eighteen chain. Go on increasing in this way till the extreme width is obtained. To decrease, if by one square only, miss the first stitch of the last row, slip the next, single crochet the next, and double crochet the third. Reverse this to decrease at the end of the row. If two or more squares are to be decreased at each end, begin with the slip stitch over the second, third, or any other. Always work in the ends if possible. This tidy will be greatly strengthened and improved by a line of double crochet being worked entirely round it. A fringe trimming is the prettiest for round or oval tidies.

EMBROIDERY DESIGNS

EMBROIDERY FOR A SKIRT

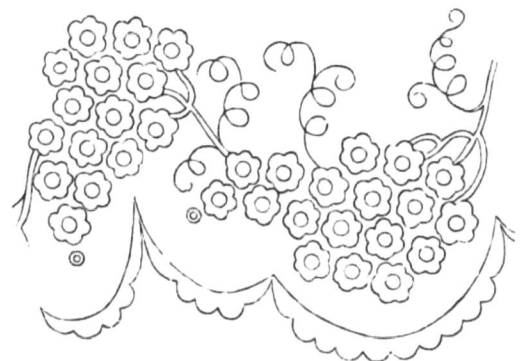

PATTERN IN BRAIDING AND BRODERIE ANGLAIS

To be worked on stout cambric, for petticoat insertion.
This fashion has now superseded the work at the bottom of slips.

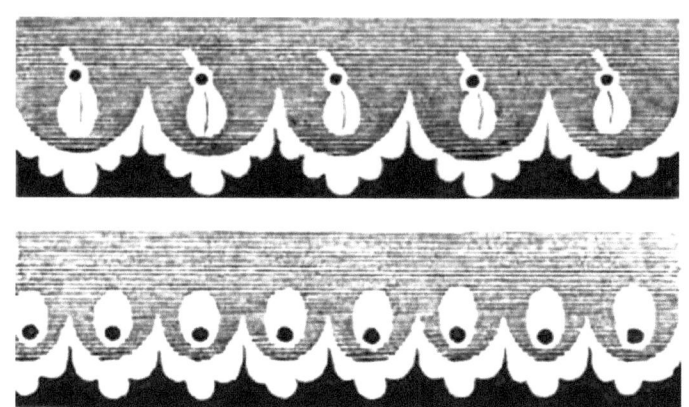

CHAPTER 6
JUNE 1861

DESCRIPTION OF FASHION-PLATE FOR JUNE 1861

Fig. 1 – French muslin dress, with seven flounces graduated. Francis 1st waistband of ribbon, richly and artistically embroidered. Coiffure of Valenciennes lace and daisies. Parasol of light green silk lined with white.

Fig. 2 – White mull spencer, puffed lengthwise and intersected by rows of black velvet sleeves to match the body, headed by two puffs, running crosswise, and an epaulette of velvet. Embroidered velvet waistband, *à la* Louis XV. Light blue *crêpe* Maretz skirt, with three rows of goffered ribbon sewed in waves at the bottom of the skirt.

Fig. 3 – *Piqué* Zouave embroidered; very full muslin skirt falling over the dress. A fluted ruff is round the neck of the shirt, and the skirt is of pink silk.

Fig. 4 – Dress formed of alternate rows of purple and mineral gray silk; Tunic skirt of the gray, edged with a narrow quilled ribbon; body low, with bretelles of gray silk, with two flounces, one of purple and one of gray silk, crossing in front and ending at the side with two falling loops and long ends. The bretelles give the dress the appearance of being square. It is a becoming style. Kid gloves, fastened at the wrist with two buttons, and having scalloped tops. Point lace barbe, trimmed with pink roses.

Fig. 5 – Rich grenadine dress, with four flounces; the upper one sewed on the body. Embroidered sash to match the dress. Long flowing sleeves and body drawn with cords to form a yoke. Coiffure of flowers and lace.

CHITCHAT UPON NEW YORK AND PHILADELPHIA FASHIONS FOR JUNE

We have given the general character of goods and toilets for the present season; they will undergo little change. The new tissues are very substantial and rich; bright or lively colors share the general favor with black and white. Among the handsomest tissues we will especially notice one having black stripes on a white ground, and powdered all over with stars; the same pattern can be had also in organdy of various colors. We note among our importation of French dresses several as excellent. One dress was white organdy, with broad lilac Chevron stipes; another the same with blue stripes. The skirts were, of course, plain, bodies made *à la vierge*, with a double shawl matching the dress, trimmed with a deep flounce. The sashes were wide white ribbons, with narrow lilac and white or blue and white ribbon quilled round them. We must not overlook one important particular, which is, that all dresses are now accompanied by a brooch bow to match the trimming of the dress.

Square muslin shawls are much worn; some of them are richly embroidered, and trimmed round with a deep frill, also embroidered; others are surrounded by a delicate wreath of embroidery, and only have bouquets in the corners. A very simple and elegant shawl may be made of muslin edged with two tucks about an inch wide and one inch apart, crossing each other at the corners and trimmed round with a frill about six inches deep, having on it a hem and one tuck to match the shawl.

Quilting dresses in all colors, with pardessus to match, are the most *distingué* walking dress for the country or seaside this season.

Zouave jackets are worn both for morning and full dress; for the former they are made of the same material as the skirt, or else of white *piqué*, braided or embroidered. We have seen some very pretty ones with a narrow vine running all round them, and large bunches at each corner in front, smaller ones being placed at the neck where the jacket is fastened, also in the middle of the neck behind, and just above the hem or scallop at the back, directly in the center. Colored braids are much used on the *piqué*, and the effect is good. Some of the shirts have a frill down the front plaited like a shirt frill and decorated with velvet. For children of both sexes, these Zouaves are all the rage; they are made of all kinds of materials, thick and thin, but the white *piqué* suit with broad, gay ribbon sash and the little turban hat with plume, makes a very pretty and stylish costume. The evening Zouaves are made of mull muslin, embroidered, with shirts to match, or figured blonde lace trimmed with ruching or narrow blonde edge; the skirt is also of lace. This last style of Zouave is quite new, particularly light and graceful, and at the same time stylish.

Surplice dresses with revers, or the dresses crossing in front and fastening at the side are much worn. Ribbons seem to be the favorite trimming. They are goffered and placed at the bottom of the skirt, either sloping or in lozenges, sometimes of two colors in alternate portions about a quarter of a yard in length. Some of the charming spring dresses are bordered by five rows of narrow satin ribbon, plaited, others are ornamented with a front trimming consisting of bows of ribbon of the same color as the dress, passing one above another from the edge to the point in the center of the corsage. A bow of the same ribbon is fixed at the top of the corsage in front. Sleeves are, of course, loose; the tight sleeve will not be resumed until fall. Puffs seem much in favor, either running the length of the sleeve or crossing it. Sleeves in the bell shape are pretty looped up in front by a strip of silk edged with lace, under which plaits are formed. Some of the sleeves are gathered at the top and drawn into puffings below. Bands piped with black and white, an inch and a quarter wide, are laid lengthwise on the full part of the sleeve between the puffs.

For young ladies, most of the dresses are made low in the neck, in order to wear the very becoming spencers now so much in vogue. These are of muslin, embroidered, or else puffed, the puffs running lengthwise or crosswise as taste may dictate, or else puffed only to form a yoke. The one in our plate is intersected lengthwise with velvet, which gives it more style; ribbons or black lace can be substituted, or the spencer can be sprinkled with small bows of ribbon or velvet. The sleeves can be long or short, but most of them are puffed to the wrist. Black and white lace spencers are also much worn, and are very pretty for evening, particularly so when worn with a Spanish corsage of black velvet or some bright tinted silk.

The Antoinette fichu, with ends crossing either behind or before, is also very much worn with muslin, *barége*, or jaconet dresses. This fichu supplies the place of a high body, and makes, with spencers, a variety in the toilet. It is composed of white muslins, sometimes of either black or white lace. A very pretty one can be made of alternate rows of black and white lace, a broader row than those employed on the fichu being set on in fullness at the edge, and a ruche of blonde with a narrow row of black velvet in the center passes round the throat and down the front.

Cloaks for watering places are made of material with a long ply on it, the ground being a bright, solid color and the raised part white, which makes the material changeable. They are circles, with a large hood lined with silk and trimmed with heavy tassels. Another style much in request just now is mostly of white, blue, or fuchsia colored cashmere, with a sleeve puffed in the fashion of Henry VIII., and trimmed with gold passementerie, which makes a very *distingué* wrap.

Indoor dresses for little girls are made with low corsage, open in front, confined by barrettes of quilled ribbon. Within the corsage is a chemisette of muslin. Sleeves formed of bouillons of muslin separated by ribbons or velvet. Thin muslin spencers, with the little laced corsage either of black velvet or of material to match the skirt, will be one of the most *recherché* costumes of the season.

For hats the turban or Tudor style prevails, and with its soft and plumy feathers, that float downwards from the hat or else curl prettily round its circumference, adds greatly to its beauty, and makes it a really graceful and becoming headdress. The round hats are, this season, almost entirely confined to riding hats. For boys the Washington and tourist's hats share the general favor with the page's cap.

Bonnets continue to be made high in front and straight on the sides, admitting of a very full trimming over the forehead. Plain and soft crowns are about equally divided among the newest styles. Black and white hair and white straws dotted with black stars or beads are much in favor, also fine Neapolitan straws. Curtains or capes of white tulle or crepe, covered with a rich black lace or *point appliqué*, are the favorites this season. Pink is recovering favor in bonnets; one of the prettiest bonnets we have seen consists of a fancy straw crown and center, with a drawn front of rose sublime silk and crepe, puffed over and fastened on the front, on each side, and on the curtain with black rosettes dotted with white; inside was a ruching of rose sublime silk.

The general form of headdresses partakes rather of the diadem and the *cîche peigne*, connected by a very slender wreath on each side. The newest wreaths are composed of two sorts of flowers; we notice some very pretty ones for young ladies; one in which violets were blended with roses. In front was a round tuft of rosebuds, and behind a similar tuft in the middle of a double cordon of violets made to part so as either to enclose the hair or to be placed underneath. Another wreath was of tea roses and pansies, and another of pinks mixed with grapes and geraniums with foliage.

Some of the summer mantles are quite straight, in the form of a scarf, others are more of the shawl shape, either pointed or square, and elaborately trimmed with borders, tassels, bows, pendants, and crochet and lace trimmings of every description. We see points, circles, and mantles in every variety of real and imitation black lace, and this season they come in a very fine quality of mohair, very stylish and light, and at the same time more durable than lace. But the most *recherché* article brought out this season is a bournous in imitation of old Honiton point, the pattern consisting of fuchsias, snowballs, lilacs, and lilies of the valley, so naturally disposed that the pendulous stem appears almost to wave.

In the midst of these groups a bird with outspread wings is darting on a butterfly half hidden among the flowers. *Barége* shawls and mantles will also be in favor, as they are a cool, pretty, and inexpensive wrap.

In parasols we notice both the canopy and the plain shape, in the former the peaked part is covered with crochet netting, terminating in points timed with tassels. The other styles are mostly black centers with a bias border of a rose sublime silk set up on the parasol, ornamented with fancy trimmings, and having the lower edge pinked. All the parasols are lined with white silk, some are trimmed with lace, a fringe of marabout feathers, or goffered ribbon.

The Josephine gloves, of a peculiar cut, and the Mathilde glove, bordered at the wrist with a row of dahlia leaves, stamped out, are to be seen on the hands of all our belles.

THE VITTORIA

From the establishment of G. Brodie, 51 Canal St, New York.
Drawn by L.T. Voigt, from actual articles of costume.

The general characteristics of the style most in vogue this season are preserved in this beautiful garment; the variation which it presents in its particular construction however, places it in a front rank with its competitors in beauty. The pyramidal creations are bordered with a corded outline of lilac silk – the garment itself being black taffeta. The upper portion is ornamented with a cape of rich black guipure lace, falling over the silk and the outer borders of the gores with an effective passementerie, which is continued at their apices by rosettes of gimp.

LATEST FASHIONS

Fig. 1 – Dress of Mozambique, grey ground, with magenta flowers. The dress is gored; body and skirt in one piece, the skirt bound with Magenta silk, and Magenta ribbon bows up the front of the dress.

Fig. 2 – Dress of gray summer poplin. Skirt plain; the body has lapels trimmed with blue silk and a linen collar turns over on this lapel. The sleeves have a blue gauntlet cuff. Sash of grey poplin, bound with blue silk.

NEW STYLE OF POINTED YOKE CHEMISE

A lilac spring silk, gored, buttoned from the throat down, and trimmed with narrow quilled ribbon. Loose sleeve with puffs laid on.

Child's dress of white muslin. Coat of buff *piqué*, trimmed with braid, and braided. White straw hat, with white plume.

DESCRIPTION OF DRESSES WORN AT THE LATE DRAWING-ROOM RECEPTION OF HER MAJESTY QUEEN VICTORIA

Mrs. Henry Willis – Rich *vert de pomme moiré* train, lined with white satin, trimmings of fine Brussels point lace, *ondé*, surmounted by wreaths of tulle and satin ribbon, *corsage à drape* with same fine lace; petticoat of rich satin blanc tulle bouillon, *en tablier*, with wreaths of fern leaves and bouquets of lilac and white azaleas. Headdress, azaleas in lilac and white, feathers, and fine Brussels lace lappets; a tiara of diamonds.

Mrs. Kekewich – Train of rich white watered silk, lined with *glacé*, and trimmed with Honiton lace and bows of violet velvet ribbon; skirt of violet and white watered silk, trimmed with tulle and ribbon. Headdress, feathers, and Honiton lace lappets; ornaments, diamonds.

Mrs. S.R. Kreft – Train of rich white broche *moiré* antique, ornamented with band of rose *du roi* velvet, bordered on each side with a fine gold band corsage to correspond, with deep gold blond fall and sabots; dress of tulle illusion, with spotted gold veil, looped up at the side with gold cables and rosettes of rose *du roi* velvet. Headdress, plume, gold cables, and veil; ornaments, gold and diamonds.

Mrs. Wilmer Wilmes – *Costume de cour* composed of a train of gray velvet, lined with silk, and trimmed with guipure and silver lace; corsage to correspond; skirts of white *glacé*, with guipure lace flounces and silver trimmings. Coiffure of ostrich feathers, veil, and diamonds.

Mrs. Richard Trench – Train of gray *moiré* antique, lined with *glacé*, and trimmed with old point lace; petticoat of *glacé*, with flounces of lace over tulle, ornamented with satin ribbon. Headdress, feathers and lappets.

Mrs. Hodson – Train of black *moiré* antique, lined with *glacé*, and trimmed with velvet; skirt of black *glacé*, trimmed with tulle and velvet. Headdress, feathers and tulle veil.

Mrs. Henry Sandford – Train and corsage of rich white *moiré* antique, ornamented with plaitings of the same; dress of rich white *poult de soie*, with tunic of fine Brussels point lace and garniture of pink ribbon and marguerites. Headdress, plume, lappets, fine flowers, &c.; ornaments, diamonds.

Mrs. L. Powys – Train of rich pink *moiré* antique, trimmed with Honiton lace, festooned over plaitings of crepe, and trimmed with white azaleas'. Headdress, feathers, lappets, and flowers; ornaments, diamonds.

Mrs. S. Christy – A train of rich petunia *poult de sole*, with garniture of fine Honiton lace, and ruches of petunia and white silks; corsage to correspond; dress of white tulle illusion, with narrow flounces and tunic of fine Honiton lace. Headdress, plume, lappets, and flowers; ornaments, diamonds.

Miss Victoria Russell – Train and bodice of rich white *poult de soie*, richly trimmed with blue taffetas and silver braid, ornamented with bows of silver; petticoat composed of alternate flounces of blue and white tulle over white *glacé*; corsage drape. Coiffure, plumes, lappets, and silver flowers.

Miss Thynne – Train of rich white *glacé*, trimmed with tulle, blond lace, and ruches of Solferino *glacé* silk; petticoat of white tulle, over silk, trimmed with ruches and bouquets of red and white camellias. Headdress, feathers and camellias; tulle veil.

The handsomest Fan in the World is probably the one given by the Jewish ladies of Algeria to the Empress Eugenie the past year. It is formed of white ostrich feathers of about fifteen inches in length. The feathers are fixed in a golden disk, which is ornamented round the outer edge with fine pearls, rubies, and emeralds and in the center with arabesques in enamels, on gold of different colors, and with rubies, emeralds, and diamonds. In the center is a Hebrew inscription, mentioning the conquest of 1830, a date not agreeable to the moors, since it was that at which their domination in Algeria ceased. The handle is in coral, fluted with gold and ornamented with fine pearls. The upper part is divided into two branches, ornamented with arabesque and having the imperial crown in gold; the other end terminates in a golden ball, studded with stars in diamonds, and bearing a ring ornamented with rubies and emeralds. On one side of the handle is a large emerald surrounded with a double triangle forming a star with six points, ornamented with arabesques, rubies, and brilliants. Three are also two circles in fine pearls relieved with arabesques, and bearing the following inscription: "Les dames *Israéllite* d Alger à S.M. *Impératrice Eugénie*, 1860. This magnificent fan is enclosed in a beautiful Arab case.

Bridal Wreaths still affect the round form, slightly elongated before and behind. The last creations of Mme. *Bonier-Cherre* were, first, one of lilac and orange-flower, coming rather low at the sides; then one of narcissuses and orange-flower; and lastly, one of orange-flower and jessamine. We have seen a few entirely of some large white flower, like the narcissus, the pink, or the primrose, and having only a tuft of orange-flowers added on one side.

NOVELTIES FOR JUNE

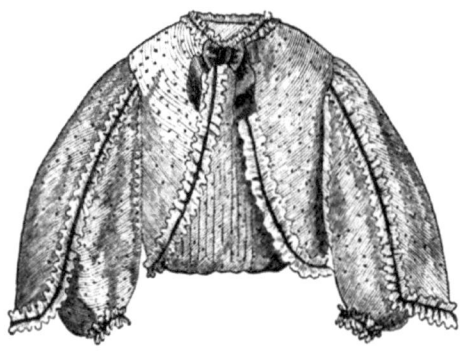

Fig. 1 - Zouave jacket and vest for dotted muslin, trimmed with a ruche of the same, through which is passed a braid or narrow velvet ribbon of some bright color, bow of the same shade. This is an extremely simple and serviceable pattern, easily done up, as the ribbon is only caught on; and as the jacket will be almost universal the present season (together with the white spencer and black velvet point), we consider the present design very serviceable.

Fig. 2 – A new style of chemise for a young lady.

Fig. 3 – Morning slip for a child just walking. To be made of dimity ruffling and narrow linen braid.

Fig. 4 – Shirt for a little boy, with worked Marseilles collar and cuffs

Fig. 5 – Cap of net and lace, suitable for a matronly lady.

Fig. 6 – Stylish cap of dotted black and white tulle. Coronet and bows of mauve colored ribbon.

Fig. 7 – Fancy muslin cap, trimmed with a full ruche of pinked silk, with large bow on the top; the ends of the bow fall over the back of the cap.

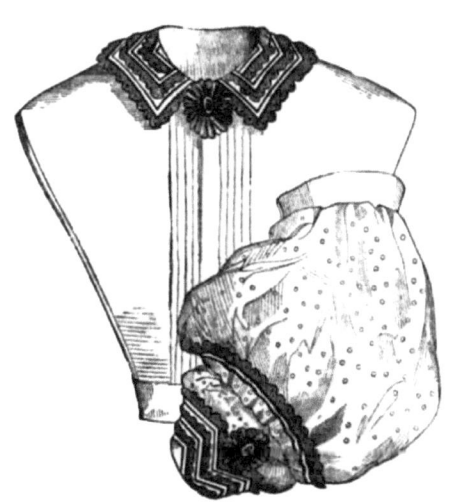

Figs. 8 & 9 – Collar and sleeve for half-mourning, very stylish and effective.

Fig. 10 – Sleeve for evening dress, also suited for undersleeve with a very open dress sleeve, in any summer material. Four puffs of Brussels net, separated by ribbon ruches, the two last terminating in bows on the forearm. Double fall of point Duchesse. This is a very suitable sleeve for the clear white muslin spencers so desirable for those to whom the Zouave jacket is unbecoming.

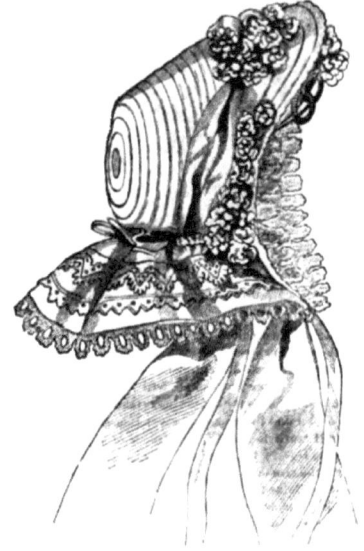

Fig. 11 – White chip bonnet, trimmed with lilac ribbon and flowers.

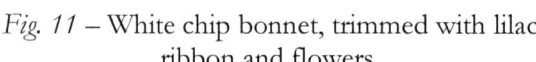

CHILD'S BRAIDED GATOR BOOT

The toe and heel are to be tipped with patent leather.

CRAFTING & NEEDLEWORKS

SOFA PILLOW IN LONG-HOOK CROCHET

Materials – Two colors of S thread or double Berlin wool (these colors should be adapted to the tint of hangings of the room); one skein of shaded double wool, either scarlet or any other hue which will harmonize. The cushion from whence the engraving is taken is composed of stone color and light emerald green (not grass green). The scroll work is scarlet; one skein of the darkest claret is necessary for dividing the pieces. A cushion of calico, the size of the crochet, cut in the same shaped pieces, then joined together, then well waxed by rubbing a lump of beeswax on the inside to prevent the feathers from coming through, and then filled with four pounds of feathers, will make a handsome cushion. A crochet hook nine inches long, and on measuring round with a piece of tape, it should measure half an inch and one-eighth over, or in other words, five-eighths of an inch.

Explanation of Stitch, which it were well to practice first on a foundation of ten stitches, and decrease every other row: *Foundation Row* – Make 21 chain as in ordinary crochet; miss the 1st chain or loop; place the hook through the next; catch hold of the wool at the back; pull it through as a loop on the hook, still keeping it on the hook. Repeat the same to the end of the chains, *still keeping all the loops on the hook*, till there are 20 loops on the hook. *1st Row* – Twist the wool over the hook; pull it through the two loops nearest the point of the hook, thus working it backwards. Twist the wool over again, pulling it through the next two, and continue working backwards till there is only one loop on the hook.

2d – On examining the work, a row of untwisted loops will be found in *front*, not *on the edge*; miss the first long loop; place the hook through the next; draw the wool through as a loop on the hook, still keep it there, and continue till there are as many loops on the hook as was commenced with. Count this row every time to see there is no diminution of stitches till the decrease. Make 21 loops; *now work 10 rows on, till 5 long loops in front can be counted; then decrease at the end of next row on left-hand side, by taking the two last of the front loops together.

Now work the row back, and take the last three loops together on the right-hand side; repeat from * until there are only four loops on the work. *But observe that, after the decrease on the right-hand side* IN THE NEXT ROW, *the hook must be inserted in the* THIRD LONG STITCH, *or there will be no decrease; and be sure to take up the last loop on the left-hand side in every row that is not decreased.* Now, with 4 loops on the hook, twist the wool over the hook; draw it through two loops again; twist over; draw through 2; then again through 2; now place the hook through 2d long in front; pull the wool through, Then again through next long, and pull the wool through; now through 2 loops backwards; and again through 2; then 1 chain, and fasten off. Now there are 43 long loops on the surface, from the point to the commencement, reckoning from the center. Now join on the wool to the broad end of the point, and at the right-hand side insert the hook in the 1st loop of the foundation; twist the wool over the hook, and pull it through; repeat this till there are 20 loops on the hook; then finish this point as the first. Now observe that on one side of the piece, at the edge, a perfect chain stitch appears, and on the other side only a slight loop.

Now, with the darkest claret wool, work a row of single crochet all-round the piece, taking up the two loops of the chain on one side, and only one on the side of the single edge. Now, with same wool, sew the pieces together, making one stitch in every loop. There must be sixteen of these divisions, which will make a handsome cushion.

BRAIDED SLIPPER PATTERN

HEART-SHAPED SCENT SACHET

These pretty little sachets should be made by every lady, to be scattered through her drawers, so as to impart a general fragrance to the various articles of her wardrobe. The trouble is very slight, and the material no more than any trifling remnant of silk of the size shown in our illustration, and three quarters of a yard of ribbon to form the bow. The little group of flowers which we have given is to be embroidered on the sides as slightly as possible; the two parts are to be laid face to face and stitched together, with accuracy, to their shape, leaving an opening at the top; after this they are to be turned and filled with fine cotton wool, impregnated with any perfume most agreeable to taste; after which the aperture is to be closed, and the rosette of ribbon laid upon the place. Ladies who are not inclined to undertake the embroidery may take any piece of fancy silk, or even such as are quite plain, and make them up in the same way, without this decoration. These little sachets make pretty presents, and it has been with reference to this that the "Forget-me-not" has been selected for its embellishment.

SCENT CASE FOR NOTE PAPER

The material on which the cover of the Scent Case is worked is satin, which may be of any rich color; royal blue, purple, ruby color, or in short, any that may be preferred. The medallion in the center is of white watered silk, but to avoid trouble this may also be left of the satin which has been chosen. The medallion is surrounded by a double row of gold beads, of which the interval between may be filled up with either clear white or black beads. When the medallion is tin white silk, this margin effectually conceals the line of its insertion. The scalloped pattern is worked in chain-stitch, in double lines; of the first row, the inner one is in light maize color, and the outer one of dark maize. The second row of scallops is in either two crimsons or two blues, according to the color of the satin. The two straight lines of the margin are in the two shades of maize, while the zigzag line between is simply a herring-bone of violet color. The group in the center is worked in maize color.

When the ornamental needle-work part has thus been completed, it will of course be less trouble to send it to the repository to be made up; but as we think some ladies may feel inclined to finish it themselves, and as we think that with ordinary care it is one of those things which come within their own power, we will go on to offer them a few further instructions.

A blotting book of the required size must be taken; within each cover must be laid a piece of wadding exactly fitting its dimensions, and sufficiently impregnated with whatever perfume the lady worker may prefer. This being neatly squared round its edges, the satin cover must be laid on the outside, brought over, and carefully tacked down, having been so arranged as to leave a margin of about half an inch all round of the plain satin beyond the needle-work pattern. This being done, two pieces of perforated cardboard are to be placed inside, just within the margin, which having been first bound with narrow ribbon, is then fastened down. Through the apertures of this perforated cardboard exudes the scent which impregnates the note paper of which the scent case is the receptacle.

EMBROIDERY PATTERN FOR THE DOUBLE SKIRT OF A LITTLE GIRLS DRESS

The pattern we are now giving has a very rich effect worked on the edges of an upper and under skirt of a little girl's dress. It is formed of heart shaped parts, which are linked within each other, and appear as interlacing; these are of two kinds, and alternate. The one has a row of open holes at each edge, the branching lines to which they are attached in the interior being sewn over. The other is filled in with leaves in the cut-out work. The flowers in the centers of the hearts may be either in well raised satin-stitch or in the cut-out work. The scallop is in clear distinct button-hole stitch. This border should be worked over a tolerably wide hem, instead of being cut out to the scallop, as the effect is better, and firmness and durability are more secure.

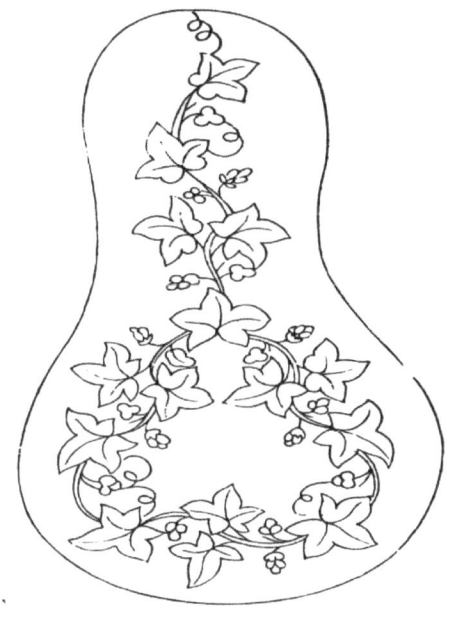

EMBROIDERED WATCH CASE
To be worked on velvet or cloth, with chenille or silk.

KNITTED ARTIFICIAL FLOWERS
(Heart's Ease)

This flower requires five petals to form it, two violet and three yellow; one of the latter must be larger than the rest, and of a deeper color. All the wool must be split.

For the violet petals, cast on ten stitches on two needles, five on each; fold the two needles so as to bring the last stitch behind the first, and double knit a piece of rather more than half an inch in length, taking one stitch from one needle, and one from the other throughout each row. When you take the needles out, run the wool through them with a rug needle, and pass a piece of double wire through the little bag which the knitting has formed, catch it at the top and sides to keep it in form, draw up the other end, and twist the wires together after having shaped the wire to the form of the petal. The yellow petals are knitted in the same way, the largest requires twelve stitches, and the last four or six rows must be done with violet wool, to form the dark spot at the top. The two smaller yellow petals only require eight stitches, with two or four rows of violet at the top; twist the wires of the five petals together, and cover the stem with green wool; a cross stitch, like herring-bone, should be made with green wool, where the petals join in the middle of the flower.

For the calyx, thread a needle with whole green wool, fasten this on the stem, at the back of the flower, and take a herring stitch at the back of each petal, making the stitch rather long, and leaving the wool loose. The buds formed by making a little tuft of yellow, violet, and green wool, mixed together; fix it on a piece of wire by crossing the wool over, and twisting the wire very tight, turn the ends of the wool down the wire, and fasten them at about a quarter of an inch down, by twisting some green split wool round, with which the little stem must be also covered.

Leaves – Cast on three stitches
Knit one row, purl one row, then
1st row – Make one, knit one throughout the row
2d – Make one, purl the row

3d – Make one, knit three, make one, knit one, make one, knit two
4th – Make one, purl the row
5th – Make one, knit five, make one, knit one, make one, knit six
6th – Make one, purl the row
7th – Cast off, or fasten off, three stitches, knit three, make one, knit one
8th – Cast off three stitches, purl the row
9th – Make one, knit five, make one, knit one, make one, knit four
10th – Make one, purl the row
11th – Make one, knit seven, make one, knit one, make one, knit six
12th – Make one, purl the row
13th – Fasten off three stitches, knit the remainder
14th – Fasten off three stitches, purl the rest
15th – Knit six, make one, knit one, make one, knit six
16th – Purl the row
17th – Knit seven, make one, knit one, make one, knit six
18th – Purl the row
19th – Fasten off three stitches, knit four, make one, knit one, make one, knit seven
20th – Cast off three stitches, purl the row
21st – Knit six, make one, knit one, make one, knit five
22d – Purl the row
23d – Knit seven, make one, knit one, make one, knit six
24th – Purl the row
25th – Cast off three stitches, knit remainder
26th – Cast off three stitches, purl remainder
27th – Knit row plain
28th – Purl the row plain
29th – Knit row plain
30th – Purl row plain
31st – Cast off two, knit remainder
32d – Cast off two, purl remainder
33d – Knit row plain
34th – Purl row
35th – Knit row plain
36th – Purl row plain
37th – Cast off two, knit remainder
38th – Cast off two, purl remainder
Fasten off the two last stitches.

It is on this principle that all kinds of indented leaves are made; by knitting more rows with increase between the castings off, they are made broader: by working more rows between the castings off, they are made longer; and by casting off more stitches at a time, the indentations are made deeper; so that the endless variety of natural leaves may be copied without difficulty.

Having completed the leaves, some wire must be sewn neatly round, following the turnings of the leaf exactly; and for the larger ones, it will be better to sew a double wire in the center of the leaf at the back, which will conceal the openings left by the increase of stitches.

One or two flowers, with a bud, and two or three leaves, are sufficient for a small branch.

PATCHWORK DESIGNS

TOP OF TOILETTE OR PINCUSSION
In embroidery, or braiding in fine gold thread

BEAD MATT No. 1

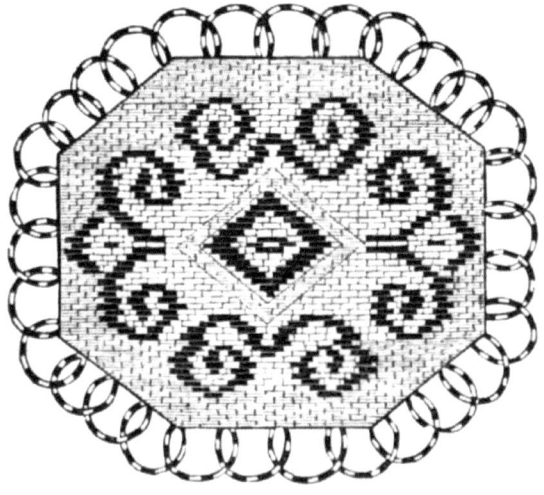

It is quickly made and very pretty. The beads are large, and of glass, white and red, strung on purse silk of a deep crimson. Make the pattern of the beads, the dark ones red, the light white, and fill up the canvas in black tapestry stitch. Take a piece of card, the shape of pattern, and sew the canvas down to it; line with crimson silk. The fringe is made of the beads fastened down in loops crossing each other.

EMBROIDERY DESIGNS

CORNER FOR A POCKET HANDKERCHIEF

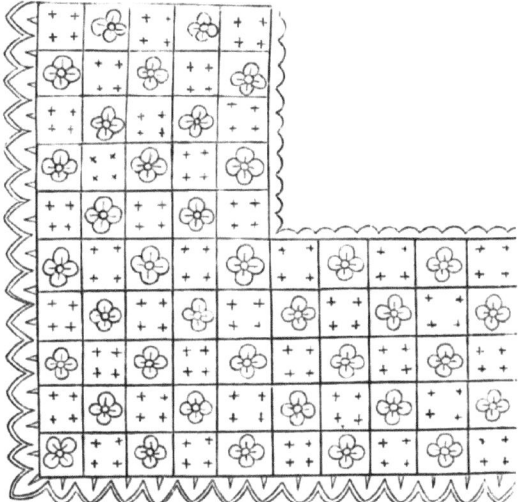

FOR PILLOW AND BOLSTER CASES

FOR A DRESS OR CLOAK

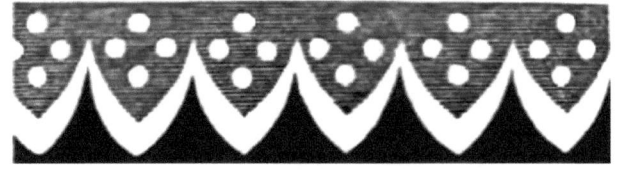

CHAPTER 7
JULY 1861

DESCRIPTION OF FASHION-PLATE FOR JULY 1861

Fig. 1 – Robe, with three skirts of pink and white tulle over a slip of white silk. The lowest skirt is composed of white tulle, and is trimmed at the edge with a narrow flounce of pink satin ribbon. Over this skirt there is a pink tunic skirt, edged with a frill of ribbon. The upper skirt is of white tulle, open, and the two ends are crossed over like a fichu, the two pointed ends being fixed to the edge of the tunic by a bouquet of water-lilies mingled with blades of grass and sprays of small flowers. The corslet is of pink satin, surmounted by folds of white tulle; it is pointed in front both at the upper and lower edge; at the back it is pointed at the top only. The sleeves are very small, composed of tulle, trimmed with a narrow frill of ribbon. The hair is dressed very low, and a wreath of water-lilies with grass encircles the head.

Fig. 2 – Zouave jacket of blue armure silk, embroidered. The shirt, with wide bouffant sleeves, is made of white muslin, buttoned up in front by a row of coral buttons or studs, and has a small standing up collar and cuffs composed of blue embroidered silk, and edged with narrow lace. Skirt of blue armure, trimmed with a band of a darker shade, having the upper edge embroidered. The waistband is of blue velvet, ornamented with gold embroidery. The headdress is the coiffure Orientale, composed of a bandeau in gold passementerie, with a rosette on each side encircled with gold beads, and having pendent gold tassels.

Fig. 3 – White grenadine skirt, ornamented with bands of green; waist and over skirt of fine French muslin; shoulder knots and sash of green ribbon;

white Leghorn hat, trimmed with black velvet and an ostrich plume.

Fig. 4 – A summer habit, consisting of a buff nankeen skirt, white *piqué* jacket trimmed with Marseilles buttons, a blue necktie, and white straw hat trimmed with black velvet and a white heron's plume.

Fig. 5 – Magenta pink grenadine skirt, made over a silk slip; white muslin spencer, composed of puffs and inserting, and trimmed with ribbons to match the skirt. Coiffure of black lace and daisies. Mathilde gloves.

CHITCHAT UPON NEW YORK AND PHILADELPHIA FASHIONS, FOR JULY

It is not to be expected that the same variety will pervade the world of fashion the present season, when there is so little encouragement for the production of novelties. The largest houses in the country give this as a reason for the comparative absence of the more perishable articles of the wardrobe that would be on hand at this moment.

Our milliners have, however, had their usual summer openings, and in many cases these were well attended, and the sales good. Not to weary our readers with passing them in review, we give some of the latest and freshest bonnets found at Mrs. Scofield's establishment, where the display was all in good taste.

A bonnet of white net, with a round crown. It was entirely covered with figured black lace, plain across the crown, but full on the sides and brim. A narrow ribbon of the pink salmon color, known as Garibaldi, encircled the extreme edge of the crown. The edge of the brim was bound by a ribbon of the same shade, richly embroidered in rosebuds, with natural colors. Quite on the front of the brim, a little to the left, was a large bouquet of jonquils and black sloes; inside the brim, a bouquet of jonquils, buds, and blossoms, with the contrast of the sloe berries; ribbon strings.

A delicate hat of white crepe, the brim quite plain, save flat loops of violet ribbon, with ends, on the extreme edge of the brim, with a few large violets in the center of the knot. About the center of the bonnet, a blonde veil was fastened by a large bouquet of violets, mounted as a heavy spray; this fell backward over the crown cape, which was plain. A full cap, the first we have seen this year, inside the brim, with a spray of violets across the forehead.

The "Zillon braid" is a new material resembling chip, still more than the Pamela. It is also much lighter than the Pamela. We saw a bouquet of this pure white material, with a soft cap crown of black and white lace. The cape was of white crepe and black lace. A diadem spray (that is, the flowers being heavy in the center, and growing less each way) of pale blue flowers on top of the crown; the same flowers with a white blonde cap inside.

In pure chip we noticed a peculiar brim, nearly one half of which appeared cut in strips an inch wide, and ending in loops of the same, fastened by pearl ornaments in the solid part of the brim. The spaces were filled with lace and blonde. The cape was blonde, with a plaiting of chip above. The bouquets on this bonnet were the liveliest combinations we have seen - jessamine, lily of the valley, stems of grass, and a handful of roses laid lightly together, while an exquisite spray of wild rosebuds strayed down, the buds and foliage looking as if just gathered from the hedge rows.

Taffeta crepe, the delicate tissue being caught in diamonds by stitches of straw, was one of the prettiest materials we noticed. The Zillon braid and white chip rival the popularity of crepes, blondes, and black lace. Black lace was never used in greater profusion, from the costliest Brussels to the plainest net. Flowers of almost native beauty and in heavy wreaths, bouquets, and sprays are found both inside and on the brim of every bonnet; those on the outside may either be very far forward on the brim, at the center of the bonnet, or far back on the edge of the crown. One of the most simple and tasteful hats we have seen, a direct importation, was of drawn crepe, a fanchon, or rather handkerchief of thread lace completely covered it, one point being turned over the edge of the brim in front, the other falling below the cape. This lace was the sole ornament, save that to the left the lace was raised by a cluster of blush roses without foliage; the same formed a diadem inside the brim. Caps are fully reinstated in favor; Parisian houses saying that their absence is too trying to ordinary faces. It will take a year or two to banish them entirely.

In dresses Stewart has a few novelties in grenadines, *barége Anglais*, and Organdies. The first is ever a serviceable material, and though costly, repays its first expense by its long wear. The rich embroideries in silk – the Jacquard lawn now rivalling the needle in every respect – are upon plain or grayish grounds; bright green, Magenta, and mauve being the favorite shades for the figures, which are leaves, pansies, rosebuds, cherries, geometrical figures, etc. The costliness of the higher grades in the material prevents their too common adoption. These dresses are trimmed with plaitings of solid colored ribbon, the shade of the embroidery. The sash should be of silk, the same color, with a plaiting of narrow ribbon surrounding it, or of embroidered ribbon to correspond. Late arrivals from Paris confirm the return of the sash into high favor. During the summer months, the Spanish bodice is more suitable for silks, though nothing can be a better contrast than a *point d la Isabel*, with the white muslin spencer we early introduced to the notice of our readers, and illustrated in our last number. All muslin, organdy, and other summer tissues, are now made with draperied waists, either *d la vierge* (baby waist) surplice, drawn into fullness by cords, or laid in plaits. No prettier design for a summer dress can be found than in Fig. 4 of our last number, though many prefer the single flounce around the bottom of the dress. For the neutral poplins, Mozambique's, etc., now worn for traveling dresses, black velvet, either in plaitings, bows, or set on plain, appears to be the favorite material. Close sleeves are very convenient and suitable for travelling, with a puff or jockey to relieve the plainness. For all other materials flowing sleeves were never more worn. We are reminded in the connection that Madam Demorest has opened an uptown establishment, more central and accessible for ladies wishing their own materials made up, and where "Garniture" is not forced mysteriously to cover four-fifths of an enormous bill. Mrs. Ellis, the head of the dressmaking department, a lady of great good taste and much experience, is hereafter to be found at the uptown establishment, 27 East Fourteenth Street, and we can heartily commend her to those of our subscribers who are strangers to the locals of New York dressmakers.

Several new styles for making up fall silks are in preparation, but we turn to a more seasonable subject – Brodie's light summer wraps, never more stylish or graceful than now, despite the pressure which has crushed other less well established houses.

There is a new material called Cashmere, a mixed cloth of wool and silk, entirely unlike the old fabric, yet light and soft, very suitable for summer travelling wear. Of this clouded gray material Brodie has made up wraps in a circular form, shaped to have a gored appearance, though quite seamless. They are hemmed around the edge, or finished with braid to correspond, *stitched on flat*, not bound, which is a feature of cloth cloaks this season. A dahlia rosette of the same cloth, with two barbe like ends, handsomely finished, is the sole ornament of the full circular riding hood attached. This hood, the veritable "Red Riding" in shape, is the most popular in silk cloaks also. Among Brodie's handsomest cloaks is one of rich plain black taffeta, with a hood of this shape edged by a rich fall of lace three inches deep. Lace was also introduced into the rosette, and edged the barbe. Another elegant summer cloak, in the same costly material, was quite plain on the back, the amplitude required for grace being obtained by square plaits on the shoulders, over which the trim line in a neat curve. This rimming consisted of a band of white silk, an inch and a half in width, covered by a guipure inserting, and edged on each side by narrow guipure lace; the silk only serving as a rich background on which to display the lace. This same style of trimming over violet silk we noticed in another style of burnouse, set on in spaces, like the quartering of an orange, from the neck to the waist line. *Length* has in all things taken the place of breadth in the whole style of figure. "The churn air is the air *distingué*", as someone cleverly says the present season. Nearly all cloaks, mantles, etc., come to within a few inches of the hem of the dress, and in walking dresses or coats they are made in many instances completely to cover them. We shall speak of lace mantles, thin shawls, children's dress, and mourning in our next.

SUMMER TOILETTES FOR THE STREET AND WATERING PLACES

Skirt of blue grenadine, made over silk, with box plaited trimming. White muslin spencer, puffed lengthwise, and three rows of very narrow velvet between the puffs. White muslin shawl with flounce. Blue drawn *crâpe* bonnet with flowers on the outside.

ORGANDY CHEVRON DRESS

Organdy chevron dress, white ground, with violet chevron stripes and wreaths of flowers between the stipes. Corsage half low, with a puffed muslin chemisette. White straw hat, one of the new spring styles, trimmed with fruit and black velvet.

THE ZOUAVE NÉGLIGÉ

The jacket and skirt are of white *piqué*, trimmed with two rows of very narrow colored braid. As the jacket is only intended for morning wear, it is much longer than the ordinary Zouave; with it is worn a shirt of plaited linen bosom, and fancy silk necktie. Tuscan braid hat, trimmed with black velvet and straw.

THE IMPERIAL

This is a circle, made of light checked woolen material, bound with black silk, corded on each edge with a thick cord of purple silk. A large box plait lay underneath in the center of the back, from the neck to the waist, causes it to fit the figure, and gives grace and fullness to the lower part of the mantle. The same style of plait is on the shoulder, which forms a very nice sleeve. Fancy bands bound with purple are on the plaits on the back and shoulder. Leghorn hat, bound with black velvet, and trimmed with velvet, wheat, and field flowers.

THE ARAGONESE

From the establishment of G. Brodie, 51 Canal Street, New York.
Drawn by L.T. Voigt from actual articles of costume.

Made of black taffeta. This outfit is made without the stuff being more than an easy fullness at the back, but is arranged with the material being pinched in broad folds upon the shoulders. This presents an imposing effect. A passementerie, with a ruched edge, ornaments the upper portion.

NOVELTIES FOR JULY

The use of breakfast caps having become much more universal of late, particularly at any public place of resort, we give several different styles.

Fig. 1 – The franchette; has a tulle crown crossed by bands of Garibaldi satin ribbon, and surrounded by a row of black French lace. This is again enclosed in a fall of white blonde, forming the real border of the cap, and supported by another row of black lace. The brides are of black lace and Garibaldi satin ribbon.

Fig. 2 – Intended for an older person, also of combined black and white lace, the ends barbe crossing the front, forming the lappets. Many ladies prefer Muslin and cambric as the material for breakfast caps, and in fact either is more suitable than lace for that purpose, as breakfast is a meal that presupposes *negligée* and simple toilet.

Fig. 3

Figs. *3 & 4* – Two very pretty styles of cap.
Fig. 3 is an elaborate example of a French cambric cap, the frills and fronds, or ornaments, being lightly embroidered.

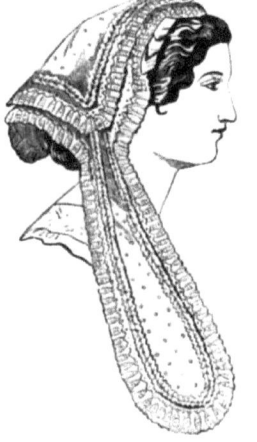

Fig. 4 – A simpler fanchon of dotted muslin, with a Marie Stewart point on the forehead; the embroidered bands that finish it are headed by a light ruche of satin ribbon, which is but caught on, and may be removed when the cap is sent to the laundress.

Fig. 5 – *Francé* undersleeve, caught up by narrow ribbons in groups of three.

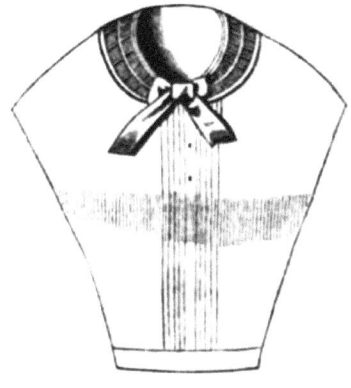

Fig. 6 – Habit Shirt – with collar for morning; the collar is of white crepe, muslin, or tarleton, made with loops, through which a violet ribbon is past. Bow of the same.

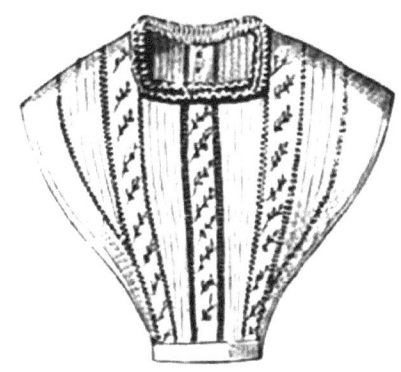

Fig. 7 – Spencer chemisette, for a rolling dress body, composed of alternate narrow plaits and widths of inserting; drawn muslin ruche round the neck, which is cut square.

PATTERNS FROM MADAME DEMOREST'S ESTABLISHMENT

The following patterns are from the celebrated Establishment of Madame Demorest, No. 473 Broadway, New York

ALFRED COAT

Cut sack style, with a slight fullness, and gored in front, and laid over in scallops, which when bound, forms a trimming; open sleeve, cut to match the body, which is confined with a belt. Designed for a child from four to seven years. Requires about two and a half yards, single width material

THE CELESTE
Flowing sleeve, the back laid over the front in points, and trimmed with braid and buttons.

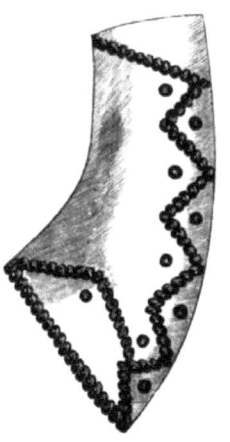

ZULEIKA SLEEVE
An elegant sleeve, in the style of the Arab hood. Decorations, tassels, and buttons.

LELIE SLEEVE
Flowing sleeve, with revers and straps, bound with velvet, and ornamented with buttons.

NIGHT-DRESS
This is a long night-dress; the front laid in plaits, with the edges scalloped, the cuffs and collar are trimmed with dimity ruffling.

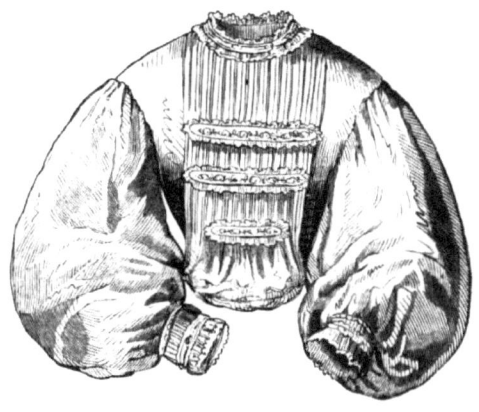

ZOUAVE SHIRT

BREAKFAST CAPS & SUMMER BONNETS

Fig. 1 – Is one of the latest shaped breakfast caps; it is made of mull. The ruffles are of lace. It is trimmed with black velvet, and is very pretty for light mourning.

Fig. 2 – Breakfast cap made of mull muslin and worked insertion. The ruffles are edged with a narrow thread lace. It is trimmed with ribbon, any shade the taste of the wearer may fancy.

Fig. 1 – Leghorn bonnet, with a wide green ribbon laid plainly over it; on the left side is a large bunch of lilacs; ruche of violet crepe in the inside of bonnet, but not extending down the sides.

Fig. 2 – Leghorn bonnet, with fancy open crown, trimmed with black ribbon and scarlet flowers; the cape and front of bonnet are bound with scarlet velvet.

Fig. 3 – Fancy straw bonnet, with edge of front bound with black velvet; the crown is open, and lined with a black cape of maize colored silk, with black lace over it; the rimming of the bonnet is bunches of yellow grass, loops of black lace and maize flowers inside.

Fig. 4 – Brown Leghorn hat, trimmed with a very full brown feather of black velvet ribbon.

NEW STYLES OF APRONS

THE POMPADOUR
Made with groseille silk, trimmed with pink ruffles and a quilling, with a row of velvet buttons down the front.

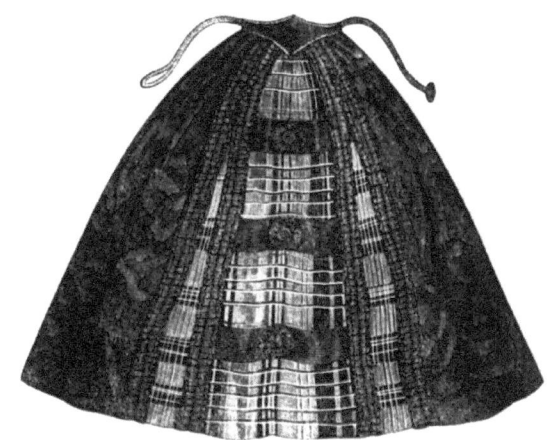

THE EUGENIE
This novel apron is made of one breadth of bright plaid silk, trimmed with lace *patés* and quilled ribbon, and a half breadth of black *moiré* antique on each side. The belt is pointed in front, both on the upper and lower edge

PATTERNS FOR WAISTBANDS AND SASHES

CRAFTING & NEEDLEWORKS

CROCHET HAIR NET

Materials – Scarlet, blue, or crimson crochet silk, medium size; gold or cut black beads. This net, which has a very beautiful effect on the head (because the hair is shown to much greater advantage through the large square holes than in the ordinary style of net, whether done in crochet or netting), is made of bands of diamond open-hem, crossing each other, and edged on each side with a border of beads. At every crossing a small crochet flower is placed. A line of diamond open-hem is carried all round; and in it an elastic may be run. It is finished with a shell-edging, which may have beads, or not, according to taste.

As the size of the net must vary according to the quantity of hair of the wearer, it is well to cut out a perfect round, in paper, of the size desired; and to work on it. Make a chain of the diameter, and work back on it in diamond open-hem. Then a line of sc on each side, dropping a bead on each of twelve stitches, and working eight without. Be careful that the beaded parts correspond at each edge. Do another piece the same length, for the center line in the opposite direction. Work four somewhat shorter lines, two to go on each side of these centers, measuring the length on the paper, so that they may just cross at the plain parts, between the beads; then four more, to go in pairs on the outside of these in each direction, and so on till sufficient are done for the net: seven each way will probably suffice. Tack those to go in one direction on the paper, fastening them at the ends only; and then weave in those which cross there, carrying them over one, and under the following, bar. Take a sewing needle, and some of the same silk, and sew them together whenever they cross. Carry a line of chain-stitch. Follow this with a line of diamond open-hem; then a bead line, then one of plain crochet.

The Shell Border - *9 sc, 13 ch, miss 12* repeat all round. Should there not be stitches sufficient to make perfect patterns, 21 being required for each, they must be increased by working two in one as often as necessary: or, if there be only a few over, instead of increasing diminish by missing one more each time, to bring it to the requisite number.

2d – 7 sc on center 7 of 9, 2 ch, 1 dc, on first chain stitch of 13, and on every alternate one, with 2 chain between; end with 2 chain * repeat all round.

3d – 5 sc on center of 5 of 7. 1 dc on every dc of last round, with 3 chain between.

4th – 3 sc on center 3 of 5. 1 dc and a picot on every dc of last round, with 4 chain between.

The Rosettes – 8 ch, close into a round. Work one round without increase, dropping a bead on every stitch. Then a round without beads, doing 2 stitches in one.

3d round - *3 ch, miss 1, sc under next, *8 times.

4th – Under each chain of 3 dc 1 sc, 3dc, 1 sc; dropping one bead on the last part of every stitch. Sew one of these rosettes at every place where two bars cross each other.

Diamond Open-Hem – has already been explained several times; but we repeat the directions for the benefit of new subscribers. Begin as for a long tc stitch, with the thread three times round the hook. Do half the stitch, put the thread twice more round , insert the hook in the third stitch from that on which you have been working; draw it through, and work as usual, only at the third movement draw through three loops. When finished it looks forked. Do 2ch, and work a dc stitch on the side of the last, putting the hook in where you slipped off three together. It then has the form of an X.

A Picot – 3 ch, insert the hook in the last stitch, and draw the thread through to form a new loop.

INSERTION IN POINTE DE LA POSTE

This extremely neat and pretty style of embroidery may be executed with great rapidity by those who have acquired facility in this particular sort of embroidery. A description of the manner in which it is worked may be of some assistance to those who are not familiar with it, but it is necessary that it should be practiced a little before commencing on the pattern intended to be worked. It will be seen that each leaf in the illustration is double; this gives a richer effect to the work than when the pattern is composed of single leaves. The size of the needle used must not be smaller than a six, and the embroidery cotton about No. 12. The needle is inserted in the muslin, and brought out at the length of the solid part of the leaf; the thread is then twisted round and round the needle ten or eleven times, pushing it up towards the eye of the needle and keeping the thumb of the left hand on it while drawing the needle through, so that the thread should not draw up and the stitch be spoilt; the needle is then put through the muslin at the top of the leaf which secures it, and is brought out at the bottom part of the leaf and another is worked in the same manner close to it, the two forming the two halves of a double leaf of beautiful regularity. The little stalk which unites the leaves is sewn over with a finer cotton. The holes in this pattern are in cut-out work, which enlivens the effect; the whole is strong, and when neatly executed produces a pattern of great richness. It is necessary for this particular kind of embroidery that the pattern should be designed expressly to suit the stitch, as those only can be worked which are arranged for it, and this is one of the reasons why this very pretty style of work is not more general

CHILDS SLIPPER

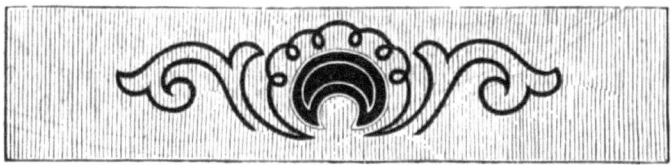

(Side of slipper)

The material is scarlet cloth; the center figure black velvet, the braid in the center figure and round it is gold color, and the other is black.

EMBROIDERED COLLAR

SUMMER DRESS AND MANTLE

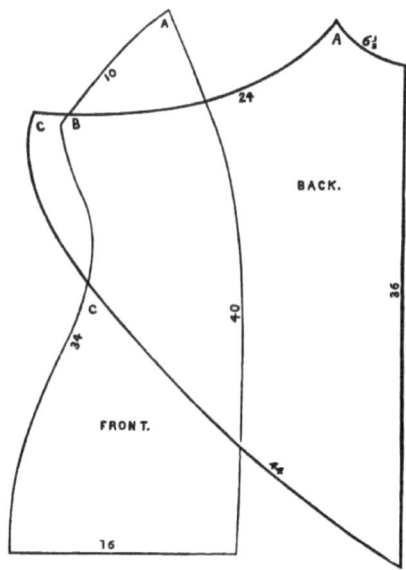

Pearl color spring silk, the body low, with high worked chemisette finished at the throat with a fluted ruffle. The skirt is trimmed with bands of ribbon sewed to the waist, and terminating near the bottom of the skirt in bows and ends. The mantle is of black silk, trimmed with a plaiting of ribbon and bands of velvet. Turban hat, with white plume.

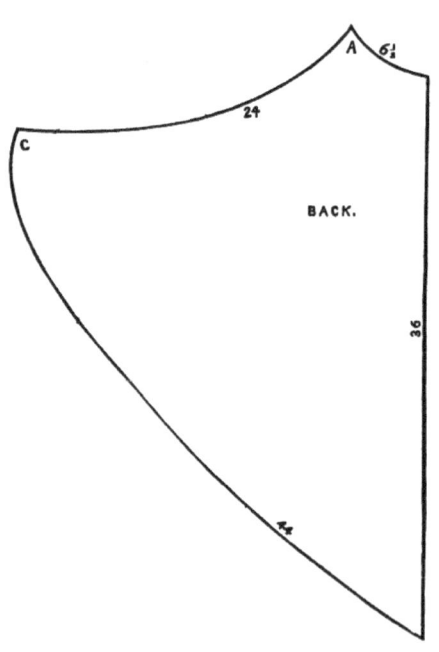

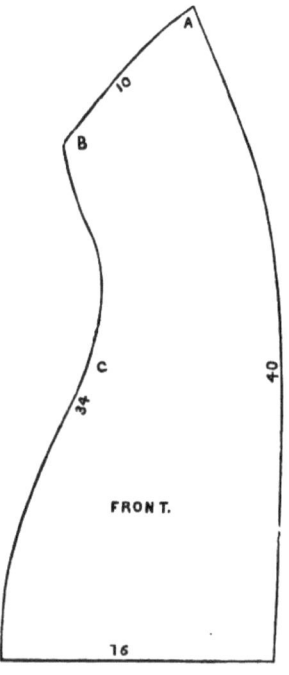

EMBROIDERY DESIGNS

CHAPTER 8
AUGUST 1861

DESCRIPTION OF FASHION-PLATE FOR AUGUST 1861
Dinner and Evening-Dress For Watering-Places

Fig. 1 – Dinner-dress of white grenadine, with trimmings of mauve colored silk and ribbon; the skirt has three *bouillonné* of grenadine, separated by narrow ruffles of mauve silk, with a narrow ornament of ribbon on the lower edge. The upper portion of the skirt is caught up by bands of mauve ribbon, laid on flat. The ribbon ornament, *en eschelle*, that edges the ruffles of the skirt, is repeated on the sleeves, which are demi long and wide. Corsage in a short, rather blunt point; *berthé* of grenadine, in *bouillonné* separated by narrow bands of mauve ribbon. Hair turned back over a cushion. Cap of blonde, flowers, and mauve ribbon.

Fig. 2 – Dress of Pompadour silk, the ground a dove color, the pattern in black and gold. Around the bottom of the skirt are four flounces, alternately of dove color and apple green, all set on with a heading formed by the flounce. The front breadth is in the very popular tablier or apron fashion, formed by alternate narrow flounces. The sleeves, which are a good shape, are ornamented with the same, and a heart-shaped *berthé* to correspond covers the upper part of the corsage. Watteau headdress of lace, with a bandeau of mauve ribbon.

Fig. 3 – Dress for a young girl. Skirt of Pompadour silk, a white ground, with Napoleon blue stripes; between the stripes are pansies in natural colors. Zouave jacket and vest of fine white cashmere, trimmed with narrow black velvet ribbon and black lace; full bishop sleeve of white muslin.

Fig. 4 – Extremely simple and pretty robe, of India muslin, in a striped pattern, made up over a slip of pale rose colored silk. It is ornamented by flat bands of the same, edged with Valenciennes. Sash and bonnet strings of rose colored ribbon.

Fig. 5 – Robe of white satin, having the lower part of the skirt trimmed with a *bouillonné* of tulle, finished above and below with a ruche of tulle, bound at the edges with blue satin ribbon. Over the upper part of the skirt descends a tunic of white tulle *bouillonné* at the edge, and nearly covered by two deep rows of black lace. The tunic is raised up on the left side by a bow with long ends of blue velvet. The corsage low, and pointed in front of the waist, is edged at the upper part with a row of white lace. In front and behind there are folds of tulle, and beneath the folds there is a ruche of tulle bound with blue satin ribbon; from the under part of the ruche descends a narrow frill of black lace. A bow of blue velvet, encircled with black lace, is placed on the ruche in front of the corsage. The sleeves are formed of two puffs of tulle, separated by a frill of black lace. The hair is dressed in frizzed curls in front, and in a bow behind. Headdress consisting of a plait of blue velvet, trimmed at the upper part with a narrow of black lace, and at the back with two lappets, also composed of black lace.

CHITCHAT UPON NEW YORK AND PHILADELPHIA FASHIONS FOR AUGUST

We have been obliged to delay noticing the novelties in juvenile wear, and will now give the nursery its due place. For infants, lovely little cap bonnets in Valenciennes medallions, lined with white silk and edged with frills of Valenciennes, have a little bow of pearled ribbon at the top of the cap or a little on one side. The cape is flowing, and also covered with medallions of Valenciennes. For country wear, tiny capellines of white cambric, lined with blue, rose-colored, or maize silk beneath the insertings are worn; or plain Marseilles or *piqué*, with the brim and edges buttonholed in small scallops, either in white or some fast color. For cloaks, dimity, Marseilles, and *piqué*, either buff or white, trimmed with an endless variety of white braid an inch broad, or several rows of narrow or the moderate width, say half an inch, put on in waved, pointed, or square *Grecque* patterns. The same materials are much used in the little suits made for the street wear of boys from two to five years old. For the house there is a large variety of sacque patterns, very wide in the skirt, so as to allow the under petticoat of flannel; they may be either high or low in the neck; When high, they are accompanied by long sleeves. They are usually cut crosswise of the stuff, which insures a better fit at the waist, and are trimmed all around with one or several rows of braid. Black velvet ribbon or flat silk gimp is largely used on un-washable materials, such as mohair, Italian (raw) silk, plaid alpaca, shepherds' plaid, and the like.

It is a good plan, for very young children, to have a tape running, put on flat on the inside, at the waist line, with a drawing-string to confine the fullness at the waist. For children of this age, in washable materials, a trimmed belt of the material is considered less stiff than one of leather. Very narrow leather belts, in fancy colors, with double clasps of enamel or mother-of-pearl. The black belts with a stamped gold pattern, or those with green, red, or Rus colored ground are the neatest. For country wear, plaid ginghams of good quality, plain linens, figured linens, plaid cottons and any of the light materials in silk and cotton; silk and wool are very suitable.

The same materials are used in the Albert street dress, which is still worn, and more popular than ever. It is a short skirt, consisting of three widths of stuff, box plaited on to a pointed band, which is attached to a Zouave vest of white cambric or linen. Over this is worn a loose jacket, rather longer behind than in front, and sloped out on the hips. In shepherds' plaid of silk and cotton or silk and wool, braided by narrow black velvet ribbon, it is a very neat and serviceable dress, readily made washed, and cared for. We must not neglect to chronicle the new Zouave suits for boys just introduced to Jacket and trousers. The cut-away jacket has long been known, and to this and the shirt above described is added, instead of the plaited skirt or the long-worn knee-breeches, full Turkish trousers, which are loose and easy to the figure, and allow full play to the limbs of the restless little being. Blue and gray flannel is very suitable for this dress, trimmed with a simple pattern in scarlet braid. We shall speak of the suits worn by lads in our next.

It may be remembered that we directed those who had been in the habit of shopping at the ever-to-be-regretted departments are continued under their original direction. We are indebted to Mrs. Myers, of this establishment, for a review of the different hats and caps in favor with the younger branches. The Tudor hat, with the high, turned-up brim, bound by black or colored velvet, with a band of the same, is a very suitable accompaniment for the above dress. It is to be had in Leghorn, split straw, and fancy braids. The half turban is also a good shape. The Continental is intended for quite a young child; its turned-up brim is tri-cornered as the name implies a point before and at each side; it is of split straw, richly trimmed with velvet and wide white ribbon; the side rosettes are of blonde velvet and ribbon. The straw caps, with patent leather visor of some light and pretty shade, and the gray Tudor felts, of the best quality, are intended for older boys.

The children's hat department, being a legitimate branch of Mr. Genin's original business, is still carried on by him in excellent taste, and with the best possible materials. All the above varieties are manufactured by him.

To return to 303 Canal Street. They have lately added a room for children's dress, where the Alfred suits, sacque, etc., already described, are to be found. We noticed in this department a pretty style for making up muslins, Chambray cambrics, etc., for little girls. The waist is full, gathered into the belt in a fan or sheaf pattern, and spreading, to the shoulders, following the outline of the gathers, is a ruffle two inches in width, placed bretelle-fashion, and running over the shoulders to the belt in front and back. The skirt and sleeves were ruffled to correspond.

Another pretty dress is *chinée* gray silk, with three small flounces, each bordered by a roll of green silk. The flounces gradually diminish in depth. The body is cut square across the top, and low, especially on the shoulders. The mantelet to match has four rows of trimming, and fastens in front by a large bow of green silk.

To accompany these low-bodied frocks very pretty Zouave chemisettes are made, plaited all over, and having lappets at bottom to prevent them from working up.

Another of these graceful dresses is made of muslin, having a white ground with mauve lozenges. The skirt is ornamented with a ruche *à la vieille*, of muslin, overlapped at each side by a ruche of mauve ribbon. The body, plaited in the sheaf fashion, is trimmed all round by a small ruche, like that on the skirt. The mantelet, laid in flat plaits, is bordered by a similar ruche, and fastens with a mauve bow.

White silk bonnets with soft crowns are sometimes made for little girls, but the round hat described in the spring (the brim set up an inch or so in the crown) are most generally worn; the trimming, velvet blended with ribbon, and a plume of feathers or straw. Black velvet and white ribbon is very popular. The brim is generally bound with velvet. For walking, Bowden furnishes half high boots of cloth; for the house, slippers of several pretty styles. For street coats – Brodie's best coat is of a light but lustrous black silk, gored to the figure and coming quite to the bottom of the child's dress. It may be buttoned closely from the chin to the waist; the seams are corded. The round pelerine, sleeves, and pockets are trimmed with a double pinked ruche of silk. The same coat is made of whit or buff *piqué*, with linen trimmings and buttons.

Brodie's elegant lace mantles are just in season. The real Chantilly laces imported by him are almost invariably in points or a half shawl, the reason being two-fold a point is always in fashion; and again, a point flowered, or a scarf with full flowers in real lace, is beyond most American purses. Some of his Pusher laces, the present season, are so admirable in design and texture as to deceive even a practiced eye.

Besides the laces, there is a scarf mantilla quite low on the shoulder; the fullness between the shoulders in double box plaits; the point is tablier; it is trimmed with a volante of medium width, the edge being hemmed with a cord. Large flat bow or rosette with long ends at the back; edge with thread lace. There are a few white grenadine and *barége* mantles corded with white silk; of a wide bournous shape. Double shawls of white muslin are also a good deal worn. They sometimes have deep flounces of the same, which round off about a point with a deep hem, or occasionally they have several rows of narrow white and black guipure and velvet ribbon. The shawls of embroidered cashmere, trimmed with lace or guipure, are worn on silk dresses and even on those of clear tissues when the color is rather dark. Lace shawls may be worn with any toilet, and are always an elegant addition. We have also seen some embroidered cashmere summer shawls, with black or carmine grounds, which, though double are light, as well as soft and warm. Summer shawls of grenadine, tissue, *barége*, etc., are quite pretty with a cloud gray center and blue, mauve, apple green, or rose sublime satin stripes on the edge; some have a *chinée* pattern in flowers.

In mourning, the distinguishing feature is a mixture of clear white with black; mauve and royal purple continue to be mingled with black also. We describe two handsome toilets in half mourning. The first, a robe of black silk, trimmed with *francés* (close *bouillonné*) of the same, fixed at equal distances by quilling's of narrow black velvet ribbon. The corsage is high, buttoned up the front, and not pointed in front of the waist. The trimming which forms the epaulette, as well as that on the ends of the sleeves, consists of *francés* similar to those on the skirt. Collar of lace. Undersleeves of tulle, trimmed with lace. Bonnets with a supple crown composed of mauve color silk. The front is edged with four frills of silk, pinked at the edges, two being formed of the same silk as the bonnet, and two of silk of a darker shade of mauve. Across the bonnet there are two frills and two border curtain. On each side is placed a quilling formed of a broad stripe of silk, of the dark shade of mauve, and the strings consist also of broad stripes of the dark silk, pinked at the edges. Under-trimming, a bandeau of white convolvuluses and white blonde at the ears.

A dress for half mourning is made of light gray silk, trimmed at bottom with three flounces of about a hand's breadth, surmounted by very small flounces of a dark gray. This dress, all the plaits of which are turned backwards, spreads handsomely in the fan shape, and presents a decided train. All the flounces are cut in festoons. The body is plain, and fastens in front with dark gray buttons. Larger buttons are put down the front of the skirt. The sleeves, wide and gathered, have a jockey formed of one deep and one narrow flounce, and end in a loose band drawn slantingly and trimmed with two of the same frills.

THE NANNETTE

Organdy dress with white muslin fichu. White straw hat, trimmed with black velvet and game plumes.

THE NINA

White muslin dress with plaited waist; finished at the throat with a lace muff.

Spanish corsage of fancy colored silk, trimmed with quilled ribbon and buttons.

THE BARCELONA

This mantle, which is exceedingly popular, presents, as the novel feature, the garment cut open at the sides and the back, and then buttoned together. The slashing at the back reaches only half its depth, as it is not carried further than to the ends of the tabs, which with the rosettes on the hood, constitute the ornament. They are made of several summer fabrics, those which are plaid being the favorite.

NOVELTIES FOR AUGUST

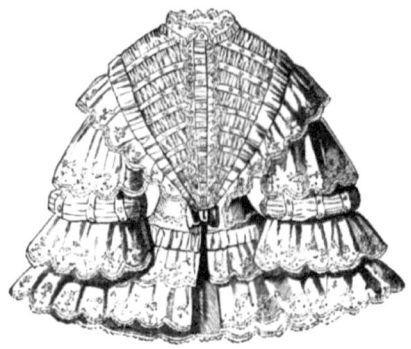

Fig. 1 - Pardessus of muslin, with embroidered flounces of the same, to be worn in the open air, above the ordinary dress, when made with a low corsage and short sleeves. The front is in the chemisette style, with alternate puffs of clear muslin and bands of work.

Fig. 2 – Tulle and blonde capelline, for the promenade of a watering place.

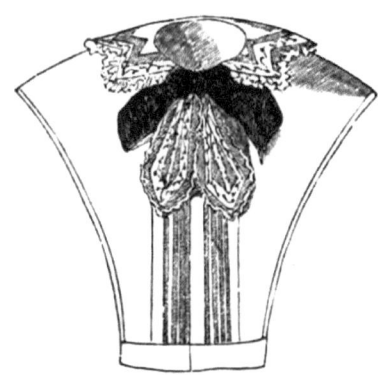

Fig. 3 – Lappet collar of Venetian point, suitable for a dowager. The bow may be of black velvet, or any suitable contrasting ribbon.

Fig. 4 – Vandyke fichu of net, with bars and points of extremely narrow velvet ribbon. Intended to be worn with a low corsage.

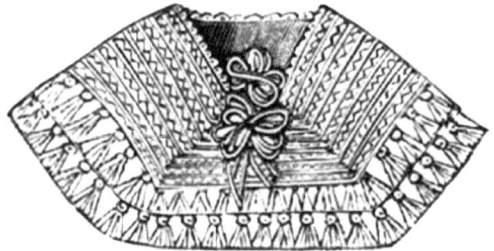

Fig. 5 & 6 – Two styles of undersleeves. *Fig. 6* is particularly good for an open sleeve

Fig. 5

Fig. 6

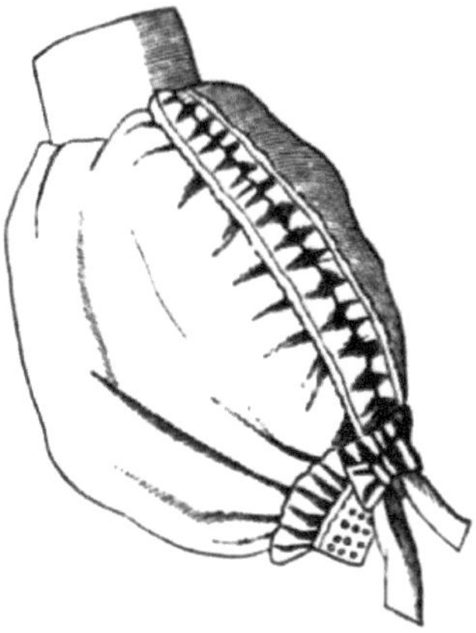

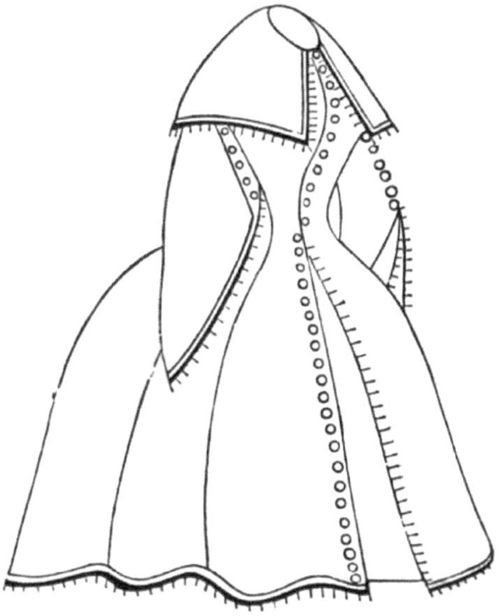

Fig. 7 – Street coat in gores, suitable for a school girl (see chitchat).

Figs. 8 & 9 – Two styles of undergarments for children. We commend *Fig. 8* as being one of the neatest and most serviceable patterns now being made up.

Fig. 8

Fig. 9

Fig. 10 – French *negligé* for a young child. To be made in cambric.

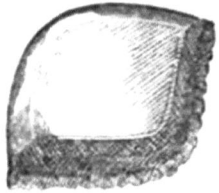 

Figs. 11 & 12 – A child's nightcap & the latest style of collar; to be had in linen or fine work.

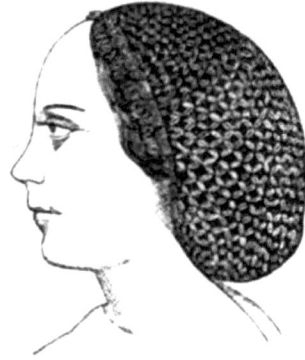

Fig. 13 – Net made of thick chenille.

PATTERNS FROM MADAME DEMOREST'S ESTABLISHMENT

THE MARIE SLEEVE

The new style of Marie sleeve is adapted to the poplins and fine French mixed cloths, suitable for fall wear. It is the half-coat shape, with a bouffant drawn into puffing's, and terminating in rounded pendants, trimmed with gimp. The cuff is scalloped and trimmed with gimp, to represent blocks, or sections, the width being little more than sufficient for the hand to pass through.

THE LADY ALICE SLEEVE

The Lady Alice Sleeve is one of the prettiest of the fall novelties. It may be made in silk, but it is best adapted to pretty household materials, and would look exceedingly well in the fine French cords, stripes, and figured cambrics, which are imported for morning dresses. The body of the sleeve consists of a small bishop, attached to a plain piece about three inches in depth at the top over which is placed a short pointed cap, trimmed with three narrow frills. The lower part of the sleeve is also gathered into a band, large enough for the hand to slip through and display the undersleeve below. Over the band is turned a cuff, divided into ornamental sections, and trimmed with braid and buttons.

THE LITTLE BEAUTY

This is a charming little apron for a child of six years. To the half waist a little pointed cape is attached, which is gathered full upon the shoulder, and falls over the short puffed sleeve of the dress. Two deep points form a polka to the skirt, back and front, and completes this little beauty, which may be made in black silk and trimmed with lace or any lighter white fabrics, braided in colors.

THE FRANCIS COAT

The back is a short jacket, with the skirt box-plaited and set under the jacket about four inches. A plain sack front with pocket and a regular coat sleeve is the outline of this coat but the ornaments are very unique — they are velvet palm leaves marked on with embroidery stitch and dots between. The edge is finished with velvet and dots in the same way. The pocket, sleeve, and back are trimmed with velvet cut in points, and marked to correspond. Suitable for a boy from four to seven years.

CRAFTING AND NEEDLEWORKS

CORAL WREATH IN CROCHET

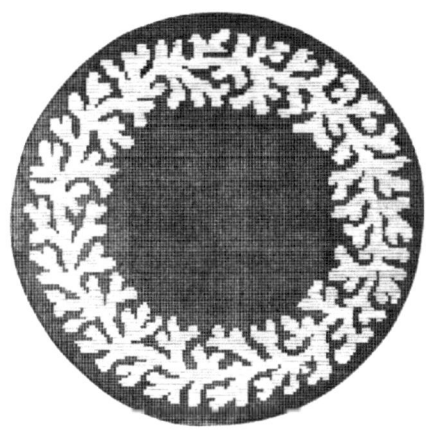

Materials — No. 12, 16, or 20 crochet cotton.

This coral wreath is to be worked in ordinary square crochet, and may be used for the Doily or cake basket, or many other purposes. A motto, or initials in crochet letters, may be placed in the center. It is equally available for darning or netting.

CHILDS BRAIDED
SLIPPER IN ONE PIECE

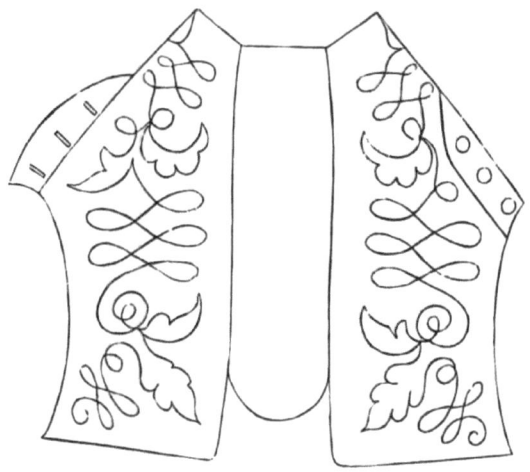

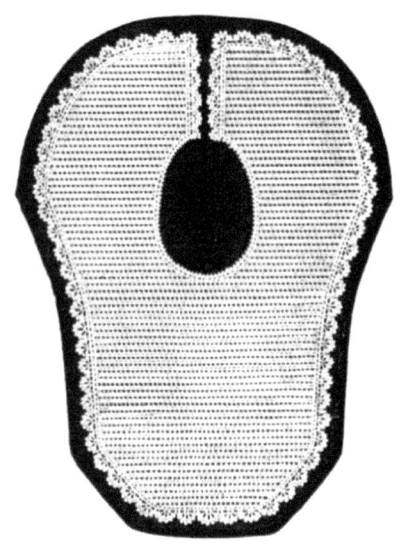

CROCHET BIB

KNITTED BRACES

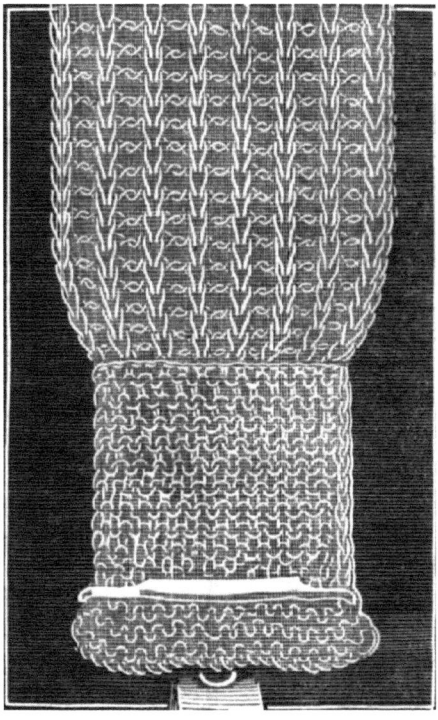

Materials – Knitting cotton, No. 6; two knitting needles, No. 15, bell gauge.

The great charm in these braces is the readiness with which they can be washed; so that they may be changed at least once a week. The only fittings required are two broad buckles, attached to loops of buckskin leather, through which are slipped leather straps having a button-hole cut at each end. There is a button-hole made in knitting itself at the other extremity of each brace; so that the only thing to be done is to detach the braces from the buckles, and replace them with a clean pair every week.

Cast on twenty stitches, and knit in plain garter-stitch about a finger-length, as tightly as possible. Begin the brioche stitch thus: m 1, slip1, knit 1. You thus increase to thirty in this row; and after it, do the ordinary brioche stitch for three and a half to four and a half finger lengths, according to the height of the wearer. Knit nearly a finger in plain stitch, contracting to the original twenty in the first row; then, for the button-hole, knit backwards and forwards ten stitches only; then the other ten only; then eight rows the entire width; after which, knit together the two first stitches and the two last except the edge stitch, in every alternate row, until ten only are left, when cast off.

To make a good edge, slip the needle in the first stitch, as if you were going to purl it; and take it off without knitting, in every row, whether plain or brioche, throughout. Fasten of the ends securely.

Those who knit very loosely should use needles somewhat finer, as it is essential the braces should be closely woven and strong.

LONG NIGHT-DRESS FOR A LADY
(NEW PATTERN)

The front is plaited in large plaits, and the yoke put on afterwards. A plain yoke behind, and sleeve fulled into a band. The ruffle or trimming is all around the yoke and neck, and on the sleeve.

SOFA OR CARRIAGE PILLOW, IN CROCHET

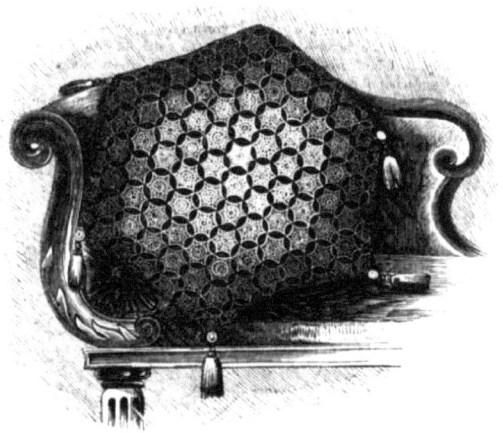

Materials – Seven shades of scarlet, four thread Berlin wool; the third shade from the lightest to be a bright military scarlet, the darkest to be nearly black. Seven shades of bright emerald green (grass green must never be used), three quarters of an ounce of each shade, except the lightest of both colors – six skeins of each of these. No 2 Penelope crochet hooks.

1st row – With lightest scarlet make a chain of 9 stitches, unite the ends; 5 chain, de *under* the 9 chain; repeat this 5 times more *(in all, 6 chains of 5)*. Cut off the wool; tie it securely at the back. *(This must be done at every row.)*

2d – Same color: 2 long under the 5 chain; 3 chain; 2 more long *under* the same; 3 chain; repeat this 5 times more.

3d – Next shaded scarlet: 2 long under the 3 chain, between the 4 long stitch; 3 chain; 2 more long under the same; 3 chain; de *under* 3 chain; 3 chain; repeat this 5 times more.

4th – Military scarlet: 2 long under the 3 chain, between the 4 long; 4 chain; 2 more long under the same; 4 chain; de on dc; 4 chain; repeat this 5 times more.

5th – Palest green: 3 long under the 4 chain, between the 4 long; 5 chain; 3 more long under the same; 3 chain; de under 4 chain; 5 chain; de under 4 chain; 3 chain, repeat.

This forms the center star.

Now work 6 more stars in precisely the same manner only varying the shades as follows: Commence with the lightest shade scarlet, and work the 2d row with next shade instead of the same; taking the next shade green for the outside row; sew with green wool these 6 stars to the points of the center star, sewing them also at the side.

Now make 12 stars, beginning with the 2d shade scarlet, making the 1st and 2d rows of the same color.

3d row – Military scarlet, same as 3d row of 1st star

4th – Next darker shade, same as 4th row

5th – Next darkest color

Sew these 12 stars round the last six, attaching them as before.

Now make 18 stars, commencing with military scarlet, making the 2 first rows in the same shade.

3d row – Next darker

4th – Next darker

5th – Next darker green

Sew these round the other stars

Make 24 stars, commencing with military scarlet, but making the 2d row of the next darker shade, instead of the same.

Use the next two darker shades in gradation, and the next darkest green.

Sew these stars round the others.

Make 30 circles, commencing with the next shade darker than the military scarlet; use the 3 darker shades in gradation, and edge with the darkest green but one. It will be observed that seven shades of scarlet are used on this side, and 6 of green: for the reverse of the cushion, 6 of scarlet and 7 of green. Damp well, and press by placing it between folded linen, with a heavy weight upon it, till dry.

Line this side with white cotton velvet, white satin, or watered silk.

For the Reverse

Make exactly the same number of stars, and worked precisely the same way with respect to the tints, but commencing with the palest green, instead of scarlet, and edging the outside row with scarlet.

This side may be lined either with white or green velvet; make a lining of strong calico, the exact size; fill with four pounds of feathers.

Trim with green silk cushion cord, and 6 shaded bullion tassels. Great care must be taken to arrange the colors precisely as the instructions given, as the effect will be to give a most intense and brilliant color, and in selecting the wools, they should be of the brightest tints.

EMBROIDERY DESIGNS

CHAPTER 9
SEPTEMBER 1861

DESCRIPTION OF FASHION-PLATE FOR SEPTEMBER 1861

Fig. 1 – Walking costume of Havana colored *moiré*, with front breadth gored, the plaits only commencing at the hips. The skirt is trimmed with plaited velvet, put on *en tunique*, brought round at the side, and finished with a large bow with embroidered ends; bows up the front of dress; body plain, and trimmed at the top with a jockey bound with velvet. Pearl colored silk hat, ornamented with *appliqué* lace and *rose* sublime flowers.

Fig. 2 – Breakfast robe of mineral gray cashmere, with embroidered spots worked on it. The robe is bound, lined, and faced with pink silk; tight waist, with small cape pointed both before and behind; rich cord and tassel. French breakfast cap, bordered with a muslin ruche. Linen collar and cuffs.

Fig. 3 – Walking-dress of rich green silk, with narrow flounce at the bottom. Two others are put on in diamonds with a band of the silk, bound on each edge with black velvet placed above them. The waist is pointed both before and behind. The upper part of the sleeve is full, but is close at the wrist. Leghorn bonnet trimmed with white feathers and lined with black velvet; wine colored strings and flowers.

Fig. 4 – Dinner dress of pearl colored silk, with three flounces headed with black velvet; round waist, half high, trimmed, *en plastron*, with black velvet; rich chemisette of muslin. The sash is of the same material as the dress. The sleeves consist of a velvet jockey, two large puffs, and a volant. Coiffure of white lace and flowers.

Fig. 5 – Wine colored silk walking dress, trimmed with narrow flounces, put on in bunches, headed with black velvet and bows, put on *á volante*; sleeves loose, and trimmed to suit the skirt. Embroidered collar and sleeves white

Eugenie velvet bonnet, trimmed with black velvet, black lace, and white flowers.

CHILDREN'S FASHIONS

Fig. 1 – Buff *piqué* suit, trimmed with black braid. Gray straw Tudor hat, trimmed with blue velvet and a tuft of feathers at the side.

Fig. 2 – Light cloth jacket, with Magenta necktie, and white pants.

Fig. 3 – Pink and white silk dress, trimmed with pink ribbon; body low, with high muslin chemisette. White felt hat, with soft curling pink plume.

Fig. 4 – White dress, with small flounces scalloped with blue; blue sash, net, and boots.

Fig. 5 – Magenta poplin Zouave and skirt, bound with white silk or poplin. Black velvet Tudor hat, with a Magenta thistle feather.

Fig. 6 – Dark blue silk dress flounced; low neck, with high muslin chemisette. Brown felt hat, bound with brown velvet, and long white plume.

Fig. 7 – Poplin dress of the new color called rose sublime, trimmed with black velvet. Hungarian hat, with a tuft of feathers.

Fig. 8 – Mauve poplin Zouave and skirt. A mauve velvet hat, with long white curling plume.

THE CORDOVAN

From the establishment of G. Brodie, 51 Canal Street, New York
Drawn by L.T. Voigt from actual articles of costume

The characteristics of these garments are so strongly marked, that no special comment is required. They are made of all fabrics suitable to the season, and the passementeries vary according to material and the price, so as to suit all requirements of different tastes and pecuniary means.

THE ALEXANDRINE

Mauve grenadine dress, trimmed with silk rushing's. Spanish corsage over a fine muslin spencer. Leghorn hat, bound with rose sublime velvet, and plume of the same color.

CHITCHAT UPON NEW YORK AND PHILADELPHIA FASHIONS FOR SEPTEMBER

There has never been a season since the Lady's Book originated a monthly fashion report in which there have been so few preparations made for the autumn. As yet there is scarcely an importing house that can show any novelties, or any manufacturing establishment that is bringing new styles into notice. Some few items may be gleaned here and there, however, by those who are at the fountainhead of the stream. First of all, there are in the ribbons intended for the fall two decidedly new colors, which will be the rage. The *Azurline*, a bright blue, as its name denotes, so intensely blue that all other shades of the same color look yellow beside it. It is the old Napoleon blue, heightened, and it will be found very becoming to an ordinarily good complexion. Brunettes will rejoice in its companion, "the Sublime", as the French call it; "Rose Sublime," as our importers have happily designated the shade. It is a ruby scarlet, an intense color, to be compared to nothing so perfectly as the shade a cluster of fully ripe currants takes when held in the sunlight. These colors are often mixed with black, to bring them out more fully, and when placed upon a black straw or crinoline bonnet, or mingled with black velvet or lace on a white one, the effect is excellent. Magenta and Solferino will be allowed a temporary rest. *Red* Scarlet contracted with vivid green, and flame color worn with black are also prominent.

For instance, a rice straw bonnet, with a wreath of scarlet geraniums and green leaves placed quite on the back of the crown and fastened by a knot of black lace, or a black lace barbe, raised by a knot of rose sublime ribbon, with a cape of the same shade in silk, covered by black lace and a bow and flowing ends of black velvet ribbon. Bonnet of black crinoline with straw stars, a trimming composed of *coques* of black lace, with flame colored ribbon between each; inside the brim black sloe berries and flame colored nasturtiums, with foliage. Belgian straw bonnet, covered with a black silk net, from which small elongated olives hang all round. The bandeau inside is composed of a large ruche of flame colored silk, pinked at the edge, supported by another ruche of black silk; voluminous tufts of large corn poppies are put at the sides so as to completely fill up the cheeks of the bonnet. Below these tulle lappets are seen. The curtain is black silk with a plaited head and a bow of black ribbon formed of two long loops and two long ends hanging down. The whole outside of the bonnet has no other ornament than the net which covers it and hangs down as a fall in front and on both sides. On one side, however, placed upon the net, there is a voluminous tuft of poppies. Strings of ribbon, black, with red edges, and a stripe of straw color in the middle. Straw bonnets trimmed with ribbon (plain black ground with bouquets of cherries worked on it), branches of cherries, white blonde and black lace. The trimming of this bonnet consists of a ribbon which goes round it and comes to the left hand side, where it forms a large bow in which branches of cherries are inserted. The end of this ribbon hangs down at the side. The curtain, of plain tulle, is covered by another, all of blonde, which forms three flat plaits; one on each side and a third in the middle. The inside of the front is covered with narrow black lace. On the forehead there is a bandeau composed of ribbon knotted in the middle and *crumpled* at the sides. Blonde down the cheeks.

Caps are made either with loose crown or a round one in the Charlotte Corday style. One of Mme. Alexandrine's caps was made of Mechlin tulle, with a deep trimming turned back on itself, a lilac ribbon crossed the head and was tied in a long bow on the left hand side, while on the right there were bunches of white and colored lilac.

One of her richest headdresses is a torsade of flame colored ribbon ornamented on the right hand side with a knot of gold wheat ears and behind by a smaller knot from which a long white feather falls towards the left. One was quite round, of camellias of equal size; another, composed of a torsade of black velvet starred with gold and intertwined with a gold cord, terminated on the right hand side in two handsome tassels and dandelion puffs spangled with gold; another was of red and white pinks mixed with fern leaves; another of large blue Hortensia's with silver hearts; another of red hyacinths with pale foliage; another of a *Magenta* velvet torsade, a Chinese tassel and gold chains; another of pansies and tea-roses; another of blue and white ribbon rolled with a silver torsade, and having two silver tassels and blonde agrafes. We have never known headdresses so universally adopted from the simple lace barbe to the artistic creations of Alexandrine or the importations of Madame Tighlman. We noticed this particularly in the review of a *trousseau* prepared recently for a lady of this city. The morning caps and headdresses formed a conspicuous and expensive part of the preparations. Each dress had its appropriate accompaniment. The mob, or Charlotte Corday cap, was the shape selected for morning wear; to be adopted as soon as mademoiselle could write herself Madame. The lingerie was of the most delicate and finished style, large use being made of grass cloth for tucked skirts, jackets, etc.; linen cambric puffs, separated by Valenciennes inserting and edge, took the place of the yokes; in the night-dresses the puffs were longitudinal and extended to the waist; collars and cuffs of Valenciennes lace. Among other novelties, the most dainty of nightcaps had a bow exactly on the top, quite forward, of mauve colored ribbon. The wedding dress was of rich white corded silk, the skirt seven yards wide, with demi train; the bottom was ornamented with a double ruche of *crêpe areophane* set on in alternate squares and points of about twelve inches deep, corsage pointed, with a *berthé* formed by two rows of rich point lace, headed by a crepe ruche, narrower point lace in the neck, drawn by a silver cord, the center ornament a spray of orange buds and blossoms; veil of tulle, very ample and entirely bordered by a corresponding ruche of crepe, which sustained it in its place. Wreath, mounted diadem fashion, of white clematis, very fine and close, a spray of orange buds in the center, and a *ciche peigné* of orange buds at the back of the head. Among the reception dresses was one of lilac silk, skirt gored, and very wide; each gore was distinguished by a band of violet colored velvet, cut crosswise, corded with white silk and edged with blonde lace. Every two bands approached each other in the center, narrowing as they rose, and were looped under each other in the form of a bow at the height of twenty-four inches from the bottom of the skirt. Corsage low and pointed, trimmed with a pointed *berthé* in violet velvet, edged in the same way. Between the point of the *berthé* and the top of the corsage was a stylish velvet bow, trimmed to correspond. Sleeves, a full puff of tulle, caught up by bands of trimmed velvet. Valenciennes edging in the neck, drawn to shape by violet chenille. A *robe de chamber* of the style called Marquise; the front is gored, *à la Gabrielle*, the back straight and full, set into a plain yoke on the shoulder by three or four square wide plaits, which are not confined by the girdle, which is a Cordelier, fastened under the arm on each side, and knotted in front. From the knee there is a single flounce, running all round, headed by a ruche of rose colored ribbon. Sleeves loose and ample, edged simply by a ruche of ribbon. Material, fine plaid of black and white silk. There were some pretty muslin spencers, with the fiat plaiting or ruche in the neck that is now so much worn, the plain place between the groups of plaits filled by bows of exceedingly narrow ribbon, also the new style of closed undersleeves, white with a tongue of black lace and velvet extending half way to the elbow, at the back of the arm. We have designs of these in preparation.

We must not forget to notice the popularity of the *Aneline* shawl and the trimmed shawl. The latter is square of lama (fine Cashmere wool) silk, French crepe, or grenadine, either plain or richly embroidered. The trimming is a deep border or flounce of lace; in winter materials, plush, velvet, and quilted satin will be used for borderings. In color they vary in every shade, black being perhaps the most popular. They are very well suited to autumn wear. The *Aneline* shawl is also of lama or grenadine; the middle of the marbled pattern and the colored border finished by a rich fringe. The *Pekin Aneline* shawl is of a soft, fine woolen texture, which drapes gracefully about the figure; the border is a real Chinese pattern, executed in light colors. The *Pekin Bournous* is a Zouave wrap for evening; the material Canton crepe, the pattern in colored embroidery, with rich silk tassels. Brodie's taste and ingenuity are already at work to supply the autumn wraps which are always worn in heavier materials.

NOVELTIES FOR SEPTEMBER 1861

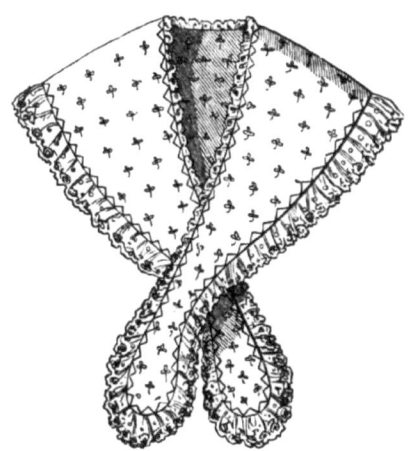

Fig. 1 – Worked muslin fichu, a pretty style

Fig. 2 – Casacque of embroidered muslin, to be worn with a muslin skirt for morning or *négligé*. Puffings of muslin, with wrought flounces, or ribbon of some light shade may be drawn through the puffs, and bows of the same fasten the garment.

Fig. 3 – Headdress of tulle *de soie*, black velvet and full blush roses with foliage. The hair is turned back from the forehead, and the headdress set well on the back of the head.

Fig. 4 – Breakfast cap of white muslin and embroidery, with knots of ribbon holding the frill back from the face.

Fig. 5 – Headdress for evening wear, a full wreath of daisies mounted with rose colored ribbon, a flat bow of the ribbon on the forehead, with a bow and flowing ends behind.

Fig. 7

Figs. 6 & 7 – Two styles of closed undersleeves. *Fig. 6* is of Cambric, with a pointed cuff, embroidered; the sleeve in a very full puff. *Fig. 7* is of lace; the cuff is finished by a puff, with edging of lace.

Fig. 6

Fig. 8 – Habit shirt and collar, for an open dress, the shirt has five narrow tucks each side the square plait in the middle. The collar is in five decided points, and between the embroidery and the Valenciennes edge is an inserting with a black velvet ribbon, bow of the same.

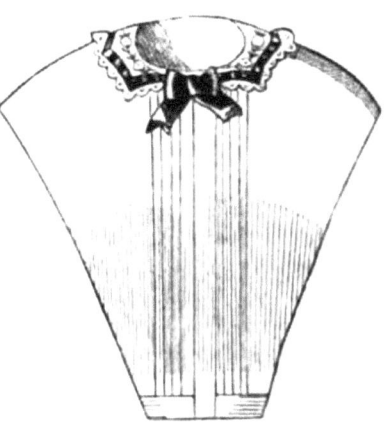

Fig. 9 – A very simple style of dress, suitable for any kind of material.

PATTERNS FROM MADAM DEMOREST'S ESTABLISHMENT

THE NINA CORSAGE

A low body for full dress, specially adapted to the elegant Pompadour silks now in Vogue. The body is plain and ornamented with a scarf of crepe, which crosses the shoulder, and gradually decreasing in width, terminates at the belt in pendent ends. Round the neck a wide pointed blonde is laid flat upon the silk, a narrow blonde edging being placed upright above it. The short sleeves consist simply of a puff and scalloped frill, edged with white blonde.

THE BELLE SLEEVE
Makes up elegantly, especially in the new light figured poplins which are so much admired. A short pointed cap, placed over a deep puff, forms the upper part of the sleeve; the lower part having a wing and cuff, ornamented with tassels, the entire effect of which can hardly be reproduced in an engraving.

THE GEORGIAN
Is an elegant sleeve in silk, grenadine, or English *barége*. It is plain, half flowing, and cut up square on the front of the arm, so as to display much of a dressy undersleeve. On the top of the sleeve are three pointed puffings, placed over a double pointed cap – the five points finished with tassels. The puffings may be gathered or laid in plaits, according to the thickness of the material.

ROBE

THE PRINCESS PALETOT
The Princess Paletot is one of the most elegant of the fall designs for misses, from ten to thirteen years. The back is fitted to the figure and cut in squares; lappets with the skirt set on underneath in box plaits. The front is a French sack shape, with a sort of cu-away over, that joins the fitted back, really giving the effect of a pretty Zouave, with the skirt so adapted as not only to make a finely fitting coat, but very stylish street wrapper for a young lady. It may be made in fine French cloth or silk, according to taste – in cloth, will require three yards.

NEW STYLES OF APRONS

MISSES APRON
This apron is of black silk, trimmed with velvet. A very pretty style.

THE MATHILDE
Made of dark blue silk with three bias folds, edged with a ribbon ruffle. The pockets are trimmed to match.

THE BEAUTY

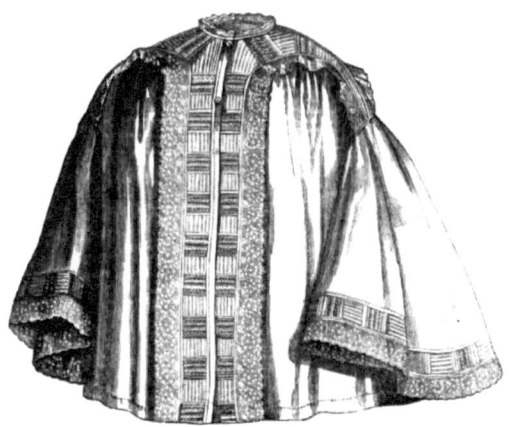

This very *recherché* night-dress is made of very fine French muslin; the yoke and front trimming is formed of insertion, small tucks, and flouncing. The style is something entirely new.

NECK-TIE OF SCARLET SILK
With black velvet inserted, and braided with gold braid

THE CLAUDIA CHEMISE

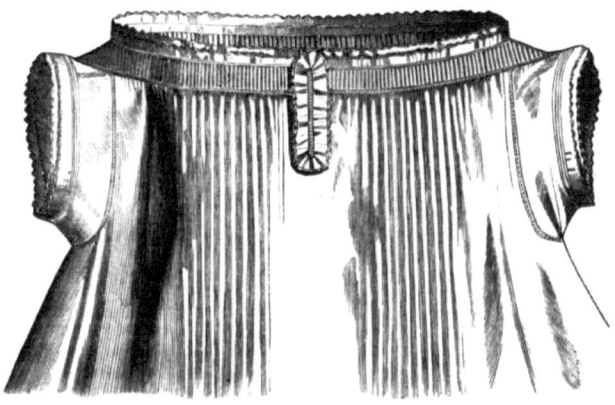

The yoke is formed of small plaits, and the edge of the band is scalloped.

CRAFTING & NEEDLEWORKS

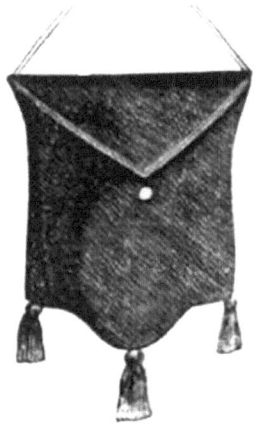

BAG OR POUCH FOR ZOUAVE JACKETS

Many of our readers having asked for patterns of the little bags, or pouches worn suspended from the waistband underneath Zouave jackets, we give a representation of one sent from Paris, which we have had engraved. These little novelties may be made in embroidered velvet, poplin, or silk, and sometimes in fur; in a word, they should be made of a material to correspond with the dress with which they are worn. Their origin is somewhat Scotch and somewhat Oriental.

BOOT NEEDLE BOOK

This is made by cutting out two shapes in cardboard of the same size and covering them with bronze kid, colored leather, or satin, velvet, or silk, any of these materials being suitable. It is ornamented with gold thread in the pattern given. A row of very small pearl buttons is placed up the front, or else a row of gold or black beads. A bow of ribbons is placed where the buttons commence. Both the shapes are worked the same, and the inside are lined with silk. The tops are finished with a fringe, and the two tied together with a bow of ribbon, having the leaves for the needles inserted between them, and leaving them so as to open.

A NEW STYLE OF INFANT'S CROCHET BIB

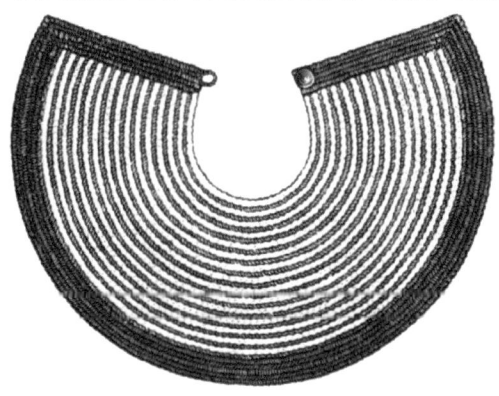

KNITTED ARTIFICIAL FLOWERS
(Michaelmas-Daisy)

This flower may be knitted, with two stitches for the width of the row, but it is much quicker to work it in a chain of crochet; it is generally variegated, either in two shades of red, or two shades of violet. The variegation is produced by working with two threads of Berlin wool, one of a deep, the other of a light shade, of the same color.

Make a chain of simple crochet, about a yard in length, then cover a piece of thin wire, as long as you can conveniently manage, with one thread of Berlin wool, and begin to sew this wire along one edge of the chain, leaving about an inch of wire at the beginning; when you have sewn about an inch, out the chain, pull the thread through the last stitch, bring your wire round, sew half the second edge, then bring round the wire that you left at the beginning, sew it to meet the other, letting the wires cross each other, twist them and the wool together tightly, to form a stalk, and turn up the two little petals, first cutting away one of the wires close to the twist, to prevent the stalk being too thick when finished.

Wind a piece of yellow wool on the end of one of your fingers, pull it out thus doubled, and twist a bit of rather strong wire over it, twist the wire very tight, and make with this wool a kind of little ball, which must be covered with a piece of common net (dyed yellow if possible), tie the net as tight as possible over the wool. This forms the daisy.

When you have made a sufficient number of petals to form two or three rows, each row being made rather larger than the first, you must sew them all round the little heart, and proceed to make the calyx as follows:

Make a chain of twelve stitches with the crochet needle, using green wool, not split; work two rows in double crochet, increasing two stitches in the second row. Sew this calyx under the petals, fasten up the open side, and gather the stitches of the lower extremity, cover the stem with green split wool.

Bud – Make a small ball of any color, then take fifteen or twenty bits of split wool, the same colors as used for the flower, each about an inch long, tie them tightly as a little bundle; fasten this on the top of the little ball, to which you must first fix a wire; bring down the ends of wool in alternate stripes of dark and light shades, tie all these ends round the wire, and cut them close. Wind a bit of green wool, as a very small ball immediately under the bud; then with green wool, not split and make a row of herringbone stitches from the little bud to about half way up the colored one. This makes a very pretty bud, looking as if just ready to bloom.

Leaf – like that of the Heart's ease.

PATCHWORK

EMBROIDERY DESIGNS

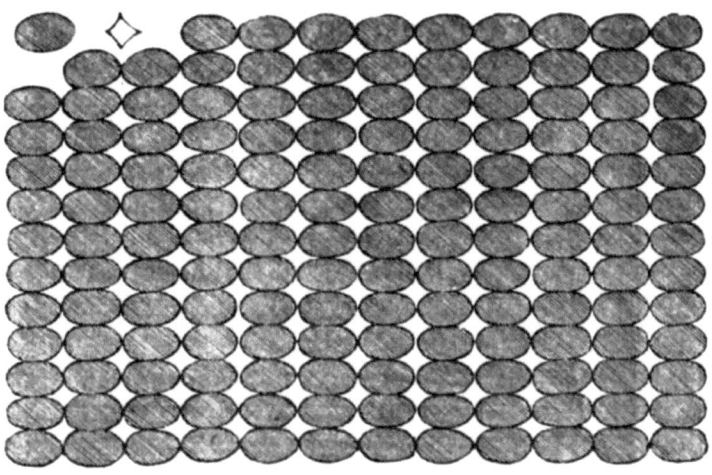

PORTION OF EMBROIDERED COLLAR & CUFF

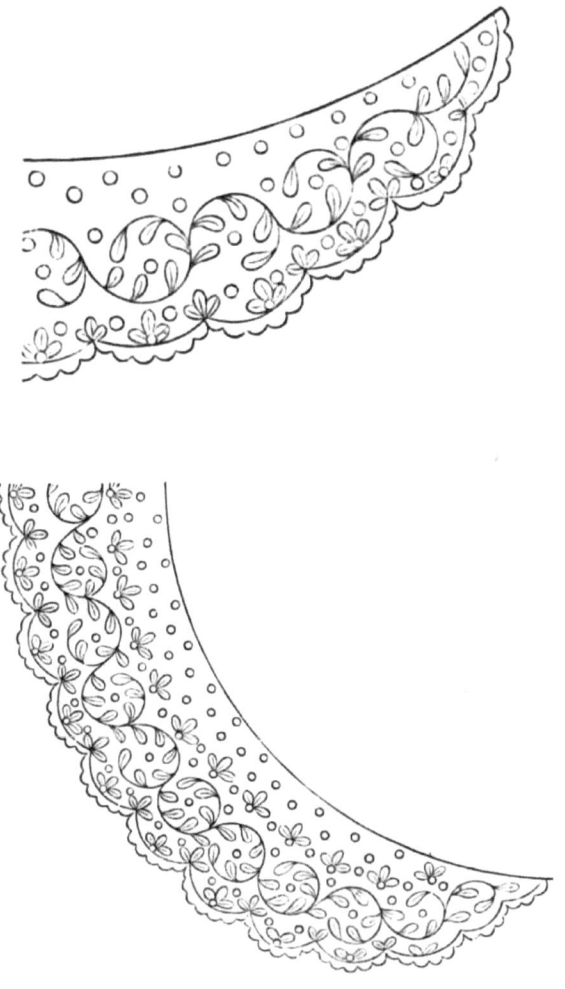

CHAPTER 10
OCTOBER 1861

DESCRPTION OF FASHION-PLATE FOR OCTOBER 1861

Fig. 1 – Walking-dress of rich green *moiré antique*. The trimming consists of black Lyons velvet, of the best description. A band, twelve inches in depth, extends around the skirt, turning back with a point, at the side, where it is met by a corresponding band, formed by the continuation of the tablier in front, and is connected with it by a lozenge of velvet. Similar lozenges connect the tablier in front, leaving a space through which the green *moiré* is visible. The velvet is edged by three rows of narrow fancy braid, and the tablier by a double row of pendeloques. The sleeves are partially gored, and with the waist, may be readily adopted where the heavy trimming on the skirt may not be thought desirable. Bonnet of royal purple velvet, the shape of the curtain being a novelty; full white plume to the right; convolvulus blossoms and leaves across the forehead; bonnet cap of tulle and blonde.

Fig. 2 – Walking dress of lavender French poplin, made quite plain, with a row of black velvet buttons down the front, and a narrow girdle of black velvet at the waist. The point of the sleeve extends from the corsage; it is edged by a good black lace, headed by velvet ribbon. There are two puffs below it, and a tight sleeve, with an ornament of black lace and velvet at the back. Drawn bonnet of black satin, with strings of rose sublime.

Fig. 3 – Evening-dress of white crepe, with a tunic skirt, caught together by sprays of eglantine; bouquet *de corsage* and hand bouquet to correspond. A single flower placed above the brow.

Fig. 4 – Carriage-dress of a good black silk; the bottom of the skirt is trimmed to the knee with bias rows of puffing, separated by pinked ruffles; a narrow ruche heads this stylish ornament. The bottom of the sleeves is trimmed to correspond. Corsage plain. Light mantle, with puffs and ruches, edged by a fall of rich black lace. Bonnet of black silk, velvet, and lace; the barbe of lace being caught inside the brim by three small crimson roses.

Fig. 5 – Dinner-dress of rich cerise colored reps silk. The sleeves in puffs; the corsage has a pointed trimming of velvet, edged by a narrow pearling of lace. The same style of velvet is used in the dashing ornamentation of the skirt, which needs no description.

Fig. 6 – Robe of dark brown silk, trimmed with rows of black velvet, are disposed so as to leave lozenge formed spaces between them. The trimming ornaments the lower part of the skirt, the corsage, and the front and back of the sleeves. The skirt has gores cut from the upper end of each breadth, so that it is much narrower at the top than at bottom, and it is set on at the waist in very small plaits. On each side there is a pocket edged with rows of black velvet. The corsage is buttoned up in front. It is rather short in the waist and not pointed. The sleeves are tight. The ceinture, which is tied on one side, has the ends square and trimmed with crossings of velvet. Collar and cuffs of lace, the latter turned up over the sleeves. Bonnet having the front composed of lavender velvet, and the crown of white silk covered with black lace. At the edge of the front there is Magenta velvet in *bouillonnés*. The crown and the curtain are covered with falls of black lace.

CHITCHAT UPON NEW YORK AND PHILADELPHIA FASHIONS FOR OCTOBER

In our last Chat we enumerated many styles for trimming fall bonnets, and have little more to add to this. There are always some part of the community who have distinct dress bonnets made for the intervening periods; these are composed of mixed materials – silk, lace, and ribbon. For instance, a bonnet with a front of Azurline blue, in lengthwise folds, shaped like a fanchon; the crown is of white net crossed with black lace, as is also the cape; crimson chrysanthemums in velvet, set in black lace, form the bandeau; the strings are Azurline blue, handsomely tied.

This favorite shade is also brought out in dress silks, quite plain, without figure or stripe. There is also the *glacé Marguerite*, a pale drab and mauve shot silk. Not being figured in any way these dresses are suited to plain or flounced skirts, and are always more lasting and more becoming to young people than a decided style. Black silks will, however, be the staple for full street wear, trimmed usually with a contrasting shade.

Black alpaca is more in favor than it has been for some time: but it must be of the best quality, soft and silky to be ladylike.

There is also a new mixed material, with a texture almost as shiny as satin, which looks extremely well so long as it is kept from the rain; water in any way ruins it. Trimmed with ruches of silk darker than itself, it has an excellent effect. Our steel plates are now so full, and so completely up to the times, as scarcely to need a letter-press comment.

In the richer silks, intended for dinner or evening dress, we may mention one of black silk, figured with satin stipes; between the stripes there are bouquets of red and green flowers. The corsage is not quite high; it is edged at the top with a ruche of silk of the three colors, red, green, and black, and under the corsage there is a chemisette of worked muslin trimmed round the throat with a ruche, also of muslin. The sleeves, which are bell-shaped, have revers, ornamented with a ruche like that on the corsage, and the skirt is trimmed with groups of flowers, three in each, alternately black, red, and green. A cap and a mantelet of black lace have been selected for wearing with the dress just mentioned. The cap is of the round form, and is trimmed with blonde, roses, and anemones of black velvet with gold centers.

An elegant dress intended for dinner costume has just been made of silver gray silk, figured with a Pompadour pattern of various hues, cerulean blue being the predomination color. The lower part of the skirt is ornamented with a trimming in blue and rose color, the two intertwined, so as to form a chain pattern. The corsage is low, and with it is worn a fichu of tulle puffs. A sash of the same silk as the dress is fastened in a bow with long ends, the rimming on the ends corresponding with that on the skirt.

A very pretty little pelerine, to wear with a low body, may be made with a plain net or muslin covered with narrow tucks; it should be made pointed behind, with ends crossing in front, and trimmed round the neck with a ruching of narrow lace, and outside with two rows of wider lace. The sleeves to wear with this pelerine should be made to correspond, with two puffings at the top, and a deep frill with a series of narrow tucks, finished off by a double row of broad lace.

There is another very pretty novelty for wearing over low bodies. It consists of pieces of velvet, not narrower than an inch, tacked together at equal distances, forming squares, and is pointed both behind and before. Sometimes white or black net is placed underneath the velvet, and sometimes a fullness of net is gathered in the top row, and drawn with a narrow velvet round the neck.

A new style of sash has appeared, made of the same material as the dress, with three ends, the middle one shorter than the others; they may be made, also of velvet rounded at the ends, and trimmed with fringe, and worked with gold or steel embroidery.

Skirts are worn as ample and full as ever, and are generally gored, to throw them out at the bottom. Stiff muslin petticoats, with flounces, or one deep flounce at the bottom, are very suitable for wearing with evening dresses, as they set the dresses out in a more graceful manner than does a very large crinoline. A moderately sized steel petticoat, and a muslin one – with, of course, a plain one over it – make a muslin dress look very nicely. We are told that the Empress usually wears one of these muslin petticoats, with a series of narrow flounces to the waist. Of course, this style would not suit everyone, on account of the difficulty and expense of washing, etc.

The best steel skirt we have ever seen has recently been sent to us from the new establishment of Madame Demorest, 27 Fourteenth Street, New York. It is of a graceful shape, enlarging gradually at the train, and though containing forty springs is a model of lightness and comfort. All steel skirts "give" as it is called, that is, grow longer by wear; in choosing them, this should be kept in mind. A skirt that exactly suits it to length at first, will trail in three weeks. Many ladies cut off the bottom springs, but this spoils the shape of the skirt entirely. In Madame Demorest's patent they are made self-adjusting, and if still too long when the whole of the cords are tied in, *the top spring may be unknotted* and removed.

The style of dress known as the "Gabrielle" will still be popular this fall for street or house dresses, for the mixed woolen stuffs especially. It is more generally known as "the gored dress." The *Impératrice* is a decided improvement on the original Gabrielle; it is more graceful and more easily worn by all figures. In front it is formed like a long casaque, widening considerably at the bottom. At the seam, under the arm, there are wide plaits, like other dresses, and the back is flat and rounded at the waist; the sleeves are with elbows and turned back cuffs.

A favorite style for trimming these dresses is a bound band of velvet placed two or three inches above the edges of the skirt, and not quite meeting in front, where the ends are pointed, and either turned back as in Fig. 1 of our fashion-plate, or held plainly in their place by a fancy button.

In a rich dark material we have seen a flounce of guipure lace, set on with slight fullness in the same way, but continued up the front on each side of the waist quite plain, so as to appear like the trimmings of a tunic skirt. From the waist the lace, which has been narrowed to shape in front, is carried up the corsage, and descends from each shoulder to the center of the waist at the back, where the two ends are crossed over the other after the fashion of lappets. A trimming of passementerie heads the lace. A row of lace buttons extends down the front of the dress. The velvet given in Figs. 5 and 6 of the steel fashion-plate will be much used as a trimming; it has a pearled edge of narrow lace; a broad width of it would be very suitable for the above trimming.

A black silk dress of good texture may be made up with a band of green or violet silk, at a little distance from the hem of the dress, and be closed up the front by green buttons of a graduated size. The sleeves are bouffant, as in Fig. 5, and closed at the wrist. A scarf mantelet of the same silk as the dress is added for street dress. The ends are crossed one over the other in front of the waist, where they are folded in. The ends of the mantelet are trimmed with a *bouillonné* and two narrow ruches edged with green silk. At the back it is trimmed by a small frill, beneath which descends a broad flounce, which falls over the arms. This broad flounce is edged with a frill having a ruched heading and bordered with green silk. Narrow flounces in groups of three are set on in festoons oftentimes; the central flounce being blue, cherry, green, or purple, or all are of black, bound with either of the above colors.

A full notice of Brodie's fall wraps which we have not had time to do justice to will appear in our November number.

THE ALBUERAN

From the establishment of G. Brodie, 51 Canal Street, New York.
Drawn by L.T. Voigt, from actual articles of costume.

The material is arranged in diverging plaits from the waist; these plaits, five in number, are, as in the plate, banded by a passementerie, which matches in style that which ornaments the shoulders. In some garments, this confining transverse piece is omitted, as the wearers taste may elect. There are slits in the circular front for the arms. The materials are various in which this style is fashioned.

LATEST FASHIONS

Fig. 1 – A breakfast Zouave, made of black cloth, and trimmed with quilted silk.

Fig. 2 – Loose sack, made of rough cloth, and trimmed with black velvet, for street wear.

NEW STYLES OF APRONS

THE ROSALIE
It is composed of Solferino silk, with a black lace inserted as a border. Tabs of lace bordered with silk are placed on each side to cover the pockets.

TUNIC APRON
It is composed of black silk, with flounces bound with white ribbon put on in tunic form, with graduated flounces on the front breadth.

FROM MADAM DEMOREST'S MAGAZINE DE MODES

Our readers can procure at this establishment either plain or elegantly trimmed patterns of every article connected with ladies' and children's apparel, either by mail or express. Hoop skirts in all varieties and of Madam Demorest's own styles.

Fig. 1 – Morning costume. Robe of rich gray taffetas broche in small bouquets, or tiny fruit, of a violet or cerise color. The skirt is gored in front, and fastened with knots of ribbon the same shade as the figure in the silk. Over this is worn a casaque of the same material, trimmed with a border of quilled ribbon, and having wide open sleeves, which display the elegant undersleeves of mull, drawn on the front of the arm with narrow ribbon to match the trimming of the dress. Full chemisette of mull muslin, and a silk net which confines the hair in a loose knot; complete a most elegant morning toilet.

THE SICILIAN

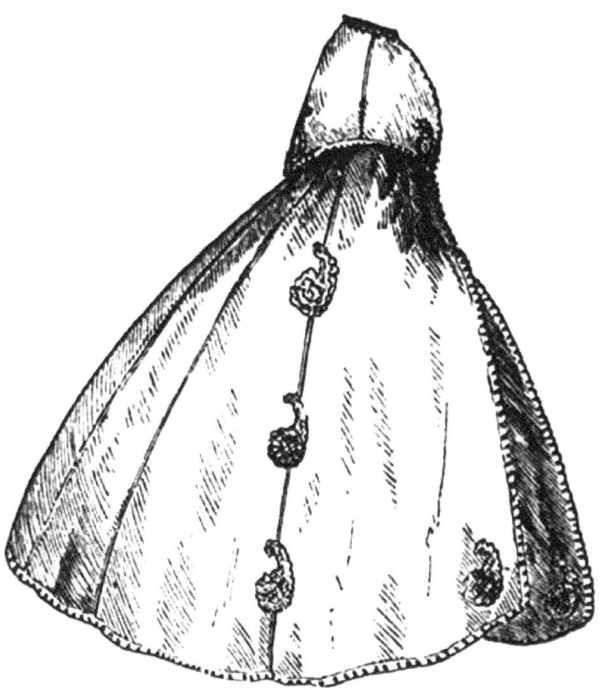

Fig. 2 – This elegant mantle takes three and a half yards of cloth one and a half yards wide, and six yards of seven-eighth silk. It is plain on the shoulders, which are covered by a pelerine cape, and gored at the back. It has no sleeve, except what is formed by the square side-piece, which comes over the arm, and composes, with the loose front, a deep, graceful drapery. The ornaments are palm leaves of crochet, or guipure. Requires four yards of cloth for the ordinary length.

Fig. 3 – This pretty Zouave suit for a boy of five years is made of light checked French cassimere; the garniture, serpentine braid and buttons. The pockets and cut of the jacket in front are seen in the engraving; on the sides where it is slit, it is laced up, and also on the back. The sleeves are full at the wrist, and laid in three large plaits, caught with buttons. Short pants, ornamented with buttons down the sides, and confined by an elastic band below the knee. Plaid stockings, low black shoes, collar, and plain tie complete the dress.

CONTINENTAL JACKET

Fig. 4 – This is a stylish little garment, and is suitable for a child of three or four years. The under waist is plain, but extends down over the hips, and to it is attached the skirt, which is box plaited on a band about an inch in width. The back of this waist has side pieces to fit the form, and is cut in quite a deep polka, which is slit and laced up like the sleeve, which is seen in the engraving. The "fly" jacket is attached only to the front, and rounds off gracefully from the under waist or vest. Two yards of material, one yard wide, are required.

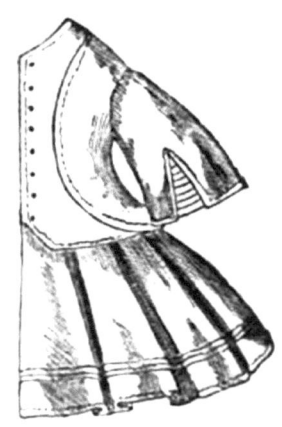

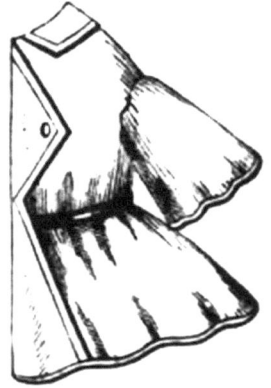

BOY'S PLAIN SACK

Fig. 5 – A lappet ornaments the front. It is simply confined with a belt at the waist. Requires three and a half yards of single width material, and is suitable for a boy of seven years.

LILLIAN DRESS

Fig. 6 – A charming dress in muslin or thin material for a girl of eight or ten years. The skirt is ornamented with a puffing, rounded from the front, and crossed with bands of any pretty contrasting color. The plain low is ornamented with a puffed cape. Back and front pointed at the waist, scalloped on the edge and extending across the shoulders over the sleeves, which consist of a puff and scalloped frill. For a Miss of the above age. Ten yards of silk will be required.

BISHOP SLEEVE

Fig. 7 – A bishop sleeve sufficiently wide to show the present style of undersleeve. A sidecap, with pendant ends, is laid on the upper part of the sleeve, and a plain band connected under the points, which confines it slightly and forms a puff.

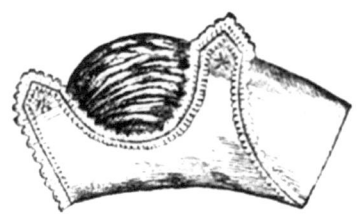

NOVELTIES FOR OCTOBER

Fig. 1 – Walking dress and jacket for the approaching cool weather; the jacket is of a woolen stuff ribbed in diamonds; the trimming is Astrakhan plush.

Fig. 2 – Light walking cloak or mantle, of brown cloth with stripes of velvet, and edged by a fringe.

Fig. 3 – A Tuscan straw bonnet, trimmed with fruit and flowers; the cape is of white silk, bound with lilac; the front of the bonnet is bound with lilac velvet.

Fig. 4 – Neat breakfast cap of plain cambric, the frills edged by a row of narrow Valenciennes lace; the little round crown is covered with Valenciennes edging sewn on in circles.

Fig. 5 – A more elaborate cap of embroidered cambric; bow and strings of colored ribbon.

Fig. 6 – Dress cap of tulle and Blonde, with bunches of blush roses without foliage.

Fig. 7 – Simple close sleeve.

Fig. 8 – Pretty close sleeve, for a dress sleeve, open in front; the puff of Swiss muslin has a worked inserting the whole length, which shirrs the sleeve to shape it to the arm. The wristlet is composed of alternate puffs and insertings.

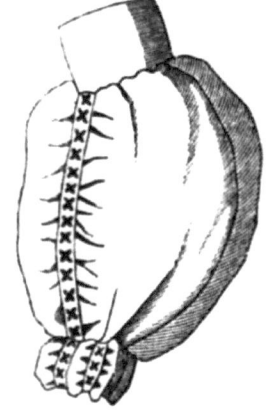

Fig. 9 – Wreath for dinner toilet, made of black lace and flowers, fastened at the back with black velvet bow and ends.

Fig. 10 – Simple headdress of black ribbon, black lace, and purple pansies.

NEW DESIGN FOR MISSES DRAWERS

POUCHES FOR ZOUAVE JACKETS

We have just received other patterns from Paris of the little pouches which still continue to be worn suspended from the waistband by a chain and hook, and sometimes by a cord. They are made of all kinds of materials, and are embroidered in gold, silver, and jet; or they are made of the same material as the dress with which they are worn, and trimmed in the same manner.

VELVET SACHET TO BE WORKED IN BEADS AND BUGLES

CRAFTING AND NEEDLEWORKS

HEADRESSES

Fig. 1

Fig. 1 - This coiffure is composed of a black velvet coronet standing high in the front, and is trimmed with black velvet leaves veined with gold, and mixed with gold tendrils or sprigs. To make the coronet, procure twenty-four inches of common chip or straw one inch wide; sew a thin wire on each side, tack over this a piece of lining, and stretch the velvet tightly over it, stitching it neatly down on the wrong side. The leaves which may be purchased in sprays, as also the gold tendrils, should then be prettily mounted on the coronet, leaving the latter without any trimming whatever at the sides. The illustration shows the back of the headdress.

Fig. 2

Fig. 2 – This headdress may be made of artificial flowers, or pearl flowers and leaves mounted on wire. The coronet is composed of black velvet, with a row of large pearls fastened on the inner edge, the flowers being tastefully arranged high in the center and narrowing towards the sides, with a full bunch behind.

DRAWING ROOM WORK BAG

A small receptacle for needlework, which may easily be carried in the hand, to convey it from place to place, or from room to room, with the few requisites which it demands, so as to keep the means of pleasant occupation always ready, that spare portions of time may not be wasted, is one of the necessary appendages of the worktable which we are now endeavoring to supply in a simple but novel style. The shape is first to be cut out in cardboard, the bottom of the bag having five sides, from which are turned up the five parts, each similar to the perfect one, as seen in the illustration. When laid flat upon the table it will appear as a five-sided piece with corresponding projections, which must be so folded as to give the whole the required shape. This being done, the under part may be covered with silk, and the sides with velvet, or the whole may be covered with velvet. The most ready way of doing this is to stitch the velvet on to the cardboard at its lower part, then to turn it up, and having folded it over the edge, to tack it all round in the same way as patchwork, carrying the velvet about half an inch over. The ornaments are very easily attached, being nothing more than those golden stars which have lately been so much used for the headdresses of ladies. In our engraving we have given the small stars as a border, with a larger one in the center of each division; but these may be varied at pleasure, as bees, butterflies, crescents, and many other tasteful forms, are now manufactured for the same purpose. When these have been fastened on in their respective places, the tacking threads will be concealed by them, and the whole shape must be laid down upon a round of silk and stitched down at each corner, the drawing in at the top having been first prepared and made ready for the strings. There will now be a vacancy between each of the five parts in which the silk will appear, and round this line, elastic is to be carried, which, while it draws up each part close to the neck, allows the bag to expand according to the quantity of material it is intended to convey. Another mode of making up is to line the shape covered with the velvet, and merely add the upper part of the bag in silk, which is in this way requires a much smaller quantity, and is done with very little trouble.

NECK-TIE WHICH MAY BE CONVERTED INTO A CAP

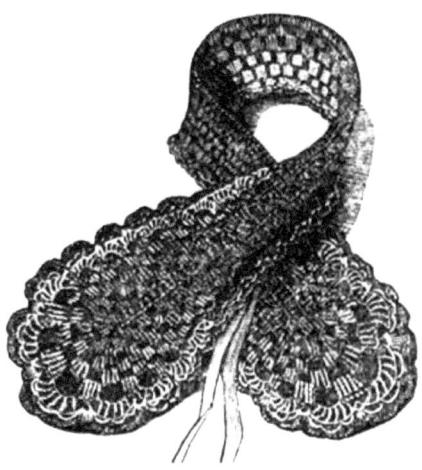

Materials – Four shades of blue 4-thread wool – six skeins of the lightest, four of the remaining shades; four skeins of white. No. 2 crochet hook.

Work 2 rows of color.

1st row – With darkest shade, make a chain of 177 stitches, turn back, work 1 long, 1 chain, miss 1 loop, *repeat*.

2d – 3 long, 3 chain, miss 3 loops, *repeat*, round the ends work 4 chain, 3 long, *under* the side of the last long stitch, 4 chain, *repeat* from beginning.

3d – 3 long *under* the 3 chain, 3 chain, *repeat*, round the ends work * 6 long with 4 chain between each, 3 long *under* the 4 chain, 4 chain, *repeat* from * again, then *repeat* from beginning.

4th – The same, working *under* every 4 chain round the ends the same as in last row.

5th – The same

6th – The same, working round the ends 5 long under every 4 chain between each 5 long.

7th – The same, making 6 long instead of 5 round the ends.

8th – *Twist the wool twice over the hook for the long stitches*, dc *under* the 3 chain, 2 chain, 5 long with 1 chain between each, *under* next 3 chain, 2 chain, *repeat* till the ends, where make 6 long *under* the 4 chain, 2 chain, and dc on center loop of the 6 long, 5 long, 2 chain, *repeat*.

9th – White, dc *under* the 2 chain, dc *under* 3 chain, dc under next 2 chain, 5 chain, dc between 2d long stitch, 5 chain, dc between next 2d long, 5 chain, *repeat*.

10th – 3 long under the 3 chain, 1 chain, dc under 5 chain, 5 chain, dc under 5 chain, 5 chain, dc under 5 chain, 1 chain, repeat.

Damp and press well.

Run a narrow satin ribbon through the first row, leaving sufficient ends to tie; it must be folded in the neck and stitched securely at the tie.

GLASS BEAD MATT

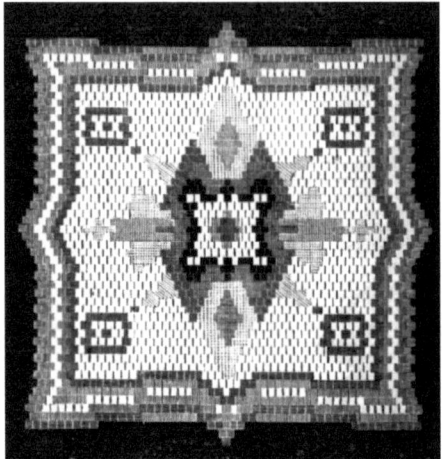

Materials — Eight rows dark blue beads, nine rows dark red, four rows light red, 2 rows dark yellow, two rows medium yellow, 4 rows light yellow, two rows green, 16 rows white, 1 row black.

This matt must be begun at A, with one dark blue bead in the middle of the thread; then take two dark blue beads, one on each needle; then pass both needles through one dark red; then take two dark red, then one dark red, two dark blue, one white, two white, one yellow, two yellow, one yellow, two yellow, one dark yellow, two dark yellow, one dark yellow, two dark yellow, one dark yellow, two dark yellow, one dark yellow, two light yellow, one black, two black, one black, two white, one light red, two dark red, one dark red; this brings to the center. Then reverse the colors, and work to the opposite side; afterwards work the two sides simultaneously with one needle only.

SAMPLER PATTERN

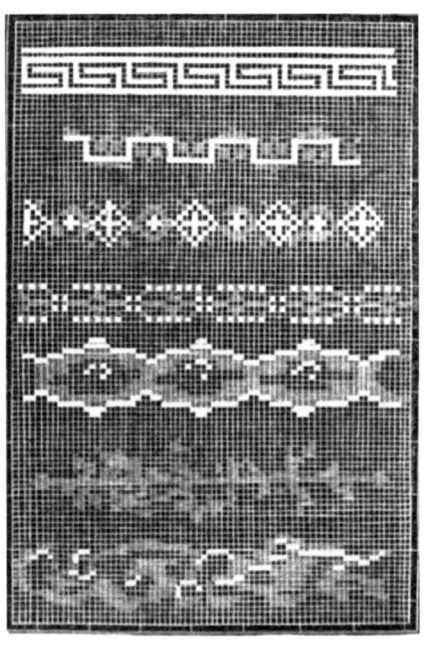

CROCHET INSERTING

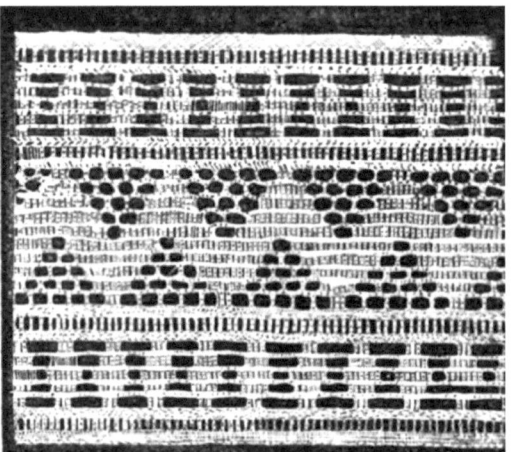

PATCHWORK

EMBROIDERY DESIGNS

BRAIDING PATTERN

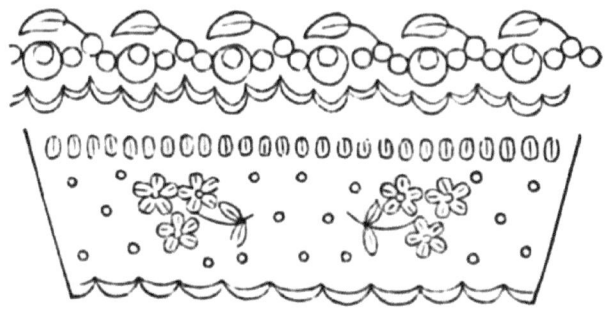

FLOUNCING FOR
A CHILDS DRESS

CHAPTER 11
NOVEMBER 1861

DESCRIPTION OF FASHION-PLATE FOR NOVEMBER 1861

Fig. 1 – Walking-dress *d la Imperatrice*. Material, rich brown poplin; the skirt has a ruche of velvet ribbon, the same on the caps of the sleeves which are plain. The body of the dress is ornamented with *patés* of green *moiré antique*, gracefully shaped, graduated in size, and surrounded by black velvet. This novel trimming is continued down the skirt. Bonnet of green Lyons velvet, with white plume.

Fig. 2 – The new pardessus, we have already given one design of, furnished by Brodie. This varies in style, but has the same marked plaits at the waist; square yoke, which, with the full sleeves, is ornamented by black lace. Fall bonnet of Belgian straw, trimmed with black plumes and damask roses, united by a ruche of black lace.

Fig. 3 – Carriage-dress of groseille reps silk; the skirt trimmed at the bottom with four narrow plaitings of ribbon, the same color. Simple mantle of Lyons velvet, corded with satin. The cape or pelerine is the novelty; it is divided into medallion lengths, each of which is ornamented by a fine pattern of embroidery; the pelerine is edged by a rich fall of black guipure. Graceful drawn bonnet, prevailing shade *tan d'or*.

Fig. 4 – Home-dress of one of those new silk and woolen fabrics which have almost the glossiness and softness of silk. The figure is in silk, raised. It is cut in the Gabrielle style, and trimmed with graduated ruches of green and maroon velvet ribbon, the two colors alternating. A novelty of the season.

Fig. 5 – Reception-dress for a bride. Material, rich mauve-colored silk, of the most delicate shade; the skirt is very full, and trimmed with a pendeloques ornament, that is a narrow plain ribbon laid on in the shape of a pendant to the long old-fashioned earrings of our mothers' time; this is headed by a handsome bow, with flowing ends; sash of the same; corsage low, and trimmed around the neck by a plaiting of the silk, "on the double" – the plaits fastened only at the bottom; tucker of tulle, drawn very full and close to the neck; sleeves in two large puffs, the upper of silk, the under of tulle. Headdress to correspond, of mauve ribbon and black lace.

Boy's Dress – Algerine sack of the new shade sublime. Material, poplin; trimming, black braid and velvet; the turned-back cuffs and sash-tie at the side are new. Hat of gray felt, pompon feather (see Chitchat), with two plumes, in white and rose sublime.

Baby's Dress – Rich robe of cambric; the tablier or front is of a richly wrought diamond pattern, separated by longitudinal puffs of cambric; sleeve and waist embroidered in the same pattern. Cap of embroidery or lace, with bows of blue satin ribbon.

CHITCHAT UPON NEW YORK AND PHILADELPHIA FASHIONS FOR NOVEMBER
Home and Walking Dress

The winter dress materials are fairly opened, and make a brilliant display upon the counters of Stewart's, Arnold's, Evans's, and other of our principal houses. There are fewer decided novelties than last year, but the bright shades of color, many of them new, which gives variety.

Plain merinos, cashmeres, and mousselines are quite behind the times; all these fabrics being printed or brocaded in small gay figures. The solid colors are of course imported, as they always will be, and chosen by a few; but they are not the style of the day. We find American mousselines greatly improved; they range from eighteen to twenty-five cents a yard, and compete in style and color, though not in quality, with the French and German goods. We notice particularly "a line", or a set, as we ladies should say of these goods, a graceful leaf, printed clearly on a black ground, in all the prevailing colors – bright purple, green, etc. American chintzes have also improved; the grounds are usually plain brown, coffee-colored, etc., with a bright clear figure. Stripes in everything have gone by, what is called "a set figure" having taken its place. Even the expensive reps in woolen and woolen and silk, that last year were all brocaded, are many of them printed in this style; the ground a dark, rich, decided color: the figure green, purple, Magenta, rose sublime, or any of these shades, toned with white and black.

The newest fabric is perhaps the *foulard de laines*, a cloth resembling alpaca, in glossiness of texture, and all wool; on it are reproduced the favorite foulard designs, chintz patterns, in very bright colors.

The variety of reps is infinite, from the cotton and woolen mixture selling at twenty-five cents a yard, to the richest finest silk and woolen, at a dollar eighty. One of the best styles in reps is a diagonal cheque, the cheque raised from the body of the stuff, and having the effect of satin; in the middle of each cheque or diamond is a small bright figure, and for instance, a black ground and cheque, with a Magenta or rose sublime figure; the effect is quite as handsome as if the material were a heavy brocaded silk, and it will be found far more serviceable. These goods have in a great measure taken the place of plain cashmeres and merinos for the street dresses, and in fact, have superseded the showy silks so unsuitable for inclement weather.

The delicacy to which the art of printing has attained is fully shown on the fine cashmeres, merinos, and mousselines of French manufacture. We have before us a specimen of one of the finest among Stewart's importations; the ground is maroon, a green leaf in the brightest of June tinting is carelessly thrown over the surface, contrasting with the same leaf reversed, showing its silver lining, as in the American poplar, etc. A tiny autumn leaf, in gray and Magenta, is added here and there to brighten its effect, and this is all, a fine artistic contrast to the gandy, nondescript figures, stretching over the whole ground, often the style of furniture chintz, which were brought out a year or two since.

Plain poplins, in all colors, are about the only plain goods that will be worn; a deep rich brown, maroon, and a deep bright shade of mauve, are the favorite winter colors; also Azurline blue, and Polish green, and a light shade of coffee-color, called by the French *Havané*. Plaids in poplin and woolen goods are used only for children's dress. The usual variety of all-wool plaids, which are manufactured with little variety from year to year, are to be found.

In making up, the gored or Gabrielle style, as we have before said, will be very popular for the materials we have named. Ribbons and bright-colored flat gimps are the most suitable trimmings for woolen goods; also ruffles, "on the double," of silk the shade of the brightest tint in the dress; ruches of silk, plaited through the middle, and pinked on the edges will also be much worn, and plain bands of silk singly, or in alternation with bands of the stuff. Velvet ribbon and bands of velvet are very suitable for reps, and other costly, weighty goods. Several new gimps have appeared, which will be described more particularly in our next; also winter silks, furs, etc.

As everyone is selecting winter wraps this month, we have made our usual *reconnaissance* at Brodie's for the benefit of our readers. First of all, there *is a tendency to shorten the length* of cloaks; all the importations are much shorter than the American taste will at present admit; for, as we are told at this favorite establishment, it requires full six months to persuade the popular taste to change materially, no matter what designs rule in Paris. We find, also, from Mr. Brodie that the cloaks which have plaitings at the back are most in favor, though there is so great a variety in shape that one can scarcely go amiss. The materials are velvet and cloth, the latter of black brown, or gray chiefly. There are several new styles of ornament, the most tasteful oak-leaves, vine-leaves and grapes, etc., cut out or rather stamped out in cloth, velvet, etc., and these are applied as *patées*. For instance, we may describe a velvet cloak made something in the old Raglan shape, but reaching to within nine inches of the hem of the dress, the sleeve large and loose, falling open so as to show a richly quilted lining in black satin. At the top of the sleeve is a passementerie ornament, a wreath of vine-leaves and clusters encircling the arm like a cap, a *patées* of the same on each side of the front. This cloak has a novel effect, given by a thick cording of gold-colored satin all around and edging the sleeve.

A brown cloth cloak, with ornaments of knots and bows, cut or stamped from cloth, fastening the plaits behind and appearing on the shoulders. A plaiting of cloth edges the front on each side.

Gray wrap, very heavy tricot cloth, wide, loose sleeve with lappets of cloth, bound with purple, and fastened by large buttons of gray with a bright purple center. A serpentine trimming, formed by a flat band of purple silk, to match the edging of the cloak, extends from the collar to the hem, with a button like those on the sleeve in each turn.

Black and white cloth wrap in the bournous style, edged by a box plaiting of broad velvet ribbon. The pelerine, which is hollowed up on the shoulder, forms a hood behind, caught by a broad bow of black velvet ribbon. The hood and pelerine edged by box plaited velvet ribbon.

Rich cloak, with wide gores of purple velvet let in, alternating with full breadths of black Lyons velvet rounded at the bottom. The deep hanging sleeve has also its broad gore of purple velvet; these gores are richly embroidered in a leaf pattern; the black velvet breadths have a Grecian chain pattern in embroidery. And are each edged by sharp plaitings of velvet ribbon, set on the edge, as are the sleeves and the hem of the garment. A graceful bertha in the fanchon shape of costly guipure on *the back* of the cloak.

Ample black velvet cloak, the hem apparently four inches deep, headed by a line of white silk. The graceful pelerine is almost in a hood shape, coming close to the throat in front and on the shoulders, deepening to the waist line behind. The center is a band of velvet, edged by white silk, the upper and lower portion rich guipure lace.

Dark brown wrap of Astrachan cloth (shaggy), with lapels turning back in front, *à gilot* (waistcoat fashion).

Shawl-shaped black cloth cloak, drooping pointed sleeves, shawl-shaped pelerine. It is bound by two rows of black satin piping, an inch apart, placed three inches above the hem of the garment, sleeves, etc.; a rich ornament in braid, the Egyptian coil, on the back of the sleeve and in each corner of the garment.

We learn from Mr. Myers, of Reynold's Bazaar, that the ruling shape for children's felt hats will be a modification of the shell-shapes and turbans so universal this summer. The shell-shape (the crown set down into the brim) has a square, or rather flat crown instead of the round one of the past season, which we think a great improvement. Black, brown, and gray felts and beavers will be trimmed with rich shades of velvet, such as green, rose sublime, Magenta, etc.; the pompon feather being used chiefly instead of plumes, though a really good plume is always acceptable. The pompon feather is also much used in bonnets. Winter bonnets in our next.

THE ALVANTE

Made of black velvet, and trimmed with rich guipure lace.

THE EUGENIA

Made of black cloth, and trimmed with fancy colored box-plaited ribbon.

THE CLOTILDE

Made of black velvet, and trimmed with a quilling of silk and velvet.

THE NATALIE

Made of black cloth, and trimmed with white braid and fancy gimp ornaments.

THE DARRO

From the establishment of G. Brodie, 51 Canal Street, New York.
Drawn by L.T. Voigt, from actual articles of costume.

This simple chaste garment is one that, whilst it commends itself to the favor of all our fair friends by its unpretending character, will prove, we incline to believe, a novelty which the younger portion of our readers especially, will seek after with avidity.

CAPS & BONNETS

Fig. 1 - Breakfast cap of mull, trimmed with inserting and Valenciennes edge, also with black velvet and cherry ribbon.

Fig. 2 - Dinner cap of spotted black and white lace, and trimmed with loops and bows of fuchsia ribbon.

Fig. 1 - Cerulean blue velvet bonnet, with white uncut velvet cape, the bonnet is trimmed with a voilette of white blonde and loops of blue velvet.

Fig. 2 – Fuchsia velvet bonnet; it is trimmed with flowers and white blonde.

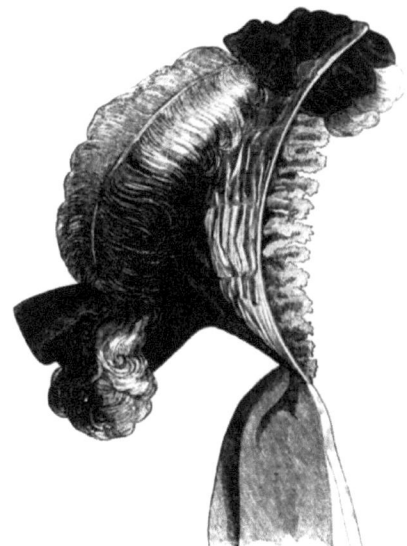

Fig. 3 – Half Mourning bonnet. The material of the crown is black velvet, and the front white tulle drawn in *bouillonnés*. A long white ostrich feather which is fixed on the front of the bonnet passes across the crown, and the tip turns over the bavolet or curtain. The under-trimming consists of a small white feather, with coques of black velvet in front, and ruches of white tulle at each side of the face.

Fig. 4 – Bonnet of dark brown velvet, ornamented with a plume of pink and white ostrich feathers, and a hcrons tuft. The bavolet covered with a fall of white lace. The under-trimming consists of coques of brown velvet and white tulle *bouillonné* strings of white sarsnet ribbon.

HEADDRESSES

Fig. 1 – Front of headdress

Fig. 2 – The coronet is composed of black velvet, with three pearl or gold stars, a large one in the center and a smaller one on either side. Two long white ostrich feathers fastened in at the side of the coronet and crossing behind, complete this coiffure. It would be equally pretty made in pink or blue velvet, with feathers of the same color, the stars being made of pearl, studded with steel.

We dare say it would be of interest to know exactly what people at court wear when they go into mourning. The Court of England last winter wore mourning for the Dowager Queen of Sweden in this fashion: the ladies were to wear black silk, fringed of plain linen, white gloves, necklaces, and earrings, black or white shoes, fans, and tippets. The gentlemen to wear black, full-trimmed; fringed or plain linen; black swords and buckles. The court to change the mourning on Thursday, the 10th January – viz. – The ladies to wear black silk or velvet, colored ribbons, fans, and tippets or plain white, or white and gold, or white and silver stuffs, with black ribbons. The gentlemen to wear black coats, and black or plain white, or white and gold, or white and silver stuff, waistcoats, full trimmed colored swords and buckles. Thursday, the 17th January, the court to go out of mourning. The whole arrangement to last one month.

NOVELTIES FOR NOVEMBER

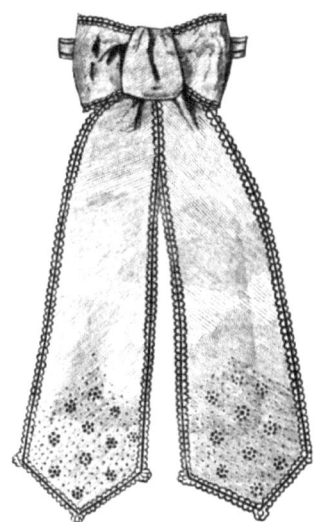

Fig. 1 – Sash bow, for a plain silk; material the same as the dress, edged with a fine satin gimp of black; the ends are prettily embroidered in single and clustered dots; the clusters may be in bugle beads, or a heavy embroidery stitch in black silk.

Fig. 2 – Headdress of lace, ribbon, and flowers, for dinner or evening wear.

Fig. 3 – Headdress for concerts, opera, or party going. The caul or net for the hair, made of pearl beads, and ornamented at the top by a loop of larger beads, fastening drooping sprays of wheat. A wreath of black silk or velvet loops starts from each side of the caul, and encircles the head; pearl beads are wound through the loops.

Fig. 4 – Headdress of braided ribbon, with a net foundation underneath to keep it in place. There is a spray of golden acorns and oak leaves in the center, and to the left, quite low down, a bouquet of crimson velvet convolvulus, with leaves and tendrils, a few golden acorns showing at one side.

Fig. 5 – Fanchon cap of delicate muslin lined with mauve colored silk, trimmed with a wrought needlework edge. The front is caught by rosettes of mauve velvet. Strings and bow of mauve-colored satin ribbon.

Fig. 6 – Habit shirt and collar for morning wear; around the neck is a muslin puff through which is drawn a colored ribbon, fastened by a tiny bow.

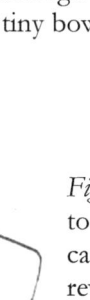

Fig. 7 – White sleeve to wear with a short sleeved dress by those who do not care to display the uncovered arm. It is of tulle with a reversed frill of blonde. It should be trimmed with ribbon, matching or contrasting with the dress.

FROM MADAME DEMOREST'S MAGAZINE DE MODES
No. 473 Broadway, New York

THE MATHILDE JACKET

This pretty jacket is very much in vogue for the matinee costume for young married ladies, and also for demoiselles. It consists of fine light blue or green cashmere, bordered with black velvet, upon which are embroidered scallops and dots in white silk. On the front of the sleeve, the velvet extends up on the arm, forming the half of a pyramidal block. A side seam gives shape to the front, and there are also seams in the lack which fit it to the waist, where the skirt is laid in a hollow plait. This jacket is very pretty in Solferino or Magenta cashmere, with a simple border of black velvet.

FAIRY DRESS

This dress made for a truly fairy child, is of blue silk, of that exquisite tint known as French blue. The waist is cut in points, two in front and two in the back, and on the hips, a scarf crosses the shoulder in plaits, fastened with buttons. The sleeve is a plain cap, with a second cap in points over it. Waist, scarf, and sleeve, trimmed with a bias quilling. Tassels on the points. The skirt has four flounces, finished with a quilling to match the waist. It is also pretty in any plain color, trimmed with a contrast. For a Miss of twelve years, would require thirteen yards of material.

DRESS FOR OUT OF DOOR WORK

At a farmers' club-meeting held at Ghent, N.Y., the ladies of the neighborhood participated in the meeting, and one of them, Miss Powell, read a very sensible original paper with the above title.

Miss Powell alludes to the decline of healthy constitutions among American women, a well-known and much to be lamented fact; and though we attribute it as much too inherited delicacy, arising from the wear and tear of nerve and brain which every American parent undergoes, doubtless it may be greatly obviated by out of door exercise, as Miss Powell suggests. We have only to look to ourselves to see that we are oftentimes hindered in this by unsuitable clothing. Embroidered skirts, open wrappers, and dressing slippers are not particularly suited to a morning walk or work in the garden. The case is still worse in the afternoon; a heavy ottoman velvet or a nice silk in winter, and thee delicate organdy and *barége* robes of summer are not improved by trailing along wet gravel walks or sloppy pavements; so we stay at home to take care of our "good clothes," instead of going out to take care of ourselves.

Every city woman should have a walking-dress as well. The walking-dress should be of a stuff stout enough for all pedestrian accidents, clearing the ground as to length, with a neat dark petticoat, and kid or kid-dressed walking-boots; these strengthen and support the ankle, and keep the stocking free from dust; in short, such a costume as a thrifty Philadelphia housekeeper wears to market. The slow, full-dress saunter in a dress that has to be carried with both hands, is of little use; it is the brisk, unimpeded walk that sets the blood coursing through the veins and brings the flush of health to the cheek.

For out of door work Miss Powell says: "I would suggest that the waist should be cut so as to give entire freedom to every muscle; the skirt for a woman or ordinary height twenty-five or twenty-six inches in length, with plain or Turkish trousers of the same material. Every woman acknowledges the benefit of such a modification in dress, and in the actress, skater, and gymnast, society respects and approves it. We commend it for all industrial pursuits, for indoor and out of door work."

A design of a dress for working in the garden, not unlike the above, appeared some time ago in the Lady's Book, the material to be of shepherd's plaid, or any woolen and cotton stuffs; made with plenty of pockets, and in every way convenient and comfortable. As for hoops, they are impossibility, and a trailing skirt would soon prove its own torment to the wearer.

One of the gentlemen present suggested "that the Empress Eugenie be memorialized to adopt a style of dress which should embody all the physiological benefits and advantages" desired, thinking that "whatever she might adopt would soon become a popular and fashionable dress." We doubt whether the dainty little lady could be brought to forego the graceful and becoming, which has very little part or lot in a really useful working garb. The lilies of the field are allowed to wear gay clothing, for "they toil not, neither do they spin;" but we, of every-day, industrial life, must be content with more serviceable garments.

A SIMPLE STYLE OF CHEMISE

A BUTTERFLY ROSETTE

A SHOE ROSETTE

LITTLE GIRLS COAT

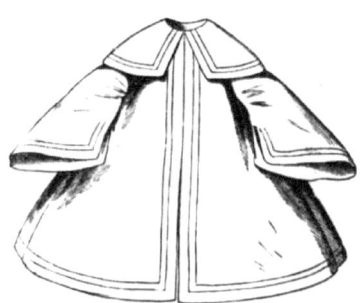

COAT FOR A BOY OR GIRL

CRAFTING & NEEDLE WORKS

SONTAG (WOOLEN HABIT-SHIRT)

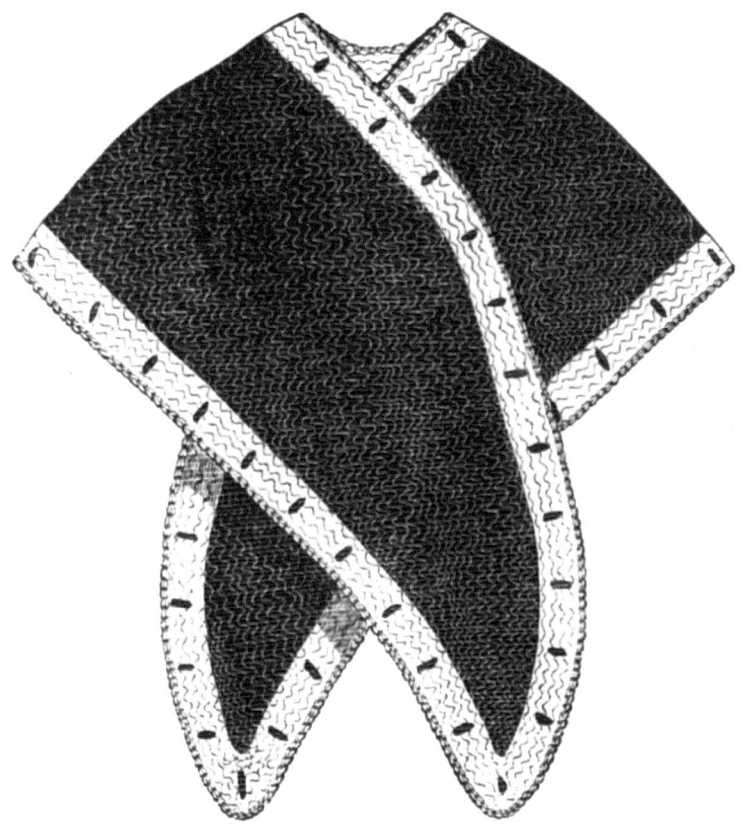

Materials — Two ounces of double Berlin wool, of any dark color, and one ounce of white ditto. Knitting needles, No. 10

This very pretty and comfortable habit-shirt is intended to be worn under a mantle or cloak; and as it gives great additional warmth, without making the figure at all clumsy, it has many advantages over shawls and other wraps.

With the dark wool cast on five stitches, and knit, increasing one stitch at the end of every row, until eighty stitches are on the needles. This is the back. Then knit only half the stitches, the others being left on the needle (which will be found much more convenient than slipping them on a separate one). Still increase one at the outer edge, in every alternate row, but decrease one at the inner edge, in the intermediate rows, so that forty remain on the needle, until you have done seventy rows, when cast off loosely. Do the other half the same. Then take up on one needle the stitches round the neck, and along these cast off ends. Knit, with white wool, ten rows, increasing one at the end of every row. Cast off loosely. Take up the stitches along the outer edge, and do the same, increasing, and joining to the inner border at the ends, and increasing also at each side of the five original stitches, that it may set square. Cast off loosely, and work small spots at intervals with the dark wool. The ends cross over the bosom.

KNITTED OPERA HOOD

Materials – Two ounces four-thread Berlin wool, of any color that may be preferred; one ounce gray and white pearl wool, half an ounce black, and ditto white; ivory needles, No. 9 and No. 7

Begin with the colored wool and No. 9 needles, casting on two hundred and fifty stitches. Knit two plain rows, and after that, cast off four stitches at the beginning of every needle for thirty rows; then cast off two only at the beginning of every row for fifty-four rows, when cast off altogether.

The Curtain – Cast on seventy stitches, and knit eighteen rows, increasing one at the end of every row. Cast off loosely.

Sew this piece along the back, in the center, slightly holding the hood in, and sewing on the ends as well as the length, as the border is carried from the points, along the sides where stitches were cast off, and along the outer edge of the curtain, in one continuous piece. For this purpose take up the stitches on the entire length; and knit with the pearl wool (No. 7 needles) twelve rows of ordinary shell pattern; then two rows with black wool, to be followed by a single plain row with white wool; after which, cast off loosely with the same.

Do another frill of ten shells, exactly the same, to sew on above the curtain, so as to cover it; and make end and tassels, which you run in along the back of the neck, to draw it in. They are put along the seam below the upper frill, which are a few rows above that seam.

A similar border is carried along the front, from point to point, and laid back; and the second (under) frill is put on a cape, sewed about six rows within the edge, so that it turns over easily, the upper frill border just covering this cape. It has seventy-two stitches cast on; and fourteen rows are knitted, with one stitch increase at the end of every row. The second border just goes the length of the head, and does not extend to the barbs.

No combination of colors is prettier for this hood than mauve, with the gray, black, and white borders.

FANCY PURSE

Made of two round pieces, worked the long open stitch, and sewed together; trimmed at the bottom with a fringe of gold beads and three tassels, A gilt clasp fastens the purse.

EMBROIDERED SCARF

Materials – A strip of black filet, No. 2, forty-eight inches by nine, cut on the square; a skein of ombre pink and violet silk, a skein of plain cherry, two of emerald green, and part of one vertislay.

This design is simply darned with the various silks on the filet, in the natural colors. The ombre pink answers admirably for the carnation, and the violet for the anemone: The vertislay for the leaves of the former, and the emerald green for those of the latter. To form the border, the filet is folded along the sides and ends, the depth of four squares, and the design is then darned on it, the stitches being taken, when necessary, through the double material. The Greek border is done in emerald green, and the stars in cherry. The fringe is knotted on the lowest row of holes, thus: Cut lengths of shaded violet and cherry, and of each green nearly half a yard long; take four strands of violet, pass them through the corner hole of the end, and tie in a knot; miss two holes, and tie in the third four strands of green, then cherry in the third from that, then the other green. Begin again with the violet: now knot four threads of violet with four green, the other four violet with four cherry; the rest of the cherry to the next violet, and green with green. Another row of knots will unite the same set of strands as at first — that is, the eight ends of violet together; then green, then cherry, then green again. This makes a very handsome fringe, and may be made richer by using six, or eight, instead of four threads.

No engraving can really give an idea of the beauty and novelty of this scarf, as the colors cannot be represented in it.

GLASS BEAD MATT NO. 2

Materials – Three rows dark red beads, seven rows medium red, seven rows light red, seven rows dark blue, eight rows light blue, one row yellow, twenty-one rows white, one row black.

This mat must be commenced the same way as No. 1, October number, at A, beginning with but two beads and working alternately two and one to the opposite side, afterwards with only one needle at each side. The white beads on the outer border of this one should be dead-white. These two mats will only require a very simple fringe.

OTTOMAN IN BERLIN WORK

Materials – Penelope border canvas, about 50 stitches in width, and of a size which will allow the beads to cover a stitch completely: amber pound-beads of two shades, rich green and claret wool; also the Mecklenburg thread No. 71

The beads are chosen of shades which contrast somewhat strongly, the darkest being of a decided orange and the others straw-color. The borders and stars are done in the dark shade: the outlines of the medallions in the other.

Fill in the medallions in green, and also the inner part of the scroll; the rest in claret in cross-stitch.

The ottoman is to be made up in alternate stripes of work and velvet, and trimmed with rich cord and tassels.

Stripes of work and velvet being also much used for *Prie-dieu* chairs, this pattern would be very effective done in straw beading and wool. It will not do to use Penelope canvas for this, as the grounding is done in tapestry stitch, that is, taken over two threads in height and one in width. Select a canvas of which the straw will cover two threads, and run a line on, across the width of the canvas in small neat stitches. Work with the wool all the parts which form the grounding, leaving the straw to represent the beads.

Each row of straw must be run on, worked, before proceeding to the next.

This design will be found appropriate for many purposes besides that for which we have given it. Carriage-bags, foot-stools, and a variety of other articles, will look well done in it.

The beads set on canvas-work being especially required to be sewed on very strongly, we particularly recommend that the thread we have indicated should be used for that purpose, to render the work perfectly secure.

HANDSOME PETTICOAT TRIMMING IN BRODERIE ANGLAISE

Materials – Fine long-cloth, and embroidery cotton, No. 14

All open-work in this design is to be simply sewed over, after being carefully traced all round. The stems are also to be sewed. The edge is done in graduated button-hole stitch, considerably raised in the center of each scallop.
Being given of the full size, the pattern may be traced from the engraving.

CHILD'S WARM SHOE, IN CROCHET

Materials – One ounce scarlet or green shaded 4-thread wool; one ounce white ditto; a skein of black and pale straw-colored ditto; a pair of cork soles; crochet hook, No. 15; a pair of knitting needles, same size; and a mesh, half-inch wide.

Begin by working the shaded wool for the shoe. Nine ch, work in single crochet on it, with three stitches in the center one. Turn, and work in single crochet, a stitch on every stitch; turn again and increase as before by doing three in the center stitch. The next row is without increase. Continue to work thus, increasing two stitches in every alternate row, until you have done eight ribs. If the child has a very high instep, it will be necessary still further to increase the size in the last three ribs, by doing two stitches, in lieu of one, in the last stitch of *every* row. In working ribbed crochet, a chain-stitch must also be made at the end of each row, that the edge may not be contracted.

Now do one side of the foot, by working as far as the center-stitch only, and then turning back. About six ribs will suffice for the heel. Work the other side in the same way, and crochet up the heel.

For the Fur – With the white wool cast on six stitches, and knit in common garter-stitch as much as will go easily round the top of the shoe. Making the fur is then done by a process exactly resembling raised Berlin work, only the ground is knitting instead of canvas. Thread a coarse rug-needle with a double strand of wool, so that you will work with *four* thicknesses. Work on the rib of knitting in cross-stitch, taking the wool over the mesh. Cut each line before you withdraw the mesh. After three lines of white only, do in the center two yellow stitches, and in the next row two black over them. When combed and cut, this makes a very pretty washable fur.

Bind the cork soles with ribbon, or strips of thin leather, and sew on the shoe, also the fur round the top. These directions, applied to 8-thread Berlin wool, with a coarser hook and a longer foundation-chain, will suffice for a lady's dressing-slipper or over-shoe.

The number of ribs may, of course be increased, according to the size of the wearer's foot.

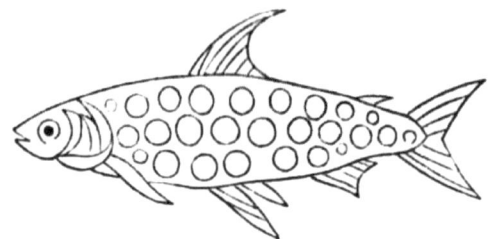

FOR CHEMISE YOKES

BRAIDING PATTERN FOR A CHILDS DRESS

PATTERNS IN CROCHET

We give this month, two patterns for the centers of antimacassars, berceaunette covers, or toilet mats. They are worked in solid or chain crochet, and are extremely durable as well as pretty. The cotton used for working them should be about No. 10. They may be finished with either a fringe or a lace. A border round them of a light, open description can be added, if they are intended for drawing-room antimacassars; but they are simpler to execute if a square is worked of the pattern, and finished with a fringe tied into every loop, a row of crochet being added all round for the purpose.

EMBROIDERY DESIGNS

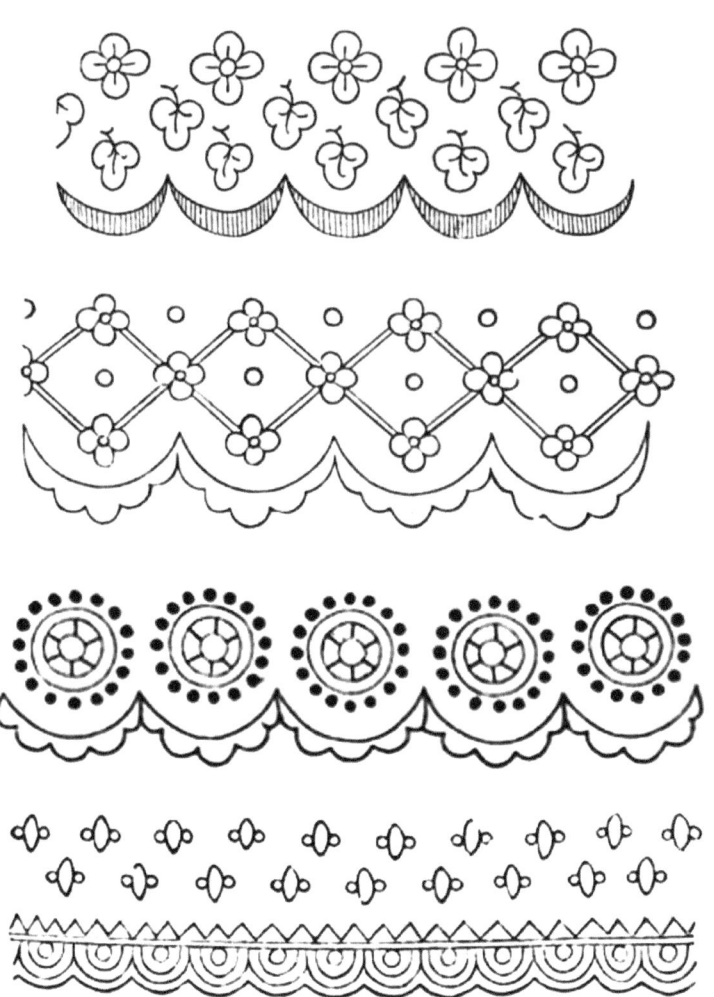

CHAPTER 12
DECEMBER 1861

DESCRIPTION OF FASHION-PLATE FOR DECEMBER 1861

Our group of brides is the first plate of the kind, we believe, ever published in this or any other fashion magazine. The variety of bridal costumes is such that the simplest and the most elegant taste may be gratified alike. We invite attention to its minutest details – the position of each figure – the admirable grouping – the effective background with delicate hangings, and appropriate floral decorations – and the artistic glimpse of the waiting friends, skillfully thrown in to add to the naturalness of the scene. Yet, apart from the picture presented, each figure is a correct costume.

Fig. 1 – Extremely rich lace robe, over white silk; it is a combination of the Brussels and *point Duchess*, the graceful design having a border of medallions, and the same pattern is repeated at the height of the knee. The sleeves and body are of white silk; the corsage high, *as is invariably the case* with French bridal costumes, since the idea of modesty and delicacy which belongs to the bride seems to require it. The corsage has a pointed *berthé* of lace in the same pattern as the border of the robe, but narrower; a double row of the same upon the long flowing sleeves, which are caught up by a knot of white satin ribbon. Sash of white satin ribbon, with silver fringe. The hair is turned lightly back from the face, and dressed low, concealing the ear; wreath of orange-buds, arranged as a diadem, a narrow cordon of buds connects the diadem with the *21. Ciche peigné*, which droops behind. Veil arranged quite back on the head, of

Brussels point, to correspond in every way with the robe.

Fig. 2 – In admirable contrast to this costly dress and veil, which could not be imported under a thousand, or fifteen hundred dollars (according to the fineness of the lace), we have one of almost nun-like simplicity, a white silk with perfectly plain corsage buttoned with ornamental pearl buttons, and a rich satin waist ribbon. Mousquetaire sleeves, the cuffs turned with a simple ruching of the material; tulle undersleeves, with a frill of lace at the wrist; plain illusion veil, with silk cord at the top of the lower hem. Wreath of orange-blossoms, mounted in clusters.

Fig. 3 – Dress of embroidered French muslin, with six flounces of embroidery running up to the left of the skirt, headed by a handsome flounce of lace. Flowing sleeves with flounces; square *berthé* to correspond; a spray of blossoms set carelessly in the left corner.

Sash of broad thick ribbon. Sprays of blossoms confine the veil, which comes low on the forehead at each side.

Fig. 4 – is given for the peculiarly novel arrangement of the veil; it is placed so as to shade the face entirely, falling in front, across the upper line of the corsage.

Fig. 5 – *A la Imperatrice*, or gored in front; the trimming, which is a broad ruching of the material (white silk), is placed *en bretelle* on the shoulders, narrowing at the waist line, and sweeping off gracefully to the hem of the skirt. A row of daisy buttons in white blonde down the front; sleeves trimmed with the ruching; a single spray of blossoms crosses the forehead, and connects beneath the roll of hair with a similar spray behind.

Fig. 6 – Muslin dress, in eight flounces edged by needle-work; sleeves headed by two flounces to correspond; full wreath of leaves and orange-blossoms encircling the head.

CHITCHAT UPON NEW YORK AND PHILADELPHIA FASHIONS, FOR DECEMBER

We would call attention to the distinguishing points of bridal costume given in this number. First, that in the true Parisian bridal costume, the sleeves are long, though flowing, and the corsage high; this would not be thought of by our American brides, but it expresses the true modesty of the sentient which, from time immemorial, has made a veil indispensable. Again, it will be seen that no person is confined to any single style or material; a bridal dress that would be becoming to a tall and slender figure, would look absurd on a dumpy person; a fabric suitable to the fortunes and probable gayeties of a person in fashionable city life, would be out of place in the quiet parlor of a country home. As to wreaths – though the diadem style is the prominent one, the coronal, the cordon, the simple wreath, or bouquets, may be worn as best suits the face. A bride of all persons should never sacrifice becomingness to the fashion of the moment. For bridesmaids, we have given some hints in our "Novelties," the present month, to which we refer our readers.

And now to redeem our promise of pointing out styles for the making up of winter fabrics, presuming that there is no specially new one imported since our last, save some rich black silks that at first glance would resemble those of the past season too much to be really new. There is this difference: the bouquets and medallions in raised or brocaded figures on the black ground are in single colors, instead of the variety of last year. As for instance, in a shamrock pattern last year, the three lines were; one in green, one in gold, and one in purple; now, all the figure is in green, or gold, or purple. The medallion wreaths, and wreath-like diagonal cheques or diamonds, are perhaps the very newest styles. Plain silks and poplins are however, the general favorites.

We have before said that the gored dresses, known as *Gabrielle* and *Imperatrice*, will be much worn. Many define the seams with a thick cord, or piping in the same, or a contrasted color; others, by flat velvet ribbons, or ruches of velvet plaits; others, again, by double silk ruches pinked at the edges, like those worn on the bonnets the past fall. Again, the velvet or ruching is placed *en bretelle* on the shoulders, and sweeps down *en tablier* on the skirt, as in *Fig. 5* of our plate. Plain black Lyons velvet of the best quality is freely used, but, instead of numerous narrow rows, one broad band is worn on the skirt, set its own distance above the hem, and frequently rising *en tablier* or *en tunic* to the skirt. The widest velvet ribbons are a little over eight inches – six and four inch ribbons are less expensive, and therefore the more frequently adopted. It may be had for .75 cents a yard – the widest is $1.20. At first glance this appears too expensive to be popular; but these broad bands on the skirt require only the exact measurement, no doubling for plaits or ruching, and are no more expensive than flouncing's of the same. We give an instance of its application. Plain rich brown silk, skirt full and long, surrounded by a band of five inch velvet, passing from left to right, it meets itself to the extreme right, and is carried upward in a curve of graduated width for a few inches, where it is caught by a large black velvet oak leaf. The sleeves are full, with flat plaits at the top, confined by an oak leaf in velvet; the bottom has a plain band of three inch velvet. There is no other trimming but a sash of five inch velvet tied in a bow at the left, the ends having a flat application of a velvet oak leaf to correspond.

Again, a Gabrielle dress, the seams and front trimmed with a four inch velvet ribbon put on in this way, three square or box plaits of the ribbon, a plain place of equal width, with a button in the center, three plaits, and plain space, etc., from the shoulder to the hem of the dress. The new daisy buttons are of chenille and blonde, or a medallion of open crochet, something in the shape of a child's pewter toy watch with handle surrounded by guipure lace. These are much used for the fronts of dresses, for looping lace, plaits, etc.

Flounces are used only on plain silks and evening dresses, and these are usually set on in groups, in waves, or points, or diagonally, with puffs between. We have seen a very striking style, in brown *Havané* silk, five or six flounces, of five inches in width, each flounce trimmed by a black satin cord at the edge of the hem; the sleeves were made in the same way; on each side of the front breadth, and on the forearm of the sleeve, a band of plain silk, edged on each side with hem and cord, is placed over the flounces, from the waist to the hem, and from the shoulder to the edge of the sleeve. On the skirt it is eight inches wide, on the sleeves five; at moderate distances apart on this plain space, bows of rich ribbon, with ends, are placed. The effect is very good. Madame Demorest makes up several of these styles; we might mention several other well-known names among New York and Philadelphia modistes.

The large velvet leaves, of which we have spoken, are among the most prominent decorations of the season. In Genin's riding-hats for ladies, which are among his very happiest creations, we notice them amid bows of rich ribbon, or *pompons* and aigrettes of scarlet and black. We instance one with a rich beaver crown, and a brim turned up, somewhat in the "old Continental style," the point in front drooping most becomingly; this is of felt, bound or faced with a broad band of velvet. Large lotus leaves in black velvet fall on each side of a scarlet and black pompon, and a black plume curls backward. At the side of the face are bows of black and scarlet velvet. Again, a double rolling brim of silk and felt crown, with Magenta decorations. This double brim, patented by Mr. Genin, is extensively used in his children's hats, as are also the lotus leaves, in their native green, fantastic scarlet, Magenta, etc., with pompons of every shade mixed with black.

In ladies' bonnets we have already given such excellent illustrations (front pages November number) that descriptions are scarcely needed. We find, from the winter openings of Mrs. Scofield, Madame Harris, and others, that the shape continues after the extreme French model, very wide, high brims, small drooping, "pinched-up" crowns; capes long, and pointed at the back, feathers playing an important part in the decorations; particularly the long, handsome ostrich feather, displaced of late years by clusters of shorter plumes; feather tips are largely introduced inside the brim, sufficient space being now allowed for their disposal. Steel-edged velvet leaves, steel-powdered clusters of grapes or berries are much worn; and the brown duller feathers of the pheasant, and all other game birds and barnyard fowls even, mounted in plumes, aigrettes, or pompons; we do not think the peacock tips will meet with general favor, as someone clearly says, "they are too suggestive of dust and fly-brushes."

We are glad to notice amid the huge *bunches* of flowers, worn on top of the brim inside and out, some plainer styles, which are to our fancy far more elegant; a plain black velvet of the best description, the only ornament three tips of ostrich feathers on the front of the brim, placed flat upon it; one in the center, one each side. Black velvet, plain crown, the front of the brim decorated by a fan shaped ornament of leaf-green velvet, in rows of box plaits an inch or so in width; the same ornament is repeated in a graduated size on the middle of the cape.

For dress bonnets, Genin's furs, boys' and babies' hats from Reynolds, boots, slippers, fans, embroidery, and Brodie's decided winter styles, in cloaks, see next number.

INVISIBLE HAIR-NETS

As there are still many ladies who value the comfort and convenience of the hair-net, and who are desirous of retaining it as long as fashion permits, we are very happy to comply with the wish of a subscriber, and give instructions for making the newest that has appeared, which is one that bears the name of the "Invisible Hair-Net." As its title implies, this net is scarcely distinguishable when worn upon the hair, as it matches it in color, and is also remarkably fine and clear, the meshes being open. The silk used is much finer than the finest netting silk, and is strong, being a sort of raw silk. Commence by making twenty loops on a mesh one-third of an inch wide, and set as many rows, thus forming a perfect square, then gather up a little portion of the center of this square, tie it round and attach it to the string of the netting stirrup, and then continue to net all-round the edge of the square until the desired size has been reached. This size must be regulated according to the convenience of the proposed wearer, and this must depend upon the quantity of hair which it is intended to confine. When completed, an elastic must be passed through the last row of loops; the net must be moistened with a little weak gum-water, stretched over a dinner plate, and left to dry. These invisible hair-nets are the best that have been introduced, and are, in fact, the only kind now worn.

THE AISSA CLOAK

Gray cloth, checked; bordered by a bias-piece of silk braided in trefoils. The ends being raised form three points for the sleeve, a small piece in the back turning towards the front.

THE EPERNON CLOAK

Of light colored cloth, edged with silk. Three hollow plaits start from the neck; one on each shoulder and one in the middle of the back. Pieces braided and terminated by a tassel are laid on each plait. This cloak is raised on the arms, and drapes amply behind.

THE ANDALUSIAN

From the establishment of G. Brodie, 51 Canal Street, New York
Drawn by L.T. Voigt, from actual articles of costume

This exceedingly graceful combination bids fair to be widely adopted. The skirt is set upon a yoke in the back, arranged in the broad middle, with two plaits upon either side of it; this is ornamented with a magnificent passementerie. The sleeves are long and flowing, trimmed to match the back, while the edge of the yoke is similarly adorned.

THE PARIS SKIRT

For the winter season, we introduce as a substitute for the Balmorals, black silk skirts, quilted with white, gold color, or crimson silk. This work is to be done by a machine, or otherwise it would be exceedingly expensive and tedious. They can be wadded or not, as the person may desire, but when worn over hoops, they are seldom wadded. Any design can be put on them and they are far handsomer and more *distinqué* than the stripped woolen skirt of former seasons. If a very rich skirt is desired, narrow bands of crimson velvet can be stitched on to form a pattern.

BONNETS FOR THE SEASON

Fig. 1 – Bonnet composed of rose sublime velvet, with white uncut velvet crown. It is trimmed with roses and a black lace barbe.

Fig. 2 – Azurline blue velvet bonnet, trimmed with white *appliqué* lace and a long white feather.

Fig. 3 – Opera bonnet, composed of Garibaldi-colored velvet and white *appliqué* lace, with a rich bird plume on one side.

Fig. 4 – This bonnet is composed of a white crepe front and raspberry-colored silk crown, and trimmed with black and white lace.

APRONS

THE HATTIE

THE ELSIE

Fig. 1 – This style of apron can be made of black or any colored silk, and is very simple, being trimmed *en tunique*, with one ruffle, and ornamented with two bows in front.

Fig. 2 – An easy apron for a child, suitable for a little party. It is made of cerise silk, trimmed with graduated ruffles, and ornamented with rosettes of silk or ribbon.

INFANTS CHRISTENING ROBE

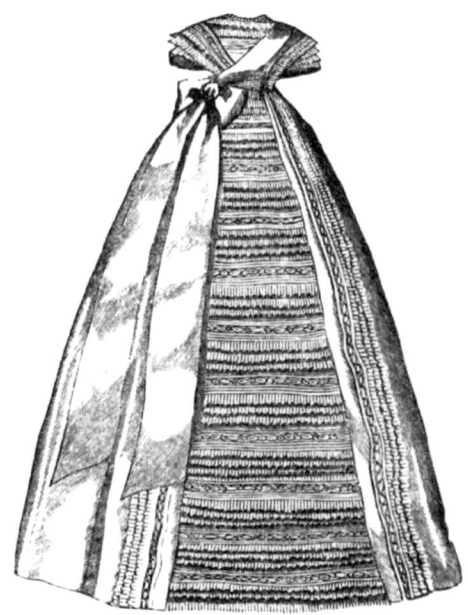

Made of fine French muslin, and trimmed with fluted ruffles and inserting. The sash is of very broad white ribbon.

BRIDAL FINERY

As this subject is never uninteresting to a group of ladies, young or old, we give, in connection with our beautiful plate, a description of a trousseau prepared by a fashionable dressmaker. The bride's toilet naturally comes first.

The veil, which is made of rich Brussels lace, is very long behind, the border is excessively handsome, and the corners are rounded; with this a wreath of orange-blossoms is worn. The dress, of white silk, is trimmed with white crepe and Brussels lace; the body is low and cut square, with a little lace pelerine buttoned in front. A small bouquet of orange-blossoms is to be placed in front of the body, where the pelerine commences. The waist is round, with a very broad ribbon sash. The sleeve is composed of a short puffing of silk, and below that a very large crepe sleeve, with a turned-back cuff in Brussels lace. The bottom of the skirt is trimmed with two rows of crepe ruches, and one deep flounce.

As will be seen from our chat, bridesmaids also have adopted the veil. This veil, which falls behind, is made of tulle, and is surmounted by a wreath of red and white roses. The dress is of white tulle, with a rose-colored silk slip underneath. The body is made low, and trimmed with a pointed bertha behind and before, which is composed of two tulle ruches, in which are placed, at regular distances, bows of rose-colored ribbon. The sleeve is very full, and descends just below the elbow, and is caught up a little in front in the bend of the arm. The bottom of the two skirts is trimmed with tulle ruches, mixed with bows of rose-colored ribbon and in putting these on the skirt they are first of all run on to a piece of double tulle, and the bows fastened in. When this trimming is completed, it merely requires running on once, and by doing it in this manner the dress is less handled than if the bows and ruches were all sewn on the tulle skirt.

Among the dresses we note a violet silk, very simple but at the same time stylish. The skirt is plain, the corsage open in front with lapels; these are trimmed with a crossway piece of black silk and edged with narrow black lace with a violet silk button at the extremity of each lapel. The sleeves have a deep turned back cuff brought to a point; the cap or epaulette is also pointed; both are trimmed to correspond with the lapels; crossways, bands of black silk edged with lace and violet buttons. The sash is very broad, trimmed in the same style – black silk and narrow black lace.

A plain dress for home wear, made of the new *poil de chevre* (a worsted and silk material very soft), of gray and lilac. The body high, closed puffed sleeves, with pointed epaulette corded with lilac, and a deep pointed wristband corded with the same.

A rich silk, with a *white* ground brocaded in black, for this mixture is as fashionable as ever. The trimming of the skirt is one of the most decided novelties of the season, a flounce ten inches in depth behind and before, but *much deeper on either side and consequently coming up to a point*. The edge of this flounce trimmed with a bright lilac ribbon, run on in the Greek pattern; the flounce is headed by a lilac silk ruching.

A plain black silk, without which no wardrobe is now complete, is trimmed at the bottom with three gathered flounces, and above these a very large ruche in pinked silk, then three flounces, and again another ruche put on in large points. The body was made with a band, and to button in front, whilst the sleeves were trimmed to correspond with the skirt; namely, with ruches and frills, only of course narrower.

NEW JEWELRY

The articles in wear for so long a time have been added to this fall – notwithstanding the pressure of the times, and the economical resolves of most families. Among them we note the rich combs of coral, ivory, silver, and gold, intended for evening wear, in full dress. To accommodate the new styles of wearing the hair, some of these have a hinged back, that is, the back of the comb opens to allow the heavy puff of hair to pass through, and closes into shape again. Jeweled pendants, to be attached to the headdress, is also another novelty; these are in various designs, as for instance, a burnished butterfly, quivering on its perch, a fine spiral wire: there are leaves, crosses, etc., all very striking in their effect, when velvet forms the background.

The gold collar is really what the name indicates, a circlet of gold for the neck, to be worn as a collar. There are several shapes, one of the prettiest modelled from the narrow bits of linen, with slightly parted and pointed ends, which have been so universal this last season. Imagine a series of flat links in this shape, fastened by an amethyst, set in gold, with a pear-shaped amethyst pendant. Others are ornamented with pearls, and the most costly with diamonds.

For fastening muslin habit-shirts and chemisettes, the spiral stud will be found very useful, as it requires the merest point of an opening, such as you might introduce and ordinary pin through; it is also more secure than the ordinary fastening.

The richest fans are ornamented with rich lace, Valenciennes and even point, set on in waves, on a silk foundation of any bright or delicate tint. The frames are richly carved, of ebony or pearl, sometimes inlaid with silver or gold.

NOVELTIES FOR DECEMBER

Fig. 1 – As appropriate to our exquisite fashion-plate for the month, we give a decided novelty – *coiffure for a bridesmaid*. Hair banded closely, a handsome ivory or silver comb, a bandeau composed of a ruche of double crepe, with bouquets of pansies, and a short illusion veil, arranged as a *cìche peigné*, and flowing gracefully down over the neck.

Fig. 2 – Headdress for a bridesmaid at a reception or wedding party; a wreath of ribbon loops, blue, pink, or rose sublime, with black lace between, terminated by a flat bow, with floating ends.

Fig. 3 – Breakfast-cap for a bride (a fashion becoming more and more universal since breakfast–caps are now made extremely *piquant* and becoming). Material spotted tulle trimmed with roses and *rose de chiné* ribbon.

Fig. 4 – Another style of breakfast-cap, of dotted black lace, over white; trimmed with a quilling and rows of violet ribbon.

Fig. 5 – Necktie from a *trousseau*, intended for a dress, *à la Gabrielle*. It is of Solferino silk, with a neat pattern in braid or chain stich of black, and trimmed with black lace.

Figs. 6 & 7 – A muslin set, from a trousseau, intended for an informal morning reception, worked in brilliant colors, a decided novelty.

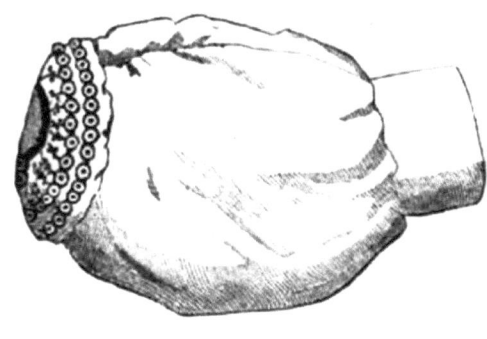

Fig. 8 – Fancy chemisette and sleeves for a child to wear with a low-necked dress.

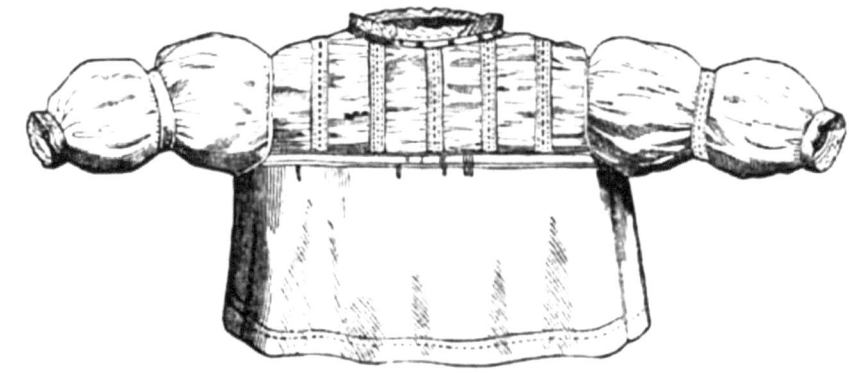

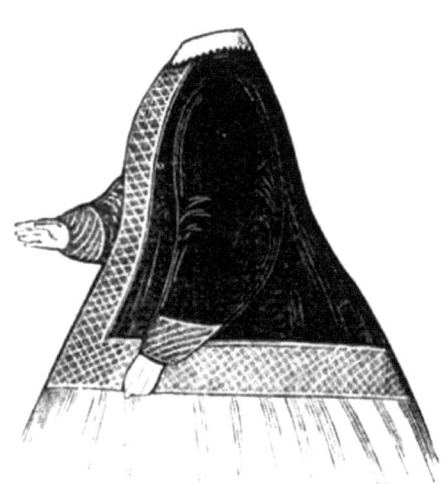

THE EIDER DOWN JACKET
Fig. 9 – Made of velvet, trimmed with quilted silk, is a most comfortable article of ladies dress for changeable weather, and can be made of any material.

THE RIFLE CORPS JACKET
Fig. 10 – Fits tightly to the figure, but allows ample space for a full and pretty lace sleeve.

THE CLEOPATRA
Fig. 11 – A very pretty style; its exquisite fit, proportions, and design are unsurpassable.

BASQUINE COAT FOR A LITTLE GIRL

To be made of cloth, and trimmed with a ruffle of fluted cloth, pinked on the edge.

MUSLIN FICHU

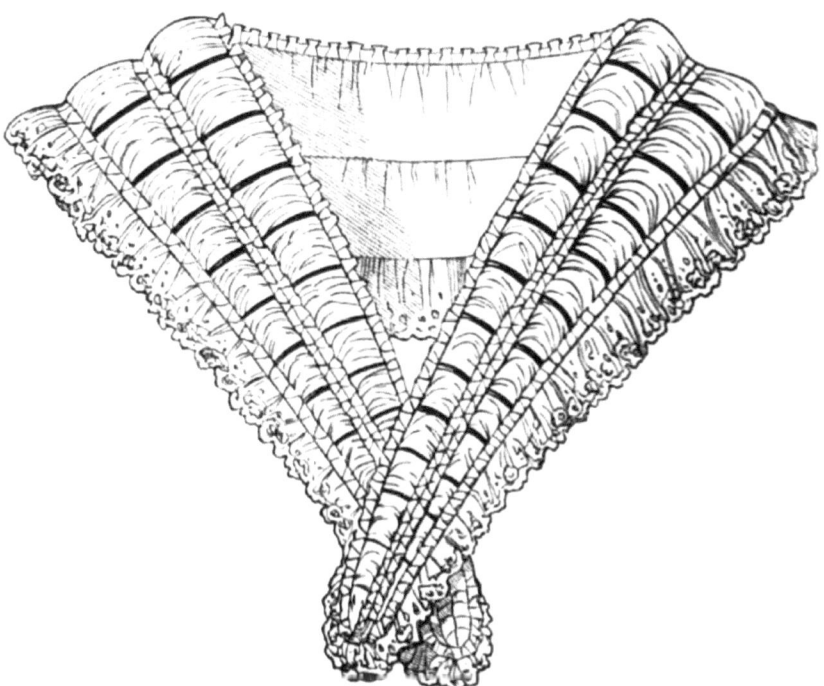

To be trimmed with black velvet, and a worked ruffle.

SHOE ROSETTE

SHOE ROSETTE

CRAFTING & NEEDLEWORKS

NETTED TIDY

Materials – Cotton No. 6, a long netting needle and flat mesh, nearly an inch wide. A large rug-needle for darning.

Begin with one stitch and increase one stitch at the beginning of every row, until there are 100 loops. *This is now the width*. Now to make it longer than it is wide, increase one stitch at the beginning of each row, and decrease one at the end of each row, by omitting to net into it, till there are 142 stitches on the long side. This is now the length of the Tidy.

To finish – Instead of increasing, take two stitches into one at the beginning of row, and still decrease one at the end of row, till there is only one stitch left. Now let the netting be well washed, starched, and pulled evenly; then left to dry (or it may be ironed).

To Darn the Pattern - for which reference must be made to the engraving, commence working exactly in the center of the Tidy. It works well to darn in just the centers of all the patterns first, and these centers are sixteen stitches apart. The dots of darning are worked round each pattern.

PURSE
Knit in blue worsted and gold thread, with small gold tassels to finish it at the edge. A very pretty purse

Coiffure composed of pieces of bias silk cut out and box-plaited

PETTICOAT SUSPENDER

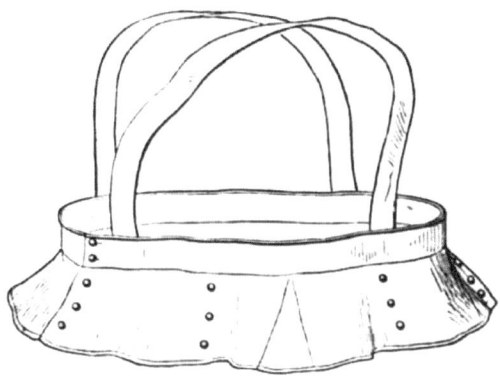

This suspender is attached to a band which is fastened round the waist, and supported by shoulder straps. It is made of some strong material, lined with muslin, and bound with muslin or tape. It can be worn to fasten in front, or on the back. The arrangement of the buttons is marked on the patterns. This suspender has been tried and found to answer very well.

GLENGARRY CAP IN CROCHET

Materials — Green crochet silk, green satin, black sarsnet, cord and tassels, and some stout material for lining.

For the band, make a chain of 380 stitches; do one row of sc.
1st row – 6 dc, 13ch, miss 13*; repeat to the end.
2d - * 2 dc, 4 ch, miss 4, 3 dc, 9 ch, miss 9, 1 dc *; repeat to the end.
3d - * 1 dc, 2 ch, miss 2, 3 dc, 3 ch, miss 3, 3 dc, 6 ch, miss 6, 2 dc *; repeat to the end.
4th – 1 dc, 5 ch, miss 5, * 3 dc over 3 ch of the previous round, 7 ch, miss 7, 3 dc, 6 ch, miss 6 *; repeat to the end.
5th – 1 dc, 2 ch, miss 2, * 3 dc, 3 ch, miss 3 dc of last row, 3 dc, 3 ch, miss 3, 3 dc, 4 ch, miss 4 *; repeat to the end.
6th – 1 dc, 5 ch, miss 5, * 3 dc, 5ch, miss 5, 3 dc, 8 ch, miss 8 *; repeat to the end.
7th – 7 dc coming on the 5 ch and a dc at each side, and 11 ch before the next dc. This is the last row of the band.

For the crown, make a chain of 140 stitches, and repeat the pattern on it as often as it will permit. These stitches form the extreme width of the crown. A piece of fourteen inches long must be made, which should require about seven repetitions of the pattern.

There now remains to be worked the piece between the band and the crown, and this is done by making a chain of 120 stitches, and doing one pattern; and three rows of the next on this, increasing three stitches at each end of every row. Then work each edge separately, doing first three patterns, then two; then one only; not decreasing all at once, but leaving a few stitches at the inner edge of every row.

To make up the cap, cut out the shape first in paper; then in fine tick, or any similar material. Cover this with black on one side, and with green satin on the other. The satin should be rather darker in color than the crochet, which is to be tacked over it. The corners of the oblong piece done for the crown must then be cut off and all sewed firmly and neatly together. A piece of enameled leather usually lines the band, and a cord and tassels finish the cap at the back of the head.

BABY SOCK

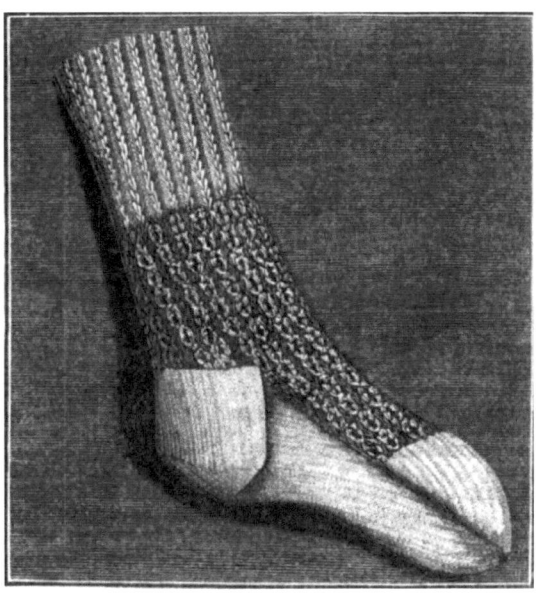

Materials – Knitting cotton, No 20
Cast on 26, 29, 26

Knit 40 rows; 2 plain and 2 purl – the odd stitch being for the seam, which is made by knitting first round plain, and next purling; so that there will be 20 purled stitches. Then commence the pattern. Purl 2; knit one; thread in front; knit 2 together.

This is the entire pattern of which ten patterns go for the leg: the seam stitch for the center of the heel. The heel is plain knitting, retaining 8 patterns in front; 12 takings-in, form the instep, after the heel is closed in the usual way. Ten patterns in front for foot. Six plain, turn beyond, and then close the toe, as is usual, by taking-in on each side of the needle, with three rows between, until 12 stitches remain; then close by casting off in the usual.

EMBROIDERY FOR A SKIRT OR TOP OF PINCUSHION

PRAYER BOOK MARKER
THE CROSS MADE OF PERFORATED PAPER
(Suitable For A Christmas Gift)

KNITTED ARTIIFICIAL FLOWERS
(Narcissus)

One or two flowers only will be needed to form a branch, neither buds nor leaves being required.

Six petals and three stamens for each flower.

Cast on one stitch in white split Berlin wool. 2d row. Make one, and knit rest of row.

3d – Make one, purl the row
4th – Knit plain row
5th – Purl plain row
6th – Make one, knit row
7th – Make one, purl row
8th – Knit plain row
9th – Purl plain row
10th – Make one, knit row
11th – Make one, knit row
12th – Knit row
13th – Purl row
14th – Make one, knit row
15th – Make one, purl row

You must now knit and purl alternately ten (seven stitches will be sufficient, if you make the flower double) rows without increase, and then begin to decrease one in the next knitted and purled rows; knit and purl one row plain; decrease one in the next two rows; knit two plain, and thus continue till you have but three stitches left, gather these with a rug needle and fasten the wool.

The next most important part of this flower is the Nectarius, which looks like a little yellow cup, edged with scarlet. The petals first made, must have a wire sewn neatly round them, and like all white flowers, will look better if washed and slightly blued before the wire is put on.

For Nectarius

Cast on six stitches in very pale yellow wool, split

1st row – Knit plain
2d – Purl
3d – Make one, knit one, repeat through the row
4th – Purl one row
5th – Knit one row
6th – Purl one row
7th – Make one, knit two, repeat through the row
8th – Purl one row
9th – Knit one row
10th – Purl one row

Take scarlet wool (or scarlet China silk), knit one row, and cast off very loosely. Sew up the open side. Make a little tuft of pale green or yellow wool, to fill the bottom of the little cup, and preserve its shape; place at the top of these, three stamens, each formed by a knot of yellow wool, fixed on a bit of wire. Then take green wool. Cast on six stitches; knit a piece about half an inch long, increasing irregularly about six stitches before you reach the top. Sew this piece under the flower, closing the open side.

The stem should be made of a piece of thin whalebone, about a quarter of an inch in width, which is better covered first with a strip of green tissue paper, and then with green wool as usual; the flowers must be fixed to the top of this, according to their natural appearance.

CIGAR CASE IN APPLICATION

Materials – Brown Russia leather, a little green and scarlet ditto; a small quantity of white, black, and scarlet silk braid, and two yards of gold ditto.

The ordinary Russia leather forms the ground of this cigar-case. The black part of the engraving represents the green leather; the inner part, engraved in horizontal lines, is scarlet leather. Both the green and scarlet are very thin, and are cut out in the forms seen in the engraving. The edges of the different leathers are sewed together closely, through a piece of linen which lines the entire case. The engraving is two-thirds the size of the original. The gold braid is marked in the engraving by a narrow double line. It will be seen that it covers the joins of the different leathers, and also forms a knot in the center. The outer line of braiding is scarlet; that on the green is white, and on the scarlet leather is black.

This sort of cigar-case is made up with a gilt frame, in the same way as the portemonnaies are usually done.

PATCHWORK

EMBROIDERY DESIGNS

EMBROIDERY FOR A CHEMISE

FOR MUSLIN EMBROIDERY

DEFINITIONS

1. À la vieille: To the old, To the historic
2. Aerophane: Fine thin silk crêpe, sometimes used for pleated and gathered dress trimmings.
3. Agrafe: A hook-and-loop fastening; especially: an ornamental clasp used on armor or costumes
4. Anti-Macassar: A small cloth placed over the backs or arms of chairs, or the head or cushions of a sofa, to prevent soiling of the permanent fabric
5. Astracan de laine: In 1861 a new rough textured trim
6. Astrakhan: lamb fleece—with heavy, curly pile. The pile may be looped or cut. Any fiber may be used; lustrous wool is common.
7. Azurline: (Azuline/Azurine); names for aniline blues, newly invented color words that combined the fashionable term "azure" with the suffix in "aniline.
8. Balzarine: A lightweight fabric made from cotton and wool, used for summer dresses
9. Barbe: a short scarf or lappet of lace formerly worn at the throat or on the head.
10. Berceaunette: Bassinet
11. Berthé: A type of lace collar attached to a low-necked dress
12. Blonde: The term blonde refers to the natural color of the silk thread. Originally this lace was made with the natural-colored silk, and later in black. Most blonde lace was also made in black.
13. Bouffantes: Baggy, puffed
14. Bouillonné: Puffs
15. Bournous: A long cloak of coarse woolen fabric with a hood
16. Bretelles: Straps
17. Cache peigné: trimming on the back part of a woman's hat either placed under the brim or attached to the edge
18. Capellines: Hat body
19. Ceinture: Broad Sash
20. Chatelaine: Chain, a set of short chains on a belt worn by women and men for carrying keys, thimble and/or sewing kit, etc.
21. Cìche peigne: Comb
22. Convolvulus: of the morning glory family, comprising twining or prostrate plants having trumpet-shaped flowers
23. Coque: A loop of ribbon or feathers used in trimming hats
24. Corsage: The bodice or waist of a dress
25. D volonté: At one's own pleasure
26. Drugget: A coarse woolen fabric felted or woven, self-colored or printed one side; a sort of cheap stuff, very thin and narrow, usually made of wool, or half wool and half silk or linen; it may have been corded but was usually plain. The term is now applied to a coarse fabric having a cotton warp and a wool filling, used for rugs, tablecloths, etc.
27. Eglantine: A sweet briar plant
28. En tablier: In an Apron

29. Fanchon: A scarf or handkerchief, folded in a triangle
30. Fluted: Groove or furrow, as in a ruffle of cloth or on a piecrust
31. Fourragéres: A braided cord worn usually around the left shoulder especially: such a cord awarded as a decoration to a military unit
32. Garibaldi: A pink salmon color
33. Gauntlet: a name for several different styles of glove, particularly those with an extended cuff covering part of the forearm
34. Genin, John: A successful clothier and hatter in New York City
35. Gimp: In reference to lace refers to the thread that is used to outline the pattern. This thread is normally thicker than that used to make the lace. It gives definition and slightly raises the edge of the design
36. Glacé: Made or finished so as to have a smooth glossy surface
37. Goffering: Treat (a lace edge or frill) with heated irons in order to crimp or flute it
38. Grenadine: A thin fabric of leno weave in silk, nylon, rayon, or wool
39. Grecque: Greek pattern
40. Groseille: Light red, or Cherry red
41. Imperatrice: Empress
42. Mantelet: A short cape
43. Marguerites: Ox-Eye Daisy
44. Modistes: A fashionable milliner or dressmaker
45. Moniteur: Instructor, teaching assistant
46. Nacarat: Mid-18th century: from French, perhaps from Spanish and Portuguese nacarado 'orange-red in color
47. Nankeen: is a kind of pale yellowish cloth, originally made at Nanjing, China from a yellow variety of cotton, but subsequently manufactured from ordinary cotton that is then dyed
48. Pardessus: Overcoat
49. Passementerie: Decorative trimming such as tassels, braid, and fringing, used on furniture and clothing
50. Patees: Straps
51. Pelerine: a woman's cape of lace or silk with pointed ends at the center front, popular in the 19th century
52. Pendeloques: Diamond shape
53. Plait or Plaiting: To pleat or fold
54. Plastrons: an ornamental front of a woman's bodice or shirt consisting of colorful material with lace or embroidery
55. Plissé: Material treated so as to be permanently puckered or crinkled
56. Portemonnaie: A wallet or purse
57. Poult-de-soie: A soft, ribbed silk fabric, used especially for dresses. Origin of poult-de-soie from French, dating back to 1825-35
58. Pusher lace: Lace made in the 19th century at Nottingham, Eng., on the "pusher" machine, the pusher machine could copy convincingly such handmade laces as Chantilly, except for the outlining thread, which continued to be hand run

59. Quilled: a band of material fluted into small ruffles so as to resemble a row of quills
60. Recherche: Defined as, 'known only to connoisseurs; choice or rare; studiedly refined or elegant
61. Reps: A cloth woven in fine cords or ribs across the width of a piece, usually made of silk, wool, or cotton
62. Robe de chamber: A dressing gown
63. Rose de Alps: Very lightest shade of fuchsia
64. Rose sublime: A ruby scarlet color
65. Ruche: A strip of fabric that is gathered or pleated down both sides
66. Sarsnet: a fine, soft fabric, often of silk, made in plain or twill weave and used especially for linings
67. Solferino: A purplish red color, so named after Solferino, a village in northern Italy, where the Battle of Solferino was fought on June 24, 1859. The color was named so because the dye of this color was discovered shortly after the battle, and supposedly the color represented how the battlefield appeared after the bloodshed
68. Soutache: Narrow flat decorative braid, a type of galloon, used in the trimming of drapery or clothing. In clothing soutache is sometimes used to conceal a seam. Often woven of metallic bullion thread, silk, or a blend of silk and wool
69. Split Zephyr: A variety of soft, fine, worsted yarn used for knitting or crocheting, and embroidery. Split Zephyr is closely twisted
70. Tablier: Apron
71. Toilette: a: formal or fashionable attire or style of dress. b: a particular costume or outfit
72. Treble: three times as much or as many
73. Velours epinglé: Terry velvet
74. Vertislay: A quiet slate-gray color
75. Voilette: Hat veil
76. Wadding: used as a layer of insulation between fabrics, most often used in quilt making
77. Watered: Now known as Moiré, a wavy (watered) appearance produced mainly from silk, but also wool, cotton and rayon. The watered appearance is usually created by the finishing technique called calendaring

www.ingramcontent.com/pod-product-compliance
Lightning Source LLC
Chambersburg PA
CBHW042129010526
44111CB00031B/34